State and Society in Brazil

About the Book and Editors

After a generation of military rule, Brazil is making the transition to democracy, and for the first time a foundation exists for creating a pluralistic and democratic political culture. Contributors to this book focus on two themes: how the enormous state apparatus inherited from the military is responding to new demands for growth and equity, for more private initiative, and for increased accountability; and how both political elites and the traditionally weak and fragmented political parties are coping with pressures for change across the social spectrum. They begin with a discussion of changes in the economic model associated with industrialization and then deal with the rise of independent labor unions and voluntary organizations. Finally, they consider how the state can be constituted to meet the challenge of new economic and political conditions and Brazil's position in a more interdependent, yet increasingly regionalistic, Western Hemisphere.

John D. Wirth is professor of history at Stanford University. **Edson de Oliveira Nunes** is director of the Brazilian Institute of Geography and Statistics in Rio de Janeiro. **Thomas E. Bogenschild** is program coordinator for the Stanford-Berkeley Joint Center for Latin American Studies.

State and Society in Brazil

Continuity and Change

edited by John D. Wirth,
Edson de Oliveira Nunes,
and Thomas E. Bogenschild

Routledge
Taylor & Francis Group
NEW YORK AND LONDON

First published in paperback 2024

First published 1987 by Westview Press, Inc.

Published 2019
by Routledge
605 Third Avenue, New York, NY 10158

and by Routledge
4 Park Square, Milton Park, Abingdon, Oxon OX14 4RN

Routledge is an imprint of the Taylor & Francis Group, an informa business

Library of Congress Cataloguing-in-Publication Data
State and society in Brazil.
(Westview special studies on Latin America and the Caribbean)
Includes index.
1. Brazil—Politics and government—1985– 2. Brazil—Economic policy. 3. Political parties—Brazil. 4. Trade-unions—Brazil. 5. Brazil—Foreign relations. I. Wirth, John D. II. Nunes, Edson de Oliveira. III. Bogenschild, Thomas. IV. Series.
JL2411.S73 1986 981'.063 87-2160

Publisher's Note
The publisher has gone to great lengths to ensure the quality of this reprint but points out that some imperfections in the original copies may be apparent.

ISBN 13: 978-0-367-28865-5 (hbk)
ISBN 13: 978-0-367-30411-9 (pbk)
ISBN 13: 978-0-429-30740-9 (ebk)

DOI: 10.4324/9780429307409

Contents

Tables

Preface

This volume grew out of a conference series sponsored jointly by the Stanford-Berkeley Joint Center for Latin American Studies and the Instituto Universitário de Pesquisas do Rio de Janeiro (IUPERJ). Entitled "Opportunities and Constraints in Peripheral Industrial Society: The Case of Brazil," the first conference was held in Nova Friburgo in July 1983 and was followed up by another at Berkeley in late January 1984. In the course of our discussions, the subject matter widened so that a new title was chosen for this book. Also, in the interim, as Brazil made the transition to democracy and returned to economic growth, many topics on the agenda for the 1980s emerged in clearer focus, so that the chapters have all been sharpened and upgraded. In the division of labor that produced this book, Nunes coordinated the project at Berkeley and in Brazil, while Wirth and Bogenschild did the editing.

Support for this project was generously provided by the Edward Larocque Tinker Foundation and by the Inter-American Foundation. The Fulbright Commission in Brazil helped with some of the air tickets, and IUPERJ handled the local arrangements in Nova Friburgo. In addition, the Tinker Foundation supported a three-year program of Brazilian Studies through the Stanford-Berkeley Joint Center.

John D. Wirth
Edson de Oliveira Nunes
Thomas E. Bogenschild

Introduction

John D. Wirth and Edson de Oliveira Nunes

On November 15, 1986 a Constituent Assembly was elected which, starting in March of 1987, will write a new democratic constitution for the New Republic. While the new constitution is not expected to be ready for at least a year after that, it will mark the closing of a long process of democratic transition which began in 1974. In fact, this transition will have lasted longer than the dictatorial phase of military rule which began with the 1964 coup. Announced by the military as a "long and gradual process of opening," the redemocratization of Brazil has followed a course marked with advances and retreats, tensions and agreement, bombs and votes, growth and recession. The recession starting in 1980 with an unfavorable international economy and a harsh decline in salaries accelerated the regime's internal fragmentation. But the opening itself was projected during the years of high growth and large public works in the Geisel government.

The first civilian administration in 21 years took power in March of 1985, the product as much as an extraordinary popular mobilization led by the PMDB opposition party as of the internal divisions in the military regime. And if the movement for direct presidential elections was defeated in the Congress, which opted instead for election by an Electoral College, the upshot of this upwelling of popular participation was to produce a coalition of the center-left strong enough to order the transition from military to civilian rule.

At the same time there is a striking parallel with the post-war democratic regime established in 1945, following 15 years of discretionary rule under President Getúlio Vargas. For one thing, just as the body of state powers from the authoritarian 1930s were carried over by the democratic post-war regime, the strong state apparatus built by the military after 1964 is largely intact, and in neither case did the military face trials or reprisals. For another, both transitions were managed from the top down, by establishment leaders -- the Tancredo Neves-José Sarney team* in this respect replaying the 1945 role of General Eurico Gaspar Dutra. Conciliation, pragmatism and cooptation, the methods by which Brazilian elites have traditionally managed change, were confirmed again in 1985 as enduring features of the political culture.

Thus there was no sharp break between the so-called Old and New Republics in 1985. Yet it is also true that in this latest opening to democracy the political base today is strikingly different from what it was a generation ago in 1964 when the military ousted the shaky populist regime of João Goulart. In the early 1980's, the strikes and demonstrations that hastened the return to democracy had little in common with the populist politics of a possibly pre-revolutionary sort that characterized popular participation before the 1964 coup. The popular campaign for direct presidential elections (which failed: Tancredo was elected indirectly) was not a mobilization for radical change. It was, in retrospect, a demand for broader economic and political participation by a society which had experienced twenty years of breakneck change under the twin forces of urbanization and industrialization, under a repressive regime. Far from rejecting capitalism, the broad majority in this new, better organized society wanted to play by democratic rules.

---

* Tancredo Neves fell ill on the eve of his inauguration. When he died some five weeks later the Vice President, José Sarney, who not many months before had bolted the military-backed PDS party to join Tancredo, became President.

The newly independent trade unions and voluntary groups are only the most visible manifestations of a society that is organizing itself massively at the grassroots level. The proliferation of voluntary organizations in the urban neighborhoods, in the unions, in the base communities of the Catholic Church and in the countryside to contest land titles is something new in scale and new in the emphasis on non-directed change. Populism has lost much of its appeal and vanguardism on the left is discredited, although traditional forms of clientelism are still pervasive in the countryside and, in the absence of strong party organizations, permeate urban politics as well.

Just how much this associational thrust will change the style and content of politics remains to be seen. What does seem clear is that Brazilian society has perhaps for the first time produced the basis for a pluralistic and democratic political culture. An evolutionary shift away from deeply rooted authoritarian patterns is occurring, although to be sure the centuries of experience starting with the long, and formative colonial period, followed by the Empire and the Republic into the 1930s which were highly stratified regimes based on vertical relationships cannot be sloughed off overnight.

Once installed, the new Sarney government continued the gradual transition, reaching out to form coalitions with the left and the right while attempting to move ahead with administrative reforms and pay its debts -- all in a difficult economic climate marked by high rates of inflation and a dangerous public debt much worsened by foreign constraints. Elections took on greater meaning, serving at once to ratify economic policies and to deepen the legitimacy of the government. In the crucial municipal elections of 1985 the PMDB suffered some unexpected defeats, notably in São Paulo where the Senate Majority Leader Fernando Henrique Cardoso lost to the old-style populist Jânio Quadros. Party fragmentation and coalition-building continued -- confirming a process that is seemingly enduring in Brazilian political culture -- while the presidency as an institution was strengthened in early 1986 by the Cruzado Plan, Sarney's bold program of currency reform and price restraints, which met with overwhelming popular support. Although it took power in difficult circumstances, the new government struck out in new directions, including accelerated spending on social programs backed by a raise in real wages. This was a striking departure from the military government, which put economic growth well ahead of social priorities and let real wages fall until the political opening was well advanced.

Sarney's growth oriented policies paid off handsomely in the November 1986 elections, enabling the government to carry all but one of the 23 state governorships while winning a massive majority in the Congress, which should allow the center-left coalition to dominate the upcoming Constituent Assembly. Just how vulnerable the government would be to the politics of redistribution remained to be seen; old style populism of the left as typified by Governor Leonel Brizola of Rio de Janeiro, or of the right as in Quadros' São Paulo victory was not expected to prevail in the more complex and better organized Brazilian society of today.

The socioeconomic base has also been transformed since 1964. Urbanization accelerated under the twin impact of economic growth and the transformation of production in the countryside. Consider the fact that by the 1980 census there were nine metropolitan areas of one million people or more. In 1965, moreover, 51 percent of the entire population could be classified as urban, but by 1983 this had risen to 73 percent, with more than half of all Brazilians living in cities of more than 500,000 people. Equally striking was the change in occupational roles, especially in the growth and proliferation of middle sector occupations which supported increased consumption. The number of manufacturing jobs also rose. And while inequality remained, and the very rich got richer after 1964, Brazilian society could not be described as a simple pyramid with a small top stratum resting atop an impoverished mass base. Living conditions on the outskirts of these mushrooming cities, where the low income groups are concentrated, are extremely precarious: 20 percent of the population lives in *favelas* or urban slums. The worsening plight of the rural poor, especially blacks, was a major impetus for migration. And it is probably still the case, as it was in data from 1972, that the top fifth of the nation controls 65 percent of the income.

To this must be added continuing social and economic disequilibria at the regional level. Economic growth has so far done little to close the gap which separates the Center-South from the rest of the nation. The relative situation of the Northeast, especially, has changed little in the last 20 years. With about one third of the national population, this long-impoverished region accounts for only 12 percent of the national income. One legacy of military rule was much better transportation and communications. But national integration only highlights the contrasts: TV transmission by satellite and direct dial telephones exist side by side with rates of illiteracy and infant mortality that are still high.

As society became concentrated, spatially, and in much better communication with itself, it became more complex and took on the characteristics of an industrial society. But this is also a society where one third of Brazilians live at the level of Western Europe while the rest must still accept sharply reduced shares. How this situation of structural inequality squares with a much more open, participatory political order will depend in large part on the performance of Brazil's very large economy.

These social transformations accompanied an economy which became both larger and more complex. Larger, in that Brazil now ranks eighth among the free market economies. More complex, in that over 70 percent of the export list is now manufactured goods. After 1967, the Brazilian economy was partially reoriented toward export-led growth. However, Brazil cannot really be described as one of the so-called "newly industrializing countries" or NICs, because so much of the economy remains oriented toward the internal market. (The share of Brazil's GNP produced by foreign trade is less than the United States.) It remains preoccupied with internal growth and large projects of import substitution, however much increased exports are necessary to make interest payments on the foreign debt and to make the large state-run sector more productive. Perhaps the biggest challenge is to ease the impoverishment of Brazil's lower classes, to create enough wealth so that what Brazilians call the "social debt" of illiteracy, poor health and low incomes can be addressed, in sum to create a more just society. For the first time in a generation, land reform is part of the national agenda.

With the exhaustion of the model of accelerated growth of the 1970s, and the rise of a new international context, especially with respect to sharply reduced capital flows, the strategy of development had to be rethought. And in the context of democratic opening, the priority ceased to be growth at any price. The Sarney government wanted to emphasize a more equitable distribution of the fruits of development. The return to growth after three years of sharp recession was the government's top priority, the goal being to attain the post-war mean of 6 percent real growth per year based on the modern and well-integrated industrial sector already in place, and on export oriented agriculture. If this historic rate of growth can be sustained, it would only be sufficient to absorb new entries to the labor market each year. The watchword was productivity -- accelerated growth using new technologies (especially in the area of informatics) in order to employ more people now that growth could no longer be obtained at the expense of wages; to service the foreign debt; and to stimulate the internal market.

Among the obstacles to be overcome in order to achieve sustained growth the financial disequilibrium in the public sector stands out. Given the speed of the foreign adjustment, the government was forced to borrow in the internal credit markets for requirements that had been met through foreign borrowing, and this drove interest rates up. This rise was the principal factor in the fall-off of investments, which declined as a percentage of GDP from 29 percent in 1975 to only 15 percent in 1984.

Furthermore, the return to private investment is essential in order for the state to redefine its functions. If the social debt is ever to be redeemed, the state must concentrate on its traditional functions in such basic areas as food policy, health, education, housing, transportation and security. Now that literacy is no longer a prerequisite for voting, the 40 percent of all Brazilians who live on the margins of society can now be heard.

All societies are the product of continuity and change, which operate together, on a continuum, but fitfully with leads and lags instead of an orderly march toward progress. What changes and what remains the same are the intertwined questions that inform the chapters in this volume. Few would deny that the Brazil of 1986 is different from the Brazil of 1964, in both the quantitative and qualitative sense. But in what fundamental ways is it different? What are the underlying forces of continuity and change?

In making the transition from military rule to a more pluralistic, open system one of the major unanswered questions is the extent to which the large state apparatus can be made more responsive to the citizens. The governmental role in production, in banking and finance, in planning and regulatory activities all increased after 1964. Through the zigs and zags of policy-making under the military an enduring theme was state directed change, with relatively little mediation by the formal political system. Congress and the courts declined as the role of new agencies run by technocrats increased. Electoral politics has now returned, but it remains to be seen how major elements of what Brazilians call "*o sistema*" can be bent to the will of elected authorities. Even more important, how can this system with its privileged access to government credit, its closed habits of operation, and its built-in patronage structures be made accountable to the popular will?

Another open question in the political realm concerns party organization. Coalition-building may be as Brazilian as rice and beans, but so is party fragmentation. This has begun again, as it did in 1946. That the post-war regime stabilized on the basis of three loosely organized political parties points to what may happen in the Nova República. However, it remains to be seen how the traditional political culture with its premium on deal-making and accommodation will respond to the new voluntary organizations. Many grass roots organizers and their followers are wary of politicians and their parties. The durability and capacity of these voluntary organizations remains untested: they are, after all, something really new. How the old actors and the new will blend their forces in party organizations is a key dynamic in the creation of responsive democracy.

Circumscribing this process, or at least conditioning it heavily is the continuance of a strong state with its military and security forces no longer ruling but in place and intact, and with its leading economic role. Finding the balance between order and progress has always preoccupied Brazilian elites. This is in fact the often-neglected corollary to *conciliação*, that central and much heralded attribute of Brazilian political culture. Authoritarianisms of the right and of the left are unpopular and discredited today, and within the context of return to democracy it would be difficult to unleash state violence against the citizens. But so far the limits of social and political action across the *democratic* spectrum have not been tested.

The economy has shifted gears from a fundamental preoccupation with growth at any cost to a relatively greater emphasis on distribution of the benefits. This is congruent with the return to open political institutions. But it also assumes a return to high growth rates of at least 6 percent, bearing in mind that the average mean rate from 1957-79 was just over 7 percent. How this can be done in the more savage and unforgiving world economy of the 1980's remains unclear, even assuming that the return to growth in 1984 that ended a three year depression will last. Judging from past experience, the export emphasis will increase, but without eclipsing Brazil's historical reliance on import substituting industrialization, or ISI. The 1984 Lei de Informática matica which reserves large sectors of the computer and information industries to Brazilian national companies is a case in point.

Taking the entire post-war period again as a guide, the clear and unmistakable trend has been for the state to gain economic space at the expense of the private sector, so much so that Brazil's neo-capitalist economy is heavily conditioned by the state. Indeed, it would be hard to imagine a substantial roll-back or divestiture of this power, given the need to allocate scarce capital across a wide spectrum of interests and demands. Holders of Brazilian foreign debt may talk of privatization, but it is unlikely to go far. The weight of tradition and established practice is, moreover, very strong. And when nationalism is involved, the public has rallied to the state. But what should be the balance between state and private sectors to regain high rates of growth is an open question for planners and the public alike. Yet in historical perspective this is not a new issue in Brazil. What has changed is the now less favorable world economy.

Addressing the social debt is a major agenda item for the new regime. In addition to a lack of funds, melioration may be even more difficult with the rise of a more complex society. Perhaps the major beneficiaries of the military years were the new middle classes, who have lost ground since 1979 but can organize to defend their interests. By contrast, organized labor has gained some ground in the real purchasing power of wages since that date. The great divide in this newly industrialized society would seem to be between the organized, and those without an effective voice. In this respect, the rash of strikes in recent years is a test of the ability of organized groups to protect and expand their interests. The direct election campaign of 1984 had the makings of a mass movement, and so must be counted an exception. But the fact remains that organized group protest is far more prevalent and pervasive than it has been. Those who are least able to protect themselves, rural blacks for example, are likely to fall further behind.

There appear to be two basic political strategies for approaching this problem. One, the more conservative stance, assumes that the basic socioeconomic model is largely in place; that what is necessary is to perfect the political institutions, especially since in light of the debt crisis there is little surplus to distribute anyway. Another, the more radical approach, believes that the only way to deal with pent up social demands and to create a more just social order is to devise a new political economy. The first approach is basically what President-elect Tancredo Neves and his successor José Sarney had in mind. The second has adherents in the ruling PMDB and in other groups on the left. But in neither faction is opinion monolithic. And it seems clear that Brazil is wedded to capitalism, but wants the capitalism of its own choice.

This book is divided into three sections, the first of which discusses changes in the economic model and analyzes the new society created by industrialism. The next three chapters, in section two, are concerned with organization -- the origin of the state, the rise of independent labor unions and the new voluntary organizations. The third and final section is about policy and perceptions: how to frame the state to meet new economic and political conditions; how Brazil might relate to a more interdependent, yet at the same time more regionalistic Western Hemisphere; and how such a fundamental role as citizenship continues to be defined by particularistic norms.

From the lead chapter by economists Regis Bonelli and Pedro Malan, to the final chapter by cultural anthropologist Roberto da Matta, the objective is to conceptualize major themes and not to attempt comprehensive coverage. (Readers wanting more discussion of politics and political parties can turn to the 1986 Westview Press book edited by Wayne A. Selcher, entitled *Political Liberalization in Brazil; Dynamics, Dilemmas and Future Prospects.* The church is well covered in Scott Mainwaring's *The Catholic Church and Politics in Brazil, 1916-1985*, published by Stanford University Press, 1986.) The chapters below focus primarily on the socioeconomic transformation of Brazil, aiming for perspective and the long view rather than the conjunctural. Taken together, however, they represent what we think are the most significant aspects of continuity and change in Brazil today.

Bonelli and Malan provide a detailed overview of the growth process since 1964, showing how it started, flourished and then ran out of steam in the changed international environment of the late 1970s. A central theme in their chapter is the struggle to contain balance of payments problems. They then explain how this traditional post-war constraint was bypassed in Brazil's dramatic return to growth in mid-1984. Having regained the high rates of growth necessary to alleviate urban unemployment, the central challenge today is to step up investment in technology and plant capacity in an international environment of constrained capital flows.

Carlos Hasenbalg and Nelson do Valle Silva, who are both sociologists, then detail changes in the occupational structure, including the new opportunities for women and the middle classes in general, while blacks fell further behind. Based on data from the 1980 census, their study does not mince words about the social costs to create this new industrial society. Their chapter speaks directly to those analysts (almost all of whom are outside Brazil) who still refer to the results of the Brazilian boom under authoritarian rule as "growth without development." Social development there surely was, but the cost was high.

The next three chapters focus on the nexus of politics and social change, with attention to organizations and institutions. Political scientists Edson Nunes and Barbara Geddes discuss the rise of the post-war state, with its vastly enlarged role and relative insulation from party politics. Bringing this sprawling apparatus under political control is high on the agenda of the new government. Political sociologist Maria Herminia Tavares de Almeida follows with an analysis of the new trade union movement and its links to the new labor party, the PT. This is followed by Renato Boschi's penetrating account of the new urban-based grass roots social movements, a chapter which is both theoretically important and based on abundant new data. Tavares de Almeida and Boschi both show how major changes in associational activity have taken place in the context of, but not at the dictates of, the enlarged state that Nunes and Geddes introduce.

In the third section, political scientist Ben Schneider and historian John Wirth address perceptions of the Brazilian polity in relation to possible structural realignments, both internal and external. Schneider examines the Brazilian state and questions how it might change. What is to be done with a state-centered polity which is informal, elitist, and lacking in accountability, but which is also pragmatic, goal-oriented, and developmentalist -- a state, in short, that is unlikely to change very much in the near term? Schneider argues that if change is to come, it will come from redefinitions of aspects of the state at the margins with civil society, especially in its dealings with the private sector. Wirth's essay on foreign relations focuses attention on regionalism, a topic which fell out of fashion in the 1970s when Brazil diversified its markets and sources of finance, developed a global economic foreign policy, and de-linked from the orbit of North American power. With the onset of the debt crisis, and in the new trade environment of more modest expectations, the theme of regional interdependence is ripe for another look. The prospect for intensifying relations with Argentina and other contiguous southern neighbors is compared with the emerging regional space of North America.

The book concludes with da Matta's spirited discussion of citizenship in a culture where relationships of family, friendships and social class continue alongside universalistic norms to govern Brazilian civic behavior. While these deep-running patterns may be breaking down, da Matta reminds us that, after all is said and done about economic growth and the new urban-industrial society, Brazil remains an integral culture with its own qualities, habits and state of mind.

PART ONE

Economy and Society

1

Industrialization, Economic Growth, and Balance of Payments: Brazil, 1970–1984

Regis Bonelli and Pedro S. Malan

The beginning of the 1980s marks the end of a unique cycle of economic growth in Brazil that lasted approximately a decade and a half. This period should be studied as a whole, emphasizing the complex set of interactions between domestic and international factors, as well as the elements of continuity and change involved in the current situation. In the early 1980s, the convergence of three crises -- an economic crisis, a political/institutional crisis, and a social crisis related to the effects of the recession and unemployment -- had implications which will continue to cast a shadow of uncertainty over Brazil in the near future. In this chapter we concentrate on the economic dimensions of the confluence of crises, emphasizing growth characteristics, aspects of industrialization, and the disequilibrium in the balance of payments. In the following chapter we bring the analysis up to early 1986, emphasizing the reasons why Brazil returned to growth in 1984 after a severe recession.

Looking back at the experience of the Brazililan economy over the fifteen-year period stretching from the late 1960s to the early 1980s, a drama in three acts can be seen, on which the curtain dropped abruptly in August/September of 1982. The first act, which took place from 1968-1973, can be described as a recovery and "boom" under the illusion of bountiful foreign exchange. The second, from 1974-78, consisted of an attempt to adjust to the first oil shock by means of further investment in the export and import-substitution sectors, which led to additional external indebtedness. The third act unfolded between 1979 and the beginning of the third quarter of 1982, when the curtain suddenly fell. This period was marked by two additional external shocks, a peculiar policy response, and, beginning in the final quarter of 1980, adjustment through recession.

THE 1968-1978 PERIOD

The decade between 1968 and 1978 is most fruitfully analyzed in two distinct sub-periods. The first is 1968-74, characterized by an accelerated expansion of economic activity in which the Gross Domestic Product grew at an impressive annual rate of 10.9 percent in real terms. The second, between 1974 and 1978, is characterized by variability and a deceleration in overall growth, in which the average annual GDP growth rate was 6.4 percent. The difference in GDP performance in these two sub-periods can be traced to the effects of a set of interrelated factors, of which the following are most important: a) the loss of dynamism in the industrial sector, where average annual growth fell from 12.2 to 7.3 percent;[1] b) the effects of the first oil crisis on the balance of payments, combined with the increase in other raw material prices (from the end of 1971) and the speculative import "boom" of 1974 and part of 1975; and c) recession and accelerated inflation in the world economy in the mid-1970s.

Despite major differences between these two sub-periods, the years from 1968 to 1978 share a common thread -- the huge increase in international liquidity, due mainly to the deficits in the balance of payments of the United States and, in part, to the recycling of petrodollars. The expansion in liquidity contributed to a notable increase in financial loans and investments from the industrialized countries to the countries of the Third World. For Brazil this meant an overall surplus in the balance of payments for all years except 1974 and 1975 (the only years between 1968 and 1978 which saw a drop in reserves), due to the overfinancing, through capital inflows, of the deficits in the current account.

The strategy of external indebtedness, coupled with a simultaneous increase in foreign exchange reserves (the supply of which was infinitely elastic given the levels of international liquidity), was based on future export potential and on accumulated foreign reserves themselves, which insured future inflows of capital. Beginning in 1979, the second oil crisis and the increase in external interest rates posed a new set of difficulties that required adjustments which differed from those that had been possible up to that time. Before moving to the analysis of the new situation, however, it is important to look briefly at the industrial "boom" which lasted until 1973-74, and the deceleration from 1974 to 1978 which followed.

The increasing integration of the Brazilian economy into the international economy, a process which had begun in the mid-1960s, produced a significant interdependence between domestic and international economic policies. Therefore the boom period cannot be analyzed without taking the international context into account. In this period favorable tendencies at both the international and national levels were reinforced by pragmatic economic policies which enabled Brazil to take advantage of them. Ever since the end of the 1950s the Brazilian economy has been able to generate cycles of investment and production that are largely determined by the behavior of its industrial sector. The years of 1963-67, in particular, were years of recession that idled capacity throughout the economy, especially in the manufacturing sector. On the supply side, one of the factors that contributed to the economic "boom" that began in 1968 was the high level of unutilized productive capacity. This permitted an accelerated productive expansion without massive fixed investment.[2] Fixed investment in industry began to accelerate after 1970, in reaction to improving prospects for prosperity in the medium run, and as the idle capacity dropped. Fiscal incentives and tariff exemptions for equipment purchases[3] also contributed to the increase in capital formation that took place during this period. In addition, balance of payments surpluses allowed for increased imports of capital goods and raw materials. On the demand side, the phase of rapid expansion was stimulated in three areas. First, expansionist monetary and fiscal policies boosted aggregate demand. Particularly important were the expansion of credit for purchasing consumer durables -- the industrial subsector that led the "boom" -- and financing for both construction and housing purchases. Second, increased public investment, including that of public enterprises, gave additional impetus to the construction industry. Third, the government created a system of incentives which promoted manufactured exports through exemptions and fiscal credits. The general prosperity of the international economy in this period should be stressed, as it was a critical factor in the performance of Brazilian exports.

As mentioned above, industry led the boom. While the agricultural sector grew at an average annual rate of 5.1 percent, this rate was possible only because of the sector's improved performance after 1970.[4] Table 1.1 summarizes the trends in GDP growth and the main sectors of the economy in selected periods, allowing for comparisons of the boom with subsequent periods.

TABLE 1.1

Real Production of the Brazilian Economy
by Principal Sectors, 1968-1983
(Average annual growth rates for selected periods, in percent)

Period	GDP	GDP per Capita	Agri-culture	Indus-try	Com-merce	Transportation and Communications
1968-74	10.93	8.05	5.13	12.20	11.42	12.69
1975-78	6.36	3.79	4.25	7.29	4.85	8.68
1979-80	7.28	4.66	5.65	7.28	7.31	10.71
1981-83	-2.00	-4.40	2.09	-5.08	-3.29	1.59
1968-83	7.10	4.14	4.40	6.93	6.39	9.28

Source: Contas nacionais do Brasil, IBGE/FGV; also *Conjuntura econômica,* Fundação Getúlio Vargas, July 1977, December 1981, February 1982, February 1983, February 1984.

The industrial "boom," lasting until 1974, was led by the durable consumer goods sector, which grew over a period of seven years at an average annual rate of 22.5 percent. This was followed by the capital goods sector, which over the same period grew at a rate of 18.3 percent per year. The intermediate goods sector, as was to be expected, grew at approximately the same rate as the industrial sector as a whole. While the non-durable goods sector grew more slowly, it achieved an annual growth rate of about 8.3 percent, and like the other sectors it surpassed the historic average rate of growth. Table 1.2 provides a breakdown of real growth in the manufacturing sector, disaggregated according to the end use of output.

TABLE 1.2

Average Annual Real Growth in Manufacturing Production
in Selected Periods by Category of Use, 1968-1983
(in annual percentages)

Category	1968-74	1975-78	1979-80	1981-83	1968-83
All Sectors	12.9	6.7	7.0	-5.5	7.0
Intermediate Goods	13.3	8.3	8.3	-4.5	7.8
Capital Goods	18.3	6.0	5.8	-16.7	6.3
Durable Consumer Goods	22.5	6.0	9.2	-8.9	10.2
Non-Durable Consumer goods	8.8	5.1	4.8	-1.9	5.3

Source: IBGE, *Indicadores conjunturais da indústria, 1971-1983;* Regis Bonelli and D.F. Werneck, "Desempenho industrial: auge e desaceleração nos anos 70," in W. Suzigan, ed., *Indústria: política, instituições e desenvolvimento,* INPES/IPEA (1978), for the period before 1971.

TABLE 1.3

Value and Structure of Brazilian Imports (FOB), 1967-1983

Year	Value of Imports ($ millions)	Structure (%)			
		Capital Goods	Raw Materials	Consumer Goods	Petroleum Products
1967	1,441	31.9	41.2	15.0	11.9
1968	1,855	33.7	41.6	13.8	10.9
1969	1,993	37.0	38.4	14.0	11.6
1970	2,507	37.7	37.0	14.4	10.9
1971	3,245	41.3	40.5	7.9	10.3
1972	4,235	41.0	38.1	10.9	10.0
1973	6,192	34.6	42.1	11.6	11.7
1974	12,641	24.8	45.2	7.6	22.4
1975	12,210	32.3	35.6	6.8	25.3
1976	12,347	28.7	33.7	6.4	31.2
1977	12,023	25.8	32.5	7.8	33.9
1978	13,639	25.8	33.1	8.2	32.9
1979	18,084	20.9	32.9	8.7	37.5
1980	22,955	19.1	39.7	5.7	44.4
1981	22,091	18.2	26.0	4.5	51.3
1982	19,397	16.9	24.0	5.2	53.9
1983	15,383	16.2	23.9	3.9	56.0
1984	13,916	15.5	29.1	6.1	49.3
1985	13,189	18.2	31.1	7.0	43.7
1986	13,300	21.1	35.3	13.5	30.0

Source: Banco Central do Brasil, *Relatórios* (various years).
Note: Figures for 1986 are estimates.

The role of the external sector in the performance between 1967 and 1974 was critical to the extent that a favorable balance of payments favored an increase of capital goods and raw material imports. Table 1.3 shows the value and structure of Brazilian imports according to four general groups of products. In 1967 capital goods imports totaled some $460 million, and raw materials imports some $590 million. Seven years later (at the end of the boom), these values had increased to $3.1 billion and $5.7 billion respectively.[5] These two categories accounted for 70 percent of all imports in 1974, suggesting that the internalization of the supply of these goods -- the strategy adopted by the government in 1974 -- could in time become the new engine of industrial and economic growth.

Moreover, as can be seen in Table 1.3, the petroleum and petroleum derivatives grouping had the least share in total imports up to 1973. In fact, the percentage of imports of these products never topped 12 percent before 1973, and in most years was less than the percentage devoted to consumer goods imports. It should be noted that import capacity grew by 150 percent between 1967 and 1973 (16.5 percent annually), while actual imports grew at an average rate of nearly 27 percent.[6] This performance contrasts sharply with that observed throughout almost the entire previous period of import substituting industrialization. During this process the import coefficient showed a secular downward trend. Growth of import capacity and the simultaneous increase in the rate of capital formation were also favorable to the purchase of capital goods abroad.

One of the most important aspects of the industrial boom up to 1974, in terms of its consequences for the future growth potential of the economy, was the substantial increase in the rate of fixed capital formation. According to the National Accounts, the ratio of gross investment to GDP was about 20 percent in 1967. By 1974 this figure rose to 25 percent. In addition, the various components of gross capital formation (construction, capital goods production and imports) behaved differently over time. During the period from 1968 to 1974 the sum of production and importation of capital goods grew at rates much higher than those for the overall level of capital formation. This relationship is inverted in the subsequent periods, as shown in Table 1.4.

TABLE 1.4

Gross Fixed Capital Formation, Production, and Importation of Capital Goods and the Construction Industry, 1968-1983
(Average annual growth rates by subperiods, in percent)

Period	Gross Fixed Capital Formation	Import and Production of Capital Goods	Construction
1968-1974	13.3	19.8	11.1
1975-1980	5.8	3.9	8.1
1981-1983	-12.0	-20.2	-7.5
1968-1983	5.9	5.3	6.3

Source: Our calculations, from figures in *Contas Nacionais* and data on importation of capital goods.

The post-1974 deceleration in gross investment is reflected in the behavior of the aggregate category "Machinery and Equipment." However, the construction industry continued to grow at relatively high rates through the end of the decade because of public investment in infrastructure, and the huge government projects of the Geisel administration.

Brazil's economic performance between 1974 and 1978 was notable for the deceleration of the rate of growth in comparison with earlier periods (see Tables 1.1 and 1.2), and for variability in the rates of growth. In particular, industry grew at about half the rate it had achieved in the 1968-1973 "boom" period. Data in Table 1.2 suggest that producers of capital and durable consumer goods were hardest hit by the reduction of rates of growth in the manufacturing sector.

These groups grew at rates only a quarter or a third of what had been achieved in the previous period. For consumer durables, this was due to a relative saturation of the market (especially in the closing years of the period), and the high elasticity of demand that characterizes these goods. In the case of capital goods it is important to emphasize that the deceleration occurred in the midst of a phase of internalizing the supply of these goods, as well as the continuation of a group of huge government projects initiated in 1974. As for intermediate goods, their growth rate above that of the industry average probably reflects increases in exports beyond increases in production for the domestic market.

The important thing to point out in this period of decelerating growth is that the economy grew as much as it did -- that is, at levels close to the historic norm -- only because the costs of adjusting to the new international situation after the first oil crisis were postponed. This was made possible by resorting to expanded external indebtedness. In fact, in a period marked by international recession in which the OECD countries experienced a substantial reduction in growth and trade (see Table 1.5), the Brazilian economy grew at an annual rate of 6.4 percent (1975 through 1978).

TABLE 1.5

OECD Indicators of Production, Trade, Prices and Unemployment in Selected Periods (in percent)

Periods	Production	Trade	Inflation	Unemployment
1960-1973	5.2	9.1	4.5	2.8
1974-1979	2.5	5.3	10.4	5.1
1980-1982	0.1	1.1	9.3	7.7

Source: OECD, *Economic Outlook* (various issues).

Thus 1974 marks an important rupture in the evolution of the Brazilian economy and balance of payments situation. Analysis of the structure of the balance of payments from 1974 to 1978 clearly demonstrates the increasing importance of what Mundell has termed "the problem of composition" between the current account and the capital account, in which the internal and external equilibrium can only be achieved by substantially increasing the amount of external borrowing.[7]

The major difference between this period and the 1968-73 period -- in which the debt represented an option and performed a critical role in the growth strategy -- was that foreign indebtedness after 1973 represented an effort to delay the costs of required structural adjustments in order to main tain growth in consumption and investment, both public and private. As a result, the net external debt grew from $6 billion at the end of 1973 to $32 billion at the close of 1978 (see Table 1.6).[8]

Writing in 1978 (the date is important because it predates the second oil shock and the increase in international interest rates), Richard Cooper, a close observer of the international economic scene, called attention to a critical phenomenon in terms worth citing at length:

> "... In many semi-industrialized and in a number of the less-developed countries there is a degree of financial precariousness that is much more widespread than at any time since at least 1950. What happened was that a number of countries took conscious and, I think, rational decisions to ride out the recession. They chose not to experience it in 1974-75, but to borrow abroad instead, to maintain growth and domestic demand, and external debt rose accordingly. They took a gamble that I think was rational and that, indeed, was very helpful from the point of view of the world economy as a whole, because they helped to limit the extent of the downturn. *But it was a gamble they essentially lost.* The recession was much sharper and much longer than was anticipated at the time, and now these

> countries face serious decisions as to how much to retreat and how to accomplish it..."[9] (emphasis added)

Paradoxically, in 1977-78 various observers considered that the game had been won and not lost, as Cooper suggested around the same time. The principal reason for this is that the problem was seen exclusively from the point of view of the current account, with special attention to the trade balance. And actually, to the hurried observer, in 1977-78 -- as compared with 1974 -- the figures did show apparent improvement.

The trade deficit of $4.7 billion in 1974 had been eliminated by 1977 through increasing exports, and by keeping imports at around $12.3 billion (1983 dollars) for four straight years (after an increase of 103 percent in 1974). The current account deficit declined from $7.1 billion in 1974 to $4.0 billion in 1977. Or, in other words, from 7.5 to 2.8 percent of GDP. Over the ten year period between 1968 and 1978, only in 1974 and 1975 did Brazil suffer losses of international reserves.[10] By 1978 it seemed to the most optimistic observers that the effects of the first oil shock on the balance of payments had been completely absorbed.

In fact, Brazil's vulnerability to external shocks did not decrease in this period, and dependence on imported oil continued, disguised by the relative price stability between 1974 and 1978. In 1978 Brazil still imported 80 percent of the oil it consumed, representing about a third of all imports, in spite of stepped-up investment in domestic production to substitute for foreign supplies.[11] Moreover, the vulnerability of the economy to increases in international interest rates grew considerably due to the fact that 70 percent of the external debt by 1978 had been contracted with variable interest rates. An increase of one percentage point in the LIBOR signified, already by 1978, an increase of about $300 million in interest payments. Thus the increase in the LIBOR (plus the *spread*) from 8 percent in 1977 to 13 percent in 1979 represented an *additional* payment of some $1.5 billion, even though the total debt had remained constant. In fact, the debt increased from $32 billion in 1977 to $50 billion in 1979.

TABLE 1.6

Balance of Payments in Brazil, 1973-1982
(in millions of 1983 dollars)

CATEGORY	1978	1979	1980	1981	1982
Trade	(1,024)	(2,840)	(2,829)	1,202	778
Exports (FOB)	12,659	15,244	20,132	23,293	20,175
Imports (FOB)	(13,683)	(18,084)	(22,962)	(22,091)	(19,397)
Services	(5,062)	(7,920)	(10,212)	(13,135)	(17,050)
Non-factors and Others	(1,085)	(3,098)	(3,515)	(3,604)	(5,128)
Interest	(2,696)	(4,186)	(5,311)	(9,161)	(11,357)
Profit & Dividend	(561)	(636)	(310)	(370)	(565)
Transfers	71	18	155	199	(7)
Current Account	(6,015)	(10,742)	1,886	(11,734)	(16,279)
Capital	10,916	7,657	9,804	12,773	7,867
Direct Investment	1,071	1,491	1,146	584	986
Loans & Financing*	13,811	11,228	11,070	15,554	12,517
Amortization*	(5,324)	(6,385)	(5,020)	(6,242)	(6,916)
Other**	1,358	1,323	2,608	1,877	1,280
Errors & Omissions	(639)	130	(408)	(414)	(544)
Surplus/Deficit	4,262	(3,215)	(3,490)	625	(8,958)
Reserves	11,895	9,689	6,913	7,507	3,994
GROSS DEBT	43,511	49,904	53,848	61,411	69,654

Table 1.6 (continued)

CATEGORY	1978	1979	1980	1981	1982
Trade	(1,024)	(2,840)	(2,829)	1,202	778
Exports (FOB)	12,659	15,244	20,132	23,293	20,175
Imports (FOB)	(13,683)	(18,084)	(22,962)	(22,091)	(19,397)
Services	(5,062)	(7,920)	(10,212)	(13,135)	(17,050)
Non-factors and Others	(1,085)	(3,098)	(3,515)	(3,604)	(5,128)
Interest	(2,696)	(4,186)	(5,311)	(9,161)	(11,357)
Profit & Dividend	(561)	(636)	(310)	(370)	(565)
Transfers	71	18	155	199	(7)
Current Account	(6,015)	(10,742)	1,886	(11,734)	(16,279)
Capital	10,916	7,657	9,804	12,773	7,867
Direct Investment	1,071	1,491	1,146	584	986
Loans & Financing*	13,811	11,228	11,070	15,554	12,517
Amortization*	(5,324)	(6,385)	(5,020)	(6,242)	(6,916)
Other**	1,358	1,323	2,608	1,877	1,280
Errors & Omissions	(639)	130	(408)	(414)	(544)
Surplus/Deficit	4,262	(3,215)	(3,490)	625	(8,958)
Reserves	11,895	9,689	6,913	7,507	3,994
GROSS DEBT	43,511	49,904	53,848	61,411	69,654

Source: Banco Central do Brasil, *Relatórios* (various issues).
* Medium and long term.
** Includes short term.

Despite the serious deterioration of the external accounts, economic policy over this period as a whole remained fairly expansionist. As can be seen in the National Accounts, the rate of gross fixed capital formation remained high over the whole five year period (1974-1978) -- a situation that stimulated the construction industry and, to a lesser extent, the domestic production of capital goods.

As for the reorientation and greater selectivity in investment approvals of the Industrial Development Council (CDI) after 1973,[12] data on projects approved by this body (see Table 1.7) show the basic developmental posture taken by the government in 1974. The amount of fixed investment in projects approved by the CDI continued at a high level between 1974 and 1978, reaching a peak in 1976. The relationship between the value of investment in approved projects (mostly concentrated in basic inputs), and the gross fixed capital formation in the Brazilian economy as a whole went from a ratio of 7.4 percent during the four year period of the boom (1970-1973) to 11.8 percent in the subsequent four year period.[13]

In part as a consequence of this attempt to adjust by means of a significant increase in investment without a reduction in real consumption, the new external debt rose dramatically from $6.2 billion at the end of 1973 (equal to the value of exports in that year) to $40 billion in December 1979. This was the equivalent of 2.6 times the value of exports in that year, which totaled $15.2 billion. (See Table 1.7).

It is important to note that beginning in 1977 the terms of trade for Brazil took a significant turn for the worse (see Table 1.8). Two years of worsening terms of trade nearly eliminated the significant gains obtained between 1974 and 1977 which depended on "mini-booms" in some commodities (primarily coffee, soya and sugar).

Despite the predictable increase in the rate of inflation to a new plateau (on the order of 35-40 percent per year through 1978), the rate of growth in output in the 1974-79 period was in real terms almost 7 percent -- which is fairly close to the historic rate of growth in the Brazilian economy.

Again, for observers reflecting only on these figures and the evolution of the external accounts, the adjustment to the first oil shock seemed, in late 1978, reasonably well handled. Brazil lost international reserves only in 1974 and 1975.

TABLE 1.7

Value of Fixed Investment in Industrial Projects Approved by the CDI and Gross Fixed Capital Formation, 1970-1982 (in billions of 1981 cruzeiros)

Year	(1) Capital Goods	(2) Basic Inputs	(3) Total (3) = (1)+(2)	(4) Gross Fixed Capital Formation	(5) (5) = (3)/(4) (percent)
1970	7.7	144.4	152.1	2.317	6.6
1971	4.6	108.8	113.4	2.691	4.2
1972	26.5	273.3	299.8	3.018	9.9
1973	29.7	263.1	292.8	3.557	8.2
1974	57.9	456.5	514.4	4.146	12.4
1975	73.6	128.2	202.8	4.172	4.9
1976	28.7	1,112.5	1,141.2	5.090	22.4
1977	64.3	249.4	313.7	5.008	6.3
1978	23.8	181.6	205.4	5.285	3.9
1979	15.0	160.0	175.0	5.511	3.2
1980	4.0	42.0	46.0	5.812	0.8
1981	6.2	124.4	160.6	5.184*	2.5
1982	0.8	101.3	102.1	4.920*	2.1

Source: CDI, *Relatórios* (columns 1 and 2).

* Our estimates are based on a regression equation where the explanatory variables are the production of the construction industry, domestic capital goods production, and machinery and equipment imports.

In the following three years inflows through the capital account more than made up for the chronic current account deficits. International reserves on December 31, 1978 reached a historic high of $11.8 billion. Brazil had balanced its commercial account in 1977 (both imports and exports were around $12 billion), and reduced its current account deficit from $7.1 billion in 1974 to $4.0 billion in 1977. The price of oil remained relatively stable in nominal terms, and therefore dropped sharply in real terms between 1974 and 1977. In 1978 various observers of the international scene and of Brazil's situation were modestly optimistic.

TABLE 1.8

Indices of International Trade and Terms of Trade, 1972-1983
(1977 = 100)

	Exports		Total Imports		Oil Imports		Terms of Trade	
Year	P	Q	P	Q	P	Q	T	EP
1972	41	76	47	70	22	61	87	72
1973	56	80	59	85	28	85	95	82
1974	71	89	91	115	93	87	78	78
1975	71	98	94	109	94	91	76	76
1976	82	99	96	108	96	101	85	88
1977	100	100	100	100	100	100	100	100
1978	92	113	107	105	101	111	86	84
1979	101	124	128	115	135	124	79	81
1980	107	152	164	115	226	107	65	78
1981	101	183	182	99	270	104	55	71
1982	95	67	176	91	261	100	54	68
1983	88	195	166	75	236	91	53	63

Key: P = prices; Q = quantity; T = total; EP = excluding petroleum
Source: Fundação Getúlio Vargas, *Conjuntura econômica* (various issues).

This illusion came to a sudden end with the second oil shock, which raised oil prices from $12 to $30 a barrel between the end of 1978 and the beginning of 1980. This coincided with the dramatic increase in international interest rates, which nearly doubled in this period due to changes in the monetary policy of the United States. The combination of these two external shocks constituted an almost mortal blow to the Brazilian economy, demanding a strategic vision for the 1980s and a coherent economic policy to execute it -- something which unfortunately has not yet happened.

EXTERNAL SHOCKS AND RECESSIONARY ADJUSTMENT, 1979-1983

The second oil shock, the explosion in international interest rates in 1978-80, the world recession over the three year period 1980-82, and the sudden contraction in international credit markets beginning in the third quarter of 1982 all led Brazil to the brink of an exchange collapse in the last four months of 1982. These changes also took Brazil into complex negotiations with the IMF, the principal international creditors, and with the United States government.

At the domestic level the new economic policy makers reacted to the situation with openly expansionist policies in the second half of 1979 and part of 1980. Economic activity remained at relatively high levels over these two years (1979-80; see Tables 1.1 and 1.2). But by the three year period 1981-83 a generalized recession hit the manufacturing industry. Nevertheless, the agricultural sector performed very well, growing by 7 percent in 1981, and this kept the GDP from falling even more that 3.5 percent in that year. In 1982 industry stagnated and continued in recession, while agricultural production fell by 2.5 percent due to poor harvests in coffee and, to a lesser extent, in soy beans. Aggregate production managed to grow by about 1 percent in 1982 thanks to growth in various sectors such as government (6 percent), transportation and communications (4 percent), and banking and finance (4 percent). But in 1983 GDP fell some 3.3 percent due to a negative industrial growth rate of 7 percent. The agricultural sector in turn presented a modest rate of 2.2 percent growth.

Considering the three year recession (1981-83) as a whole, we note that the largest decreases of all industrial groupings were registered in the durable consumer goods and capital goods sectors (see Table 1.2). In the case of consumer durables, the drop came mainly in 1981, while capital goods production suffered in all three years. The production of non-durable consumer goods decreased much less than other sectors: 1.9 percent per year over the three years, with the sharpest drop in 1981. This prevented a larger reduction in overall industrial growth than the average -5.5 percent per year rate that was actually observed.

The most direct origins of the crisis date from immediately after the second oil shock in 1979, in the wake of which domestic inflation took off. The rate of inflation, which had hovered around 35-40 percent since 1974, began to increase dramatically in the first half of 1979 and was up around 80 percent by the end of the year. The new policy adopted in November 1979 of readjusting salaries every six months to compensate for previous losses in real wages gave an added inflationary impulse that was exacerbated by the maxi-devaluation of the cruzeiro against the dollar (30 percent) in December 1979.[14] The rate of inflation accelerated unabated and reached around 100 percent in the middle of 1980, 110 percent by the end of the year, and 120 percent over the period February to May 1981, reflecting the corrective inflation at the close of 1979 and the beginning of 1980. That is, the *rate* of increase in prices tripled in about two years. In the latter part of 1981 inflation decreased, falling to 95 percent in December 1981, and remained at about this level through 1982. With the maxi-devaluation in February 1983 (again of 30 percent), the rate of inflation rose even more, reaching 130 percent in mid-1983 and 210 percent by year's end.

The increase in the inflation rate in 1980 was also related to an increase in the rate of domestic interest due to the imposition of a tax on financial operations, which in turn reflected a defined goal of economic policy.[15] Indeed, the vital necessity to attract external resources (through money loans) in order to equilibrate the balance of payments indicated that it was necessary that the internal rate of interest be greater than the external rate, plus the expected rate of devaluation. This policy was followed despite an enormous increase in the international rate of interest which followed the economic policy of the new Republican administration in the United States, raising the rate of interest charged domestically even higher. Since the Brazilian economy is dominated by oligopolies, the pressures caused by increased financial costs due to increased interest rates were quickly recouped by raising prices, adding additional fuel to the inflationary process. The pressure on interest rates was also reinforced by the "open market" policy of the Central Bank. In order to finance the budgetary deficit, new treasury bills were floated which could be sold only if they carried an interest rate that was competitive with other financial papers.

Nonetheless, since at least 1979 it was recognized that the basic limiting factor to the expansion of the Brazilian economy was the balance of payments crisis, and not the inflationary process. Given the need to increase the trade surplus, economic policy makers adopted the solution of reducing the level of economic activity as a means of constraining imports and increasing exportable surplus. Thus liquidity in the economy contracted sharply in the second quarter of 1980. This monetary squeeze is shown by the fact that the money supply in real terms dropped 29 percent by May 1981 in relation to May 1980. In turn, this monetary squeeze must also have given more impetus to the increse in *domestic* interest rates.

Despite these pressures, evidence is accumulating that given the extent of indexation in the economy, major prices in Brazil were formed independently of current expectations of future aggregate monetary expansion. Salary increases were based on the Index of Consumer Prices, and reflected *past* inflation. Imported raw material prices for any level of international prices depended on the exchange rate. This rate, in turn, depended on mini-devaluations which reflected present inflation. Rents and financial income depended on the evolution of the value of the ORTN (adjustable rate treasury bonds), and also varied according to inflation. As for government administered prices, nothing indicates that these were set according to the goals of monetary policy. They seemed to be based, instead, on past price increases. Hence, given that industrial prices in an economy dominated by oligopolistic firms are set by the addition to direct costs of a mark-up (which does not seem to depend much on demand conditions),[16] monetary policy cannot do much in the short run to affect the course of inflation. And the best predictor of the future rate of inflation is past inflation (aside from possible external shocks), not the monetary policy announced by the government. According to Edmar Bacha:

> "... This point is crucial because it implies that monetary policy in the Brazilian case is incapable of reducing inflationary expectations and, hence, of reducing the rate of inflation in the short run...
>
> "... Strict monetary policy *per se* could only curb inflation by means of a prolonged recession, or as an ex-minister said, 'by means of the purging impact of the lack of demand' which by idling machinery forces businessmen to lower their profit margins, and the mass unemployment induces laid off workers to accept lower wage compensation."[17]

Clearly, the concern of Brazilian policy makers was with external problems, not with inflation. The reaction of the productive apparatus to the monetary contraction which began in 1980 was concentrated in the industrial sector, since the agricultural sector still had access to subsidized credit. As was to be expected, production began to fall towards the end of 1980. Progress in reducing inflation was minimal in 1981 and nil in both 1982 and 1983. The results for the international *commercial* balance, however, were surpluses of about $1.2 billion in 1981, $0.8 billion in 1982, and $6.5 billion in 1983.[18]

It is worthwhile to take note of the timing of the recession, particularly in relation to the manufacturing sector. For the sector as a whole, the annual growth rate of output was on the order of 9 percent between October and December 1980, when the recession began. In February 1982 industrial output was shrinking at an annual rate of nearly 14 percent. In other words, in the 14 months between December 1980 and February 1982, the rate fell from a positive 9.5 percent to a negative 14 percent. This represents an extremely severe contraction. Through the rest of 1982 there was some recuperation, but this resulted in practically no growth at all in December -- stagnation relative to 1981. A slight recuperation occured in mid-1982, but ended in the first quarter of 1983. For this year as a whole the "growth rate" reached a negative 6 percent.

This pattern is almost the same for the subgroups of the industrial sector. Consumer non-durables grew at a rate close to 5 percent up to the end of 1980, but by February 1982 had turned to a negative 2 percent. At the end of 1982 this sector revived slightly to a positive 2 percent, but by the end of 1983 it fell again to a negative 5 percent.

Durable consumer goods, which had been growing at an annual rate of 18 percent at the end of 1980, fell to a negative 28 percent in February, 1982. At the end of 1982 they showed an extremely rapid recuperation -- led by the automotive industry -- reaching a positive growth rate of 8 percent, but by December 1983 they had a regressed to a negative rate of 4 percent. The most severely affected group was the capital goods sector. From rates slightly above 8 percent per year at the end of 1980, production began to fall in the following months to a rate of contraction of 23 percent per year in April/ July, 1982. Recuperation from this point on was much weaker than that of the other sectors. At the end of 1982 the annual rate was still a negative 13 percent, and fell again to a negative 20 percent in December 1983.

It cannot be denied that the industrial recession of 1981-83 had internal roots.[19] On the one hand, there was a drop in public investment due to the termination, suspension or reduction in the construction of several projects inherited from the previous administration, as well as the cost-cutting that characterizes the current phase of austerity. On the other hand, there was an enormous increase in both internal and external interest rates after 1980 that has forced the selection of a small number of profitable investments. Linked to this there was a large expansion of the *financial* investments of the most capitalized firms, and a reduction of the internally generated resources of the most indebted firms. The acceleration of the inflationary process itself could have something to do with discouraging private investment, given the uncertainty that higher rates of inflation would have adverse affects on the expected profitability of investments. No less important, given the weight of personal consumption in total spending, is the reduction in average personal income due to the wage legislation enforced after 1979. Combined with the reduction in the level of employment this contributed to the drop in aggregate demand, thereby deepening the recession.

But in essence, all of these factors, in one way or another, are consequences of the basic structural constraint that confronted the Brazilian economy: the limitation imposed by the strangulation in the external accounts which was reinforced by the second oil crisis, the international recession of 1980-82, and the increase in international interest rates after 1979. The situation through 1983 was not a matter of an "internal demand crisis" as it was in the mid-1960s. The internal equilibrium could not be restored because it ran up against external constraints. Generalized and unplanned idle capacicity in industry could not be utilized until the domestic industrial structure was itself capable of producing the the raw materials and equipment which have up to now been imported. Concerning the internalization of the supply of raw materials and machinery and equipment, it is important to remember that this challenge has already been overcome (and has subsequently re-emerged) more than once in the past. Nevertheless, it is worth stating that this internalization has always occurred due to strong industrial policy incentives, and always in periods of expansion in aggregate demand.

Keeping in mind the roots of the recession outlined above, we should emphasize one element that contributed decisively to the reduction in the rate of industrial growth from the end of 1980: the sudden contraction of liquidity and credit that began in the middle of that year. From that point on monetary authorities imposed a severe control on the expansion of the monetary base. The stock of money (paper money plus demand deposits in commercial banks) shrank drastically in the following quarters, as did loans from the Banco do Brasil and commercial banks to industry. Table 1.9 illustrates the results of this monetary contraction in terms of the money supply, credits to industrial activities, and interest rates (working capital). Credit to industry, generally short term loans for working capital, exhibits a contraction from the last quarters of 1979 up to the middle of 1981. During this period interest rates more than doubled.[20] Credit balances were kept at these low levels all through 1982, and showed another reduction during 1983. Interest rates on working capital loans rose again during this year.[21]

In 1980 factors *internal* to the Brazilian economy forced a change in policy stances. One factor was linked to the effects of the mistaken policy adopted from the end of 1979 to the middle of 1980;[22] in particular the pre-setting of the rates of change for 1980 for the exchange rate (40 percent), and monetary correction 45 percent) in January 1980, when a rate of inflation *at least* equal to that of 1979 (about 80 percent) was foreseen, in part as a consequence of the maxi-devaluation of December 1979.

Inflation in 1980 actually reached 110 percent. The "spread" paid on external loans increased from 0.75 percent to 2 1/8 percent, and the question of short term external debt took on a role of growing importance after June of 1980, in the wake of a radical reorientation in economic policy. This reorientation was intended to restore lost credibility with the international financial community, and aimed at reducing the level of economic activity following the commercial deficits of $2.8 billion in both 1979 and 1980, as well as the losses of international reserves in these two years, which were greater than $6 billion.

TABLE 1.9

Money Supply and Loans to Industry* in Real Terms** and Nominal Interest Rates, Quarterly Evolution from 1979 to 1983 (in billions of 1977 cruzeiros and percent per year)

Year	Qtr.	Money	Index (1980 2nd qtr = 100)	Loans to Industry	Index 1980 2nd qtr = 100)	Interest Rates % yearly
1979	First	263.4	107	222.1	112	62
	Second	259.0	106	219.9	111	64
	Third	256.0	105	218.2	110	61
	Fourth	263.4	107	209.1	105	57
1980	First	242.4	99	199.0	100	58
	Second	245.4	100	198.8	100	77
	Third	220.5	90	183.9	93	92
	Fourth	217.8	89	173.3	87	108
1981	First	184.1	75	159.8	80	145
	Second	175.6	72	162.2	81	141
	Third	167.7	68	166.7	84	142
	Fourth	188.8	77	169.7	85	152
1982	First	168.2	69	164.4	83	151
	Second	158.4	65	160.2	81	149
	Third	149.7	61	157.6	79	161
	Fourth	163.1	66	164.4	83	173
1983	First	144.3	59	161.5	81	171
	Second	131.5	54	155.9	78	191
	Third	112.7	46	129.1	70	182
	Fourth	104.4	43	127.0	64	202 ***

Source: Banco Central do Brasil, *Boletim Mensal* (various issues). For interest rates, unpublished tables from the Central Bank, DIFIN/SEFIN.

* Quarterly average of month end balances. Loans include Banco do Brasil and Commercial Banks.

** Deflated by the General Price Index.

*** Refers to October 1983.

Concern shifted from the medium and long run to an analysis of the cash flow of convertible currency. Monetary authorities had to subtract the short-term liabilities associated with loans made in order to avoid a liquidity crisis from reserves. Brazil's short, medium and long term external debt in 1980 was already over $61 billion, though the official government estimate for long and medium term debt was $53.8 billion. Table 1.10 provides evidence of the deterioration of the international liquidity position between 1978 and 1980.

TABLE 1.10

Gross Reserves, Monetary Authorities' Liabilities, and Net Reserves, December 1978 through December 1980 (in millions of dollars)

	Period	Gross Reserves of Monetary Authorities	Short-Term Liabilities of Monetary Authorities	Net Reserves	Ratio of Net Reserves/ Imports (%)
1978	December	11,895	1,613	10,282	71.1
1979	December	9,688	1,763	7,925	36.1
1980	March	7,951	2,883	5,068	23.1
	June	6,575	3,147	3,428	14.9
	September	6,487	3,329	3,158	13.1
	December	6,912	3,413	3,449	15.4

Source: IMF and the Banco Central do Brasil.

Economic policies implemented from mid-1980 until mid-1982 can be seen as an attempt to "avoid going to the IMF" by means of adopting a recessionary policy that led to a severe reduction in real output in 1981. This was especially sharp, as we have seen, in the industrial sector where the rate of decline was nearly 10 percent in real terms. Three digit inflation continued, due to the well-known mechanisms of indexation. Given the deterioration in the terms of trade and the increase in net income sent abroad, the drop in per capita national income in real terms in 1981 was absolutely unheard of in Brazil's statistically recorded history. What purpose did the recession serve in the midst of inflation in 1981?

The balance of payments situation did actually improve and the trade balance shifted by $4 billion, from a *deficit* of $2.8 billion to a surplus of $1.2 billion, due to a considerable expansion in exports (15 percent) and a reduction of imports (from $23 to $22.1 billion). In the meantime, the *deficit* in the current account was only reduced from $12.4 billion in 1980 to $11.0 billion in 1981, of which $9.2 billion were due to interest payments on the external debt. Inflows through the capital account allowed a slight recuperation in the level of international reserves which increased by about $600 million. The external debt -- including short term debt -- topped $70 billion by the end of 1981.

Encouraged by these external results, the government presented its Plan for the External Sector for 1982. The plan projected a commercial *surplus* of $3 billion (exports of $28 billion and imports of $25 billion), a reduction in current account deficit of $11 billion in 1981 to $10.1 billion in 1982, and an overall equilibrium in the balance of payments without change in the level of international reserves. Once again there was an excess of optimism considering the contraction in world trade (which declined about 2.5 percent in real terms in 1982), the recession in OECD countries where production declined 0.3 percent in real terms, and, beginning in the second quarter of 1982, the contraction in international lending by private banks concerned about their "exposure" in developing countries. This contraction, as is well known, accelerated in the third quarter, reaching a near panic with the Mexican moratorium in August. The situation was further exacerbated by frustration caused by the American posture of relative negligence towards the international financial crisis displayed in the annual meetings of the IMF and the World Bank in September.

For Brazil, this crisis capped a 15 year policy of external indebtedness at fluctuating interest rates which were contracted, at times, without an adequate perception of the vulnerability of the Brazilian economy to unfavorable international conditions. In more than one sense, September 1982 marks an important turning point in the evolution of the external accounts of the Brazilian economy, and the beginning of a process of "voluntary adjustment" marked by renegotiation of the external debt with the banks, and by recourse to the IMF, something that Brazil had tried desperately to avoid two years earlier.

SUMMARY AND CONCLUSIONS: PERSPECTIVES ON THE REST OF THE DECADE

From the analysis of the 15 year cycle 1968-1982 it is possible to extract several lessons. From the period 1968-73 we learn that growth euphoria had its costs, the most serious being the illusion that the secular constraint imposed by the balance of payments on the economy had become a thing of the past, and that the Brazilian economy was destined to reproduce patterns of consumption characteristic of contemporary affluent societies. It is true that the magnitude of the first oil shock, which closed the period at the end of 1973, was unforseeable at the time, but ever since the beginning of the 1970's various observers noted that the patterns of growth and distribution of the period could not have been maintained for the rest of the decade.

From the second period, 1974-78, we learn the lesson that the decision to avoid recession by means of abrupt adjustments to new relative prices and to new and adverse international conditions was essentially correct, yet erred by not perceiving the need for selectivity in investment planning. As in the previous period, it was impossible to foresee the second oil crisis and the shock of increased interest rates that marked the end of this period in 1979. But it was possible to foresee the increase in the vulnerability of the economy to changes in international conditions (even discounting the energy crisis) due to the increase in debt at floating rates of interest.

From the third period, 1979-82, we can extract the general lesson that the performance of 1968-73 cannot be repeated, as well as specific lessons from errors committed in the management of short term economic policy *that lacked both a strategic vision and an adequate examination of international conditions.* Between March and August 1979 one observes the outlines of an attempt to readjust the economy to new international conditions through a deceleration in growth. This orientation was abandoned in August 1979 in favor of an expansionist policy, which in turn was abandoned at the end of 1980 when a long contractionary phase began. It was a recession produced to restore the credibility of Brazil vis-a-vis the international financial community and to avoid having to turn to the IMF. The recession was rendered useless by the disarticulation of the international system of private credit after September 1982. Brazil was then obliged to turn to the IMF to renegotiate its debt with the banks.

This renegotiation was marked by four mistakes. The first was the expectation that international credit markets would quickly return to normal conditions, and resources would again start flowing to Brazil as soon as an agreement was signed with the IMF. The second consisted in the undue haste to arrive at an accord in the belief that it would not be enforced, and that there would be a political decision on the part of the Fund not to demand adherence to the performance criteria originally agreed upon. The third analytical error, related to the first two, was underestimating the amount of new resources that Brazil would need in 1983. The fourth was that the problem of the Brazilian debt, of $86.3 billion on December 31, 1982 (of which nearly $17 billion were loaned for less than a year), could be dealt with in terms of a Gregorian calendar: once the year of 1982 was "closed," then the financial requirements for 1983 could be discussed, and so on into the future.

The lesson of the epilogue (September 1982 to September 1983) is that the arduous process of renegotiation necessarily requires a longer term horizon, a more realistic evaluation of the need for new resources, and a viable and more definite agreement with the IMF and the banks. This agreement must link the transfer of real resources to the rest of the world (through commercial surpluses) to new lending, to the international context, and to the performance of Brazilian exports. It is necessary, desirable and possible to avoid a confrontation, but it is a mistake not to assess the economic and political costs of strict punctuality in the payment of contractual obligations associated with the debt. *Any* solution will have to be negotiated with the blessings of the IMF, with the banks and governments (especially with the United States); but the payment of the debt cannot be allowed to overly compromise the future growth of the Brazilian economy.

This paper is critical of the austerity policy that takes domestic recession as the only solution, waiting until something positive happens in the international arena. As long as the question of Brazil's cash flow in convertible currency is not dealt with satisfactorily through a more comprehensive renegotiation, the space for maneuver in economic policy will be extremely reduced. We need to deal with other issues that are at least as important -- or more so -- as the external debt. One example is the recuperation of public and private investment, without which the inflow of nearly one and a half million new entrants per year into the labor market will not be absorbed.

While we see an inherent potential for growth in the Brazilian economy, we must ask *how much* the long term growth trajectory was reduced by the two successive supply shocks, the reduction in the contribution of external savings, and the apparent increase in the capital/output ratio given the nature of investments undertaken in the 1970s. With what speed will it be possible to return to a long term growth trajectory -- however one defines it? And what is the relationship between output and employment in the economy? What are the prospects for reducing unemployment in the near future?

There are no simple and uncontroversial answers to questions of this type. Nevertheless, preliminary analysis suggests that: a) a long term growth trajectory for the economy -- with investment around 20 percent of output -- is about 5.7 percent annually, and a restoration of the "historic" rate of growth of seven percent would require an increase in the rate of investment to about 25 percent of output; b) working with reasonable rates of growth in output and investment, unplanned idle capacity in the Brazilian economy would be nearly 24 percent in 1984/1985; and c) given the elasticity of employment in relation to output, estimated econometrically at about 0.4, the ratio of employment to the economically active population (EAP) would decline from 98 percent in 1980 to somewhere between 83 and 86 percent in 1986. Just absorbing the annual inflow of new entrants into the workforce requires an average rate of GDP growth of around 6 percent per year, given that the EAP is growing at an annual rate of approximately 2.4 percent.

Despite the recognized precariousness of these calculations, there appears to be no doubt that the Brazilian economy will have to undergo significant modifications in the composition of output and of investment under the threat of an escalation in the already serious problem of urban unemployment, coupled uneasily with an inflation rate absolutely unheard of in Brazil's contemporary history (until 1985: see Chapter 2).

Writing from the perspective of 1983, we stressed the imperative necessity of resolving the problem of the balance of payments as the condition *sine qua non* for overcoming present difficulties. Leaving aside the possibilities of expanding bilateral trade through special agreements, we felt there were only *five* possibilities -- not mutually exclusive -- for confront-ing the situation in the mid-1980s. A reconsideration of the argument is given in Chapter 2.

Two of them have to do with the *uses* of convertible currencies: imports and debt servicing. Three have to do with the principal *sources* of convertible currency: exports, new loans, and direct investment. The reduction of imports caused by a recession will last only as long as the recession. Even those who remember the experience of the 1930's, when the difficulties in importing stimulated domestic industry in the substitution of imports, should keep in mind that we are now talking about a reduction in imports of nearly 50 percent in *real* terms (excluding oil and wheat) between 1980 and 1983. It would be very difficult for this to represent a stimulus of domestic industry in the absence of an industrial policy that merits the name.

As for exports, any serious observer knows that in the current framework the only alternative is to promote exports in any manner possible, bearing in mind the indirect effects of such a policy and the necessity of longer term support policies. Regarding the possiblity of new loans, it is well known that for now the collapse of the international private credit market makes it difficult to count in any significant way on access to this source of funds without special negotiations. The third source, direct investment in Brazil, could take the form of new undertakings or of simple transfer of real assets already existing in the country. The prospective volume of such resources is limited relative to the magnitude of the problem to be resolved. And there are severe political constraints to such a policy.

What is left? Clearly, what is needed is a renegotiation of the terms under which the past debt was contracted, and a rediscussion of the program agreed to with the IMF and the banks. A moratorium will not be necessary, but certainly a more determined and positive posture will be necessary in the next rounds of negotiations on the part of those responsible for economic policy making. What seems certain is that Brazil will have to move towards more comprehensive solutions, negotiated bilaterally and multilaterally, that allow for the resolution of the current exchange strangulation and the progressive return to economic development.

Given the extent of integration of the Brazilian economy with the world economy, it is evident that any discussion of the prospects for the domestic economy in the rest of the decade have to include an assessment of the prospects of world trade and the international economy. Space does not allow an adequate discussion of this issue. But based on the effects of the recovery of the U.S. economy we can anticipate rates of growth in real output in the OECD countries in the range of 3 percent per year, and an expansion in world trade of around 4 to 4.5 percent annually. It is important to put these figures in historical perspective so that we do not delude ourselves by thinking that the good old days will return: between 1960 and 1973 the real output of the OECD countries grew at an annual rate of 5.2 percent in real terms, and international trade expanded at a rate of nearly 9 percent. *Those* good old days are not likely to return in the years remaining to finish out the century. A country like Brazil has no choice but to look ahead and frame a coherent development strategy.

NOTES

1. For the manufacturing industries these rates reached 12.9 and 6.7 percent.

2. See Pedro S. Malan and Regis Bonelli, "The Brazilian Economy in the Seventies: Old and New Developments," in *World Development* January/February, 1977.

3. The system of incentives for capital formation prior to 1972, however, penalized the domestic production of machinery and equipment in favor of imports. This explains the relative delay in the internal production of capital goods (*cf.* Suzigan, *et. al.*, 1974.), and the emphasis upon import substitution of these goods that characterized the administration of economic policy after 1974.

4. The average annual growth rate in agriculture between 1967 and 1970 was only 3 percent, compared to 6.7 percent in the following four year period. The poor performance in the two years 1981-82 was due to poor harvests of coffee and (secondarily) of soybeans.

5. For capital goods the real growth in imports between 1967 and 1974 reached 367 percent, or 24.6 percent annually in real terms. Considering that the annual average growth rate in domestic production of these goods was 18.2 percent, one gets an idea of the acceleration in capital formation in the economy. As for raw materials, a good part of the external purchases in 1974 were purely speculative.

6. See Malan and Bonelli, *op. cit.*, 1977.

7. R. Mundell, "The appropriate use of monetary and fiscal policy under fixed exchange rates," IMF Staff Papers, March 1962.

8. It should be remembered that Brazil's net external debt at the end of 1967 was on the order of $3.3 billion, slightly less than the gross debt since the level of reserves was only $199 million.

9. Richard Cooper, "Comment," in R. Dornbusch and J. Frenkel eds., *International Economic Policy: Theory and Evidence*, (Baltimore, 1979), p.325.

10. However, in 1978 these reserves increased by more than $4 billion due to the overfinancing through the capital account of the current account deficit.

11. Nevertheless, there was little emphasis on pricing policies for petroleum derivatives. In fact, the adjustment of domestic prices did not incorporate the incrase in crude oil prices, and substitution with domestic resources was concentrated principally in alcohol.

12. See W. Suzigan, "Política industrial no Brasil," in *Indústria: política, instituições e desenvolvimento*, IPEA/INPES (1978), for a discussion of industrial policy and the changes it underwent after 1973.

13. A large proportion of the projects consisted of huge

undertakings with lengthy maturation periods. It is also admitted that there was little selectivity in the approval of projects in the face of dificulties in the external sector of the economy that were already visible.

14. The maxi-devaluation of the cruzeiro at the end of 1979 was coupled with the prefixation of the monetary and exchange rate corrections (40 and 50 percent respectively) in the following year. In 1980 the rate of inflation was over 100 percent.

15. In adition, domestic interst rates grew much more than was necessary to attract foreign capital. This was basically due to the prefixation of 1980. Some authors also cite subsidization as a possible cause of higher interest rates. Also see note 20.

16. In fact, the relationship between the industrial mark-up and demand conditions constitutes a subject around which there is no consensus. Some authors defend the conter-cyclical variations hypotheses, while others defend the pro-cyclical variation hypothesis of the mark-up.

17. Edmar Bacha, "Inflação: uma agenda não monetarista," in M.C. Tavares and M.D. David (eds.), *Economia-política da crise*, (São Paulo, 1982).

18. Due to an increase of 16 percent in exports and a small restriction of imports. In fact, this was the largest surplus ever registered, which turned back a deficit of $2.8 billion in 1980. If 1982 had not been an election year, the restriction of imports would have been greater than 12 percent. Exports, in particular, fell nearly 13 percent in 1982 as a result of the world recession. The trade surplus was expected to reach $9 billion for 1984.

19. One observes that the reduction in industrial production -- around 10 percent in 1981 -- occurred despite a large increase in manufactured exports in this year, of about

25 percent in real terms. Already in 1982 these exports were reduced by 10 percent in relation to 1981, while in 1983 they grew 21 percent.

20. According to some observers, the elevation of interest rates is associated with loan expansion ceilings imposed by the government, and also by the compartmentalization of credit: only a fraction of loans are made at the market rate, while most loans are subsidized (as are small and medium sized businesses, agriculture, exports). An increase of the market rates would be a form of compensating for the rates which benefit the other sectors.

21. Nominal market interest rates roughly follow the rate of inflation. The relevant *real* interest rates should refer not to past inflation but to future (or expected) inflation. In this sense, real rates during 1981 were on the order of 20-25 percent. Towards the end of 1982 they became negative, due to the acceleration of inflation in 1983.

22. See P. Malan, "Financial Integration with the World Economy: The Brazilian Case," in R. Ffrench-Davis (ed.), *External Financial Relations and Their Impact on Latin American Economies* (In press).

2

Industrialization and Economic Growth: Current Policy, 1984–1986

Regis Bonelli and Pedro S. Malan

Although the post-1984 Brazilian economy shares many characteristics with the previous period, it has clearly experienced significant change since the crisis of the early 1980s. These changes are discussed below in an attempt to indicate the extent of the shift that took place, and to draw out implications for the near future.

From mid-1984 onward, there was a gradual recovery in the level of economic activity. Industrial output rose by 5.9 percent, mainly due to the production of intermediate goods for export, while consumer durables actually fell by 4.5 percent, and non-durables increased only by a modest 1.2 percent (see Table 2.1). Consumption was still depressed due to continuing real wage reductions, while open unemployment did not diminish as the policy of monetary restraint was maintained.

This renewed growth in output was possible despite a reduction of $1.5 billion in total imports. Moreover, the trade surplus in 1984 reached $13 billion, with the current account representing a surplus of a half a billion dollars (see Table 2.2). Even excluding oil and refined products, the growth rate of imports was virtually zero in real terms, while exports of manufactured products expanded by 27 percent. Although inflation continued at levels slightly above 200 percent per year, it seemed clear that after three years of adjustment some progress had been made.

This adjustment was based on the realignment of relative prices, as witnessed by the large increase in the ratio of the exchange rate to the wage rate, notably since 1982. It was also based on the adoption of expenditure policies that accomplished an unprecedented fall in imports -- nearly 50 percent between 1980 and 1984, excluding oil and wheat -- and a severe reduction of government expenditure resulting in a more than 30 percent decline in gross investment. Real imports of capital goods had fallen by 54 percent between 1981 and 1983, and in 1984 would fall by another 17 percent.

TABLE 2.1

Real Rates of Growth, 1984-1985: Main Sectors

	1984	1985
Gross Domestic Product (GDP)	4.5	8.3
GDP per capita	2.0	5.8
Agriculture and livestock	4.2	8.8
Industry	5.9	9.0
Intermediate goods	6.0	8.5
Capital goods	12.8	12.3
Consumer durables	4.5	15.1
Consumer non-durables	1.2	7.9

Source: FIBGE; Fundação Getúlio Vargas.
Note: In the first half of 1986, the rate of growth of the manufacturing industry was 12 percent, with the following breakdown: intermediate goods (8.7%); capital goods (24.6%); consumer durables (40.5%); consumer non-durables (8.8%).

TABLE 2.2

Balance of Payments: Main Accounts, 1983-1985
(US$ millions)

	1983	1984	1985
Trade Balance	6,470	13,089	12,470
Exports	21,899	27,005	25,639
Imports	(15,429)	(13,916)	(13,169)
Services (Net)	(12,720)	(12,732)	(12,350)
Interest	(9,555)	(10,203)	(9,589)
Other(a)	(3,165)	(2,540)	(2,761)
Transfers	108	171	154
Balance on Current Account	(6,142)	517	275
Capital Account	3,477	6,114	268
Direct Investment	664	1,076	710
Loans(b)	15,124	16,932	12,195
Amortization(c)	(10,061)	(7,816)	(10,533)
Other(d)	(2,250)	(4,078)	(2,104)
Errors and Omissions	(699)	403	(529)
Surplus or Deficit	(3,334)	7,304	13
Reserves	4,563	11,995	11,608
Gross Registered Debt(e)	81,319	91,091	93,511

Source: Banco Central do Brasil, *Relatórios* and "Brasil: programa econômico" 10: February 1980.

(a) Of which profits and dividends represent $796 million in 1984 and $1,140 million in 1985.

(b) Medium and long term.

(c) Of which U.S. $5,656 million (1984) and U.S. $8,138 million (1985) was refinanced through the Paris Club.

(d) Includes short-term capital.

(e) Inclusion of non-registered debt would increase total to $91.6 billion (1983), $99.8 billion (1984), and $100.8 billion (1985).

Although the objective of the adjustment had been to generate trade surpluses large enough to make interest payments on the foreign debt, the recent performance of industry indicates that something else has been accomplished. In 1984, gross domestic product (GDP) growth reached 4.5 percent due to two main factors: agriculture's good performance (+9.5 percent) and the expanded output of manufactured intermediate goods (+10 percent) made possible both by the recovery of the U.S. economy -- once again the principal market for Brazilian exports -- and by the enhanced competitiveness of Brazilian industry. At the end of 1984, however, except for a few export industries, most manufacturing industries still had significant margins of idle capacity.

Growth continued in 1985 and 1986, with GDP growing by 8.5 percent in 1985 and an expected rate of over 7 percent in 1986, but it was based on a different set of factors. In contrast to the recovery of 1984, more recent growth has resulted largely from an expanded domestic market based on real wage gains of 10 percent in 1985 and on increased employment on the order of 1.5 million more jobs. Output in agriculture increased by 12 percent in 1985, and in industry by 8.5 percent, with consumer durables growing 15 percent and non-durables nearly 8 percent. Even higher rates are expected for 1986 as far as industrial production is concerned, but agriculture will lag behind because of droughts in the Center-South. However, investment levels have been modest and recovery has been based on using existing plant capacity. Thus so far it has been a consumption-led recovery. As mentioned above, recent production of capital goods has not yet reached the levels attained in 1980 at the onset of recession.

Perhaps more important than the results achieved domestically is the behavior of the foreign accounts, which in 1985 was clearly favorable: a trade surplus of $12.5 billion, a current account surplus of $275 million, overall equilibrium of the balance of payments, and a reasonable level of reserves. Foreign debt did not increase. Perspectives for 1986 are equally good, for a trade surplus of $13.5 billion is predicted.

Imports continued to fall in 1985, by almost $800 million. Even excluding oil and refined products, nominal imports rose only 5 percent, and about the same is expected for 1986 (although non-oil imports are expected to rise). This is in part a consequence of falling international interest rates, lower oil prices, and the dollar's devaluation.

Keeping in mind that the elasticity of real imports to GDP is on the order of at least 2, the results of the years 1984 to 1986 seem puzzling: real GDP grew nearly 20 percent, while non-oil imports alone rose less than half that rate. Recently, most, if not all, analysts believed that as soon as the recession ended, the growth rate of imports would be far greater than aggregate income growth -- and much higher than predicted by historical elasticities. Clearly, something has changed.

There are two competing views that attempt to explain this puzzle. One of these, widely accepted, emphasizes the role of a favorable exchange rate/wage ratio and the improved competitiveness of Brazilian industries. It should be mentioned here that manufactured goods now represent more than 70 percent of all exports. In addition, recession changed the product mix so that, even excluding the obvious case of crude oil imports, industry now requires less imports per unit of output than before. In short, this first view stresses the role played by the aggressive exchange rate policy after 1982. Before that, recession made for lower imports.

The competing view stresses the consequences of the large projects of import substitution that began in 1974.[1] Being investments of long maturation, only in the early 1980s did these new extractive programs and industrial plants begin to operate. Take for example crude oil, where offshore development accelerated only after 1979. Oil production had stagnated at a level of 170-180,000 barrels per day during 1973-1979, some 15 to 17 percent of consumption. It reached 470,000 barrels per day in 1984 and is expected to be higher than 600,000 in 1986. Alcohol is another case in point: the pro-alcohol program was created in 1975 but only gained momentum after 1979. The same can be said for coal.

The same argument is made for manufacturing industries as well. Beginning in 1974, high investment rates in a small group of high technology and capital intensive industries aimed for intense import substitution. The results began to appear early in the 1980s in the form of a surprising improvement in the balance of payments, an improvement which according to this view cannot otherwise be attributed to the recessionary economic policy. The examples given are industries such as non-ferrous metals, chemicals, steel products, paper and pulp, and fertilizers. Imports of these goods did in fact decrease by 60 percent between 1980 and 1983.

Proponents of this view say that contrary to conventional wisdom, the economy did not face only two choices after the first oil shock -- financing through additional external borrowing or adjustment. They maintain that a third choice was actually followed, and this was structural change through import substitution. Instead of postponing urgent problems, the military government in fact attacked them. Thus, the government made extensive use of incentives to stimulate investment in highly capital-intensive projects such as energy, basic (strategic) inputs, and capital goods. More than just a demonstration of political will, the Second National Development Plan of 1974 was a strategy of structural change that was economically rational and laid the foundations for a promising future.

According to this view, the expansion of productive capacity that resulted from the so-called "large sectoral programs" of the second half of the 1970s reached its peak in 1983-84. This timing could not have been better. The foreign exchange savings made possible by import substitution in crude oil and the five product groups mentioned above are estimated to be on the order of $7.4 billion in 1984, 60 percent of which was in oil. As for capital goods, the estimate is $2.2 billion. This means that other things being equal, the trade surplus for that year would have been only $3.5 billion and not $13.1 billion, the actual total, had import substitution not taken place.[2]

We believe that both these views contain elements of truth in explaining the adjustment process still in progress.

Aggressive devaluation of the exchange rate and the realignment of relative prices *did* make for cheaper and more competitive exports. Import substitution investment -- however costly in domestic and foreign resources -- *does* help to explain why real imports have not increased as growth resumed in 1984. The fact that both views exaggerate certain aspects does not detract from their explanatory power, in combination.

A source-of-growth approach may help to clarify the discussion. Industrial output grew by 42 percent between 1974 and 1980. About 77 percent of this increase is explained by expanded domestic demand: in fact, exports accounted for 14 percent and import substitution for only 8 percent. But industrial output decreased by nearly 17 percent between 1980 and 1983. Contraction of domestic demand caused 138 percent of this decrease, but the effect was partially offset by a contribution of 22 percent due to the growth of exports and of 16 percent due to import substitution.

These estimates suggest that non-oil import substitution clearly represented a relevant source of growth, but certainly less than what the proponents of the "post-1974 import substitution" view are willing to accept. As for crude oil, their view seems correct, although no measure of the cost has been provided. And as we know, a strategy cannot be evaluated only by reference to its benefits. In assessing the merits of the "recession and aggressive devaluation" view, one must realize that any attempt at analyzing the adjustment process without reference to previous import substitution is biased. It lacks a longer term perspective. Furthermore, such attempts serve better to explain the growth of exports than the reduction of imports. This is why an adequate explanation of the adjustment and return to growth must combine some elements of both views. This combination of views[3] is important because the consideration of the requirements for sustaining the present recovery is leading to a lively debate about the appropriate industrial and trade policies now to be followed by Brazil.

In 1986 however, the return to growth is occurring under the aegis of a new stabilization program -- the so-called

Cruzado Plan -- the initial results of which are favorable, with inflation running at an accumulated 4.5 percent in the Plan's first five months. The Cruzado Plan is based on a number of measures coupled with a hypothesis on the character of recent Brazilian inflation.*

The first measure was to freeze all prices of goods and services at the levels of February 27, 1986, although there had been some adjustments since then, some higher and some lower. Another basic measure was to convert all salaries (and prices) by the average of their real values since the last readjustment, as a way to synchronize salaries and prices. It was then widely believed that inflation had taken on a preponderantly inertial character: owing to indexation, and in the absence of shocks, to the fact that current inflation tended to reproduce past inflation. Given current conditions (and with high agricultural prices, for example) it was not necessary to have a maxi-devaluation of the exchange

---

* Editors' note: Skyrocketing consumer demand for such things as consumer durables, meat and other items on the export list threatened to reduce drastically Brazil's export earnings in the last semester of 1986. To dampen this demand the Sarney government, fresh from electoral victories across the board, in November 1986 raised taxes on automobiles and fuel, among other items. The so-called Cruzado Plan II hit the middle classes hard, and led to widespread protests coupled with renewed demands to reduce interest payments on the foreign debt in order to protect necessary investment for economic growth. To stem the hemorrhaging of reserves, in February 1987 Brazil declared a moratorium on interest payments on the commercial debt, a move that was also designed to give the Sarney team maneuvering room in its dealings with the new Constituent Assembly. As this book goes to press, Brazilian economic policy-making is in disarray and the Sarney presidency, having reaped major political benefits from the initial success of the Cruzado Plan, has yet to master the new policy environment created by its flawed implementation.

rate, or an increase in government administered prices. Moreover, the synchronization of salaries was accompanied by an 8 percent bonus to wageholders, and a 15.5 percent increase in the minimum wage. Unemployment insurance was also created, along with a "trigger" mechanism that would readjust wages automatically if inflation reached 20 percent before one year. There was also an automatic adjustment of wages in the proportion of 60 percent of accumulated inflation at the base-date of wage contracts, when wage increases would be freely negotiated. The upshot is a program which, in concept, is essentially neutral in terms of income distribution, and which does not compromise economic growth. In addition, it bolsters confidence in Brazilian capacity to formulate and implement a stabilization program without foreign interference.

Although present worries are concentrated on the problems involved in the implementation of the Cruzado Plan, three basic issues affecting future growth loom large on the agenda. First, there is the critical problem of financing structural public deficits which, albeit under control, may reach 3 to 5 percent of GDP in 1986 and 1987. Second, there is the fact that no permanent solution for the external debt has yet been found, although perspectives seem to have become less pessimistic with recent balance of payments results. Third, and perhaps most important, are questions about the low levels of investment. How are we to finance a rate of gross capital formation of some 23 percent of GDP, the rate it would take to return the country to its long-run growth trajectory of 6 to 7 percent per year? After the recession, the rate of gross capital formation has remained between 16 and 17 percent of GDP. In addition, we know that recent investment has been aimed at modernizing industrial plants rather than adding to productive capacity.

From the point of view of financing, in the early 1970s the share in total investment was, in percentages, 69 percent from the private sector, 23 percent from government, and 8 percent from foreign savings. (This overstates private savings because in the National Accounts state enterprises are part of the private sector.) After 1974 the share of foreign savings increased at the expense of government savings. If foreign savings accounted for 27 percent in 1982 while the government's share slipped to 2 percent, in 1983 foreign savings were nearly zero while government savings were negative. Currently, both sources of savings are negligible. Even state enterprises have had their savings restricted both by price controls and by interest payments on the foreign debt.

It will be difficult to re-establish investment rates on the order of magnitude deemed necessary to put the economy back on its long-term growth path. It is believed that the Cruzado Stabilization Plan will create an environment favorable to the resumption of higher rates of private investment. But in the short run it is unlikely that the private sector by itself would be capable of bringing the ratio of investment to GDP to over 20 percent. This increase in the investment rate -- and the efficiency with which investment, public and private, is undertaken -- may be the greatest challenge facing the Brazilian economy during the rest of this decade and well beyond.

NOTES

1. See A.B. Castro and F.E. Pires de Souza, *A economia brasileira em marcha forçada*, (Rio de Janeiro, 1985).

2. *Ibid.*

3. As in Albert Fishlow, "A Tale of Two Presidents: The Political Economy of Brazilian Adjustment to the Oil Shocks." Working Paper, Department of Economics, University of California, Berkeley. February, 1986.

3

Industrialization, Employment, and Stratification in Brazil

Carlos A. Hasenbalg and Nelson do Valle Silva

In the context of rapid structural change that took place in Brazil from 1968-1980, the transformation of employment patterns by job sector was especially significant in social terms. The redistribution of the economically active population (EAP) among various sectors can be attributed to two basic factors: the high rates of economic growth that characterized the period, and the accelerated pace of urbanization that shifted the work force out of the primary sector and into industry and services. These changes had multiple implications for work relations, and included new roles for women, a reordering of class relations, and changes in patterns of income distribution. Patterns of social stratification were also transformed with respect to social mobility, a subject to which this chapter will turn after first discussing the structural transformation of employment.

INDUSTRIALIZATION AND THE STRUCTURE OF EMPLOYMENT

Despite the strong cyclical oscillations that characterized the Brazilian economy in the period 1960-1980, there is no doubt that the overall balance sheet of economic growth was clearly positive. While relatively stagnant in the period 1962-1967, the economy maintained an average annual growth rate of 3.7 percent in its gross domestic product (GDP).

In 1968 the country began a phase of rapid economic expansion that would last until 1974 -- the "miracle" years. In this period real GDP grew at an annual average of 11.2 percent, led by an industrial sector that expanded at an average annual rate of 12.7 percent. Between 1975 and 1979, although in a phase of cyclical decline, the economy continued growing at annual rates of 6 to 7 percent (see Chapter 1).

In the 1960s Brazil became a predominantly urban country. In 1960 the 38.6 million inhabitants of rural areas constituted 55.1 percent of the total population. Between 1960 and 1970 the rural population continued growing in absolute terms to 41 million, but by 1970 it represented only 44.1 percent of the total population. In the following decade the pace of urbanization was even more rapid. The rural population declined both in absolute terms, falling to 38.6 million, and in relative terms, representing but 32.4 percent of the total population in 1980.

The relationship between the growth of the economically active population (EAP) and the total population changed dramatically in the period under review. In the 1960s, when demographic growth reached average annual rates of 2.89 percent, and economic growth was slower than it would be in the 1970s, the total population grew more rapidly (32 percent) than the EAP (29.9 percent). In the 1970s, which were characterized by a decline in demographic growth (to annual averages of 2.49 percent) and more rapid economic growth, the inverse phenomenon occurred: the EAP grew by a substantially larger proportion (48.1 percent) than did the total population (27.8 percent). Although the EAP includes the unemployed, people who are seeking work for the first time, and the difficult-to-quantify category of the underemployed, these figures lead to the conclusion that the 1970s generated more jobs, particularly in the urban sectors of the economy.

Before analyzing in greater detail the redistribution of employment among the various sectors of economic activity, it is appropriate to present an overall picture, based on the classical distinction among primary, secondary and tertiary sectors. The proportional distribution of the EAP among these sectors for 1960, 1970 and 1980 is given in Table 3.1.

TABLE 3.1

Distribution of Economically Active Population by Sector, 1960-1980

	1960	1970	1980
Primary	54.0	44.3	29.9
Secondary	12.9	17.9	24.4
Tertiary	33.1	37.8	45.7
Total	100.0	100.0	100.0

Source: FIBGE, Tabulações Avançadas do Censo Demográfico 1980, I, Tomo 2.

These figures indicate substantial decline in the primary sector (agriculture) over the past two decades, manifesting a 9.7 percent loss between 1960 and 1970, and an even larger share of the workforce, 14.4 percent, between 1970 and 1980. By 1970 this sector was absorbing the greater share of the EAP, but by 1980, when its relative share fell to approximately 30 percent, it lost this place to the tertiary sector (services). In absolute terms, the EAP of the primary sector still experienced a slight growth between 1960 and 1970, going from 12.3 million people to 13.1 million but then it stopped growing, ending up in 1980 at practically the same level as in 1970.

The secondary sector (manufacturing) grew most rapidly in relative terms, almost doubling its share between 1960 and 1970. In this period it absorbed a little more than half of the proportional reduction of the EAP in the primary sector. In absolute numbers, employment in the secondary sector increased 80.1 percent between 1960 and 1970, and doubled between 1970 and 1980, growing from approximately 2.9 million in 1960, to 5.3 million in 1970, and 10.7 million in 1980.

Finally, the tertiary sector, which absorbed a third of the workforce in 1960, expanded consistently until it included 45.7 percent of the EAP in 1980. In absolute numbers the tertiary sector included 7.5 million individuals in 1960, 11.5 million in 1970 and 20 million in 1980, which means a growth of 48.3 percent in the 1960s and 79.1 percent between 1970 and 1980.

Data in Table 3.2 allow us to analyze the trends of employment by subsectors of the secondary and tertiary labor force. Regarding the latter sector, we will adopt the distinction introduced by Paul Singer between production services (retail and wholesale trade, real estate and securities, credit insurance and finance, and transportation and communications), individual consumption services (personal services) and collective consumption services (public administration and social services).[1]

Contradicting pessimistic perspectives concerning the low capacity of the industrial sector to absorb growing numbers of workers in the peripheral capitalist countries, the secondary sector in Brazil is the area that has showed the greatest dynamism in the generation of new jobs. Between 1960 and 1970, manufacturing increased its relative share of employment from 8.6 percent to 11 percent, reflecting a gross increase of 66 percent in the number of people employed. In the next decade the pace of expansion accelerated, and the number of those employed in this sector nearly doubled, inreasing its relative share to 15.7 percent of the workforce. In the 1960s the expansion of employment in the manufacturing sector was due primarily to the dynamism of modern industries. In fact, between 1960 and 1970 the number of workers in occupations directly linked to production in traditional industries (textiles, leather, wood and furniture, foods, ceramics and glass) increased only slightly from 1,599,805 to 1,655,745. In the 1970s, together with the continued growth of employment in the modern industries, there was a rejuvenation of employment in those traditional industries, where the number of workers linked to production grew to 2,865,559, an increase that seems to have corresponded to the heightened pace of economic growth and to the expansion of demand in urban markets.

TABLE 3.2

Activities of Economically Active
Persons Ten Years of Age or Older, 1960-1980

	1960		1970		1980	
	N	%	N	%	N	%
Agriculture, Vegetal Extraction, Fishing	12,276,908	54.0	13,087,521	44.3	13,109,415	29.9
Manufacturing Industries	1,954,187	8.6	3,241,861	11.0	6,858,598	15.7
Construction Industries	781,247	3.4	1,719,714	5.8	3,151,094	7.2
Other Industrial Activities	204,808	0.9	333,852	1.1	665,285	1.5
Wholesale and Retail Trade	1,478,270	6.5	2,247,493	7.6	4,111,307	9.4
Transportation and Communications	977,345	4.3	1,167,866	3.9	1,815,541	4.1
Personal Services	3,028,933	13.3	3,925,001	13.9	7,089,709	16.2
Social Services	755,043	3.3	1,531,563	5.2	3,044,909	7.0
Public Administration	712,904	3.1	1,152,341	3.9	1,812,152	4.1
Other Activities	580,383	2.6	1,150,012	3.9	2,138,753	4.9
EAP TOTAL	22,750,028	100.0	29,557,224	100.0	43,796,763	100.0

Source: Same as Table 3.1.

The construction industry, where the number of employees increased most rapidly, quadrupled the number of people employed during the two decades, going from a 3.4 percent to a 7.2 percent relative share of the EAP. This industry, whose rapid growth is linked to the increasing urban population, to the establishment of the financial System for Housing (Sistema Financeiro da Habitação) and to the expansion of public works, maintained an average salary close to the minimum wage and may have played an important role in the incorporation of male migrants of rural origins into the labor market.

The rapid pace of industrialization and economic growth, which deepened the process of the social division of labor, leads us to expect a relative increase of employment in production services. In fact, this did occur in wholesale and retail trade but not in transportation and communications.

With respect to wholesale and retail trade, it should be noted that employment grew at a pace a good deal higher than the total EAP, increasing its relative share from 6.5 percent in 1960 to 7.6 percent in 1970, and 9.4 percent in 1980. It could be argued that the sector is heterogeneous and that not all of the employment generated in this sector is a result of economic development, since large numbers of people are involved in trade of low productivity who do not manage to enter the capitalist labor market. This was unquestionably the case in 1960, when 43.7 percent of those who were working in this sector did so on their own or without remuneration. However, this form of underemployment or disguised unemployment declined considerably between 1970 and 1980, as the contingent of self-employed and unpaid workers fell from 42.7 percent to 30.8 percent, consequently increasing the proportion of jobs in the formal labor market.

Instead of growing, the transportation and communications sector maintained a stable position in its relative share of employment -- about 4 percent -- during the period studied. A look at the quantitive evolution of the occupations of this sector demonstrates that this relative stability of employment resulted from divergent tendencies among activities. While the more recently established activities, such as air transport, urban and highway transport, and communications showed considerable increases in the number of people employed, the more traditional activities, corresponding to the period of agro-export growth, experienced a stagnation or even an absolute decline in the employed. This is the case for maritime and river transport, as well as port and railroad services.

The employment behavior of the remaining production services (real estate trade and securities, credit institutions, insurance and finance) cannot be observed directly because they are included in the residual category of "other activities." Still, it is not difficult to imagine that a good portion of the rapid growth of the proportion of persons employed in these "other activities" is due to the expansion of employment in those services.

Individual consumption services, represented by the sector of personal services, can be considered "traditional" services, in the sense that they predate the process of industrialization and economic development. As Browning and Singelman point out, despite the relative heterogeneity of the sector, all of its activities have in common an orientation toward the individual consumer. In this sense the demand for personal services is more dependent on the income of individuals than social or collective consumption services.[2]

In countries like Brazil it is to be expected that this sector would have a substantial relative share in the total of the active population, among other reasons because of the extent of domestic employment. In fact, the provision of personal services absorbed 13.3 percent of the total EAP in 1960 and 1970, rising to 16.2 percent in 1980. However, the share of the provision of personal services within the tertiary sector is declining: it represented 40.2 percent of the tertiary sector in 1960, 34.1 percent in 1970 and 35.4 percent in 1980. Moreover, its growth in relative share of the EAP between 1970 and 1980 results in part from a reclassification of occupations in the 1980 census, which counted in this category doormen, watchmen and janitors, who had all been previously included in "other occupations." Eliminating these occupations to maintain comparability with previous censuses, the proportional share of personal services in the tertiary sector in 1980 would fall to 28.9 percent. With respect to domestic employment, the 947,000 people so employed in 1960 represented 31.3 percent of the personal services sector and 4.2 percent of the total EAP; this figure grew to 1,697,000 people in 1970, constituting 43.2 percent of the personal services sector and 5.7 percent of the total EAP, going to 2,396,000 people in 1980, which amounts to 33.8 percent of the sector and 5.4 percent of the total EAP. The continuing existence of a huge contingent of domestic servants in Brazil, in contrast to the historical tendency of the advanced capitalist countries, indicates that this sector represents an important mechanism for the insertion into the labor market of women with low educational and professional qualifications, performing a function similar to that of the civil construction sector for men. Paid domestic workers were the occupational group employing the largest proportion of women (fluctuating in this period between 19 percent and 27 percent of economically active women). For those familiar with the conditions of domestic service in Brazil, it would not be difficult to find lines of historical continuity between the domestic slavery of the past and the present situation. The difference is, however, that domestic service today increasingly assumes the subsidiary function of easing the entry of women into higher socioeconomic positions.

Collective consumption services, particularly social services (education and health) have been defined as "new services" in the sense that their mass consumption is something relatively recent. Notwithstanding the differential access to social services on the part of different socioeconomic groups, we presume that the consumption of these services depends less and less on the individual capacity to pay for them.[3]

The tendency in the period under analysis was for a relative increase of employment in collective consumption services, particularly in the case of social services, which, along with civil construction is the sector that grew most rapidly. It quadrupled in number of people employed and increased its relative share of the EAP from 3.3 percent in 1960 to 7 percent in 1980.

The expansion of employment in public administration reflects the growth of the regulatory functions of the state in social and economic life. The public administration sector (which includes only direct public administration and national defense) grew at a faster pace than did the total EAP, but only gained one percentage point in its relative share of employment, going from 3.1 percent in 1960 to 4.1 percent in 1980. That people employed in the state and mixed enterprises are not included in the sector means that the generation of employment as a result of state intervention in the economy is thereby underestimated.

Summarizing the evolving trends of the tertiary sector as a whole, it can be seen that it not only consistently increased its share of employment during the period studied, but also changed its internal structure, the share of production services and collective consumption services increasing at the expense of individual consumption services. The evidence relating to the tertiary sector in the 1970s confirms the conclusions reached by Paul Singer in relation to the period prior to 1970:

> "... The accentuated growth in the relative share of the tertiary sector can be explained in part by the structural transformations resulting from development. There is no sense in regarding the relative growth of the tertiary sector *a priori* as 'proof' that it is tending to become ever more 'bloated,' in the sense that a large part of this increse in employment occurs in areas that are socially unproductive (domestic service) or of very low productivity (street vending, personal services). Unless data becomes available to confirm this tendency, the increase in employment in the tertiary sector can only be regarded as the expected outcome of development.[4]

It should be noted that these changes in the structure of employment are accompanied by important modifications in the relations of production. Some indications of this can be gleaned from the distinction that demographic censuses make among various positions in the employment of economically active persons.

For the labor force as a whole, there was a rapid expansion of capitalist relations of labor, as indicated by the proportion of employees in the total work force. In this sense, employees, who represented less than half of the EAP (47.9 percent) in 1960, increased their relative share to 54.8 percent in 1970, and constituted fully two thirds (66.7 percent) by 1980. This global process of extending capitalist relations of labor conforms, in large measure, to the urbanization of the occupational structure of the country and to the rapid relative decline, in terms of employment, of the primary sector, where the largest contingents of self-employed and unpaid workers are concentrated.

Traditionally, Brazilian agriculture has been characterized by its low degree of mechanization and the presence of archaic forms of labor relations. The fact that slightly more than 70 percent of rural workers in 1960 and 1970 were self-employed or unpaid is indicative. At the same time, the development of capitalist and mechanized agriculture in the most recent period has not been translated into any great capacity of the primary sector to absorb labor. In fact, in the 1970s alone changes of some importance occurred in the relations of production in agriculture, as indicated by the decline of self-employed and unpaid workers to a 58 percent share and the increase of employees, between 1970 and 1980, from 25.4 percent to 38.4 percent respectively.

With respect to urban economic activities, these were already predominantly capitalist in 1960, when employees constituted 74 percent of the urban active population. In the next two decades, the predominantly capitalist character of the urban labor market became more pronounced, the proportion of employees increasing to 78.1 percent in 1970 and 79.1 percent in 1980. Throughout the whole period there was a relative decline of self-employed and unpaid workers from 23.5 percent to 17.7 percent. Finally, it is interesting to note that in the 1970s a considerable increase occurred in small businesses, mainly in retail and wholesale trade and in personal services, as indicated by an increase in the number of urban employers from 236,000 in 1970 to 780,000 in 1980.

Also important in the overall modifications in the structure of employment was the evolving administrative and scientific-technical component. Table 3.3 shows the relative share of administrative occupations (distinguishing the subgroups that make them up, namely, proprietors, administrators, and bureaucratic and office functionaries) and technical, scientific and related occupations within the total economically active population.

TABLE 3.3

Administrative, Technical, and Scientific Occupations as Percentage of Total Economically Active Population, 1960-1980

	1960	1970	1980
Administrative occupations	8.0	10.1	12.3
Proprietors	(3.8)	(4.0)	(2.5)
Administrators	(0.5)	(1.3)	(1.8)
Bureaucratic and office functionaries	(3.7)	(4.8)	(8.0)
Technical, scientific and related occupations	3.1	4.7	6.8
Other occupations	88.9	86.2	80.9
TOTALS	100.0	100.0	100.0

Source: Same as Table 3.1.

With the partial exception of the proprietors, it should be noted that these two groups of occupations can be seen as a proxy for the middle occupational strata or for the so-called new middle class. They grew continually from a limited initial level in 1960 (11.1 percent), reaching a much larger share (19.1 percent) by 1980. As a consequence of the expanding state functions, the concentration of capital and the growing weight of large public and private enterprises there has been, among the administative occupations, a decline in the relative share of proprietors and a very rapid growth in the group of administrators, whose proportional share more than tripled during the period. Routine bureaucratic occupations and scientific and technical occupations grew rapidly as well, more than doubling their proportional share between 1960 and 1980. In order to have a precise idea of the quantitative expansion of these administrative and scientific-technical occupations, one notes that those occupying such jobs grew from 2.5 million in 1960 to 8.2 million in 1980.

As for changes in the class structure, we noted above the tendency for those engaged in simple commodity production and other self-employed workers to be incorporated into the ambit of wage labor. To this tendency we can now add another, consisting of the bureaucratization of labor through the growth of an increasingly differentiated stratum of administrators and bureaucrats interposed between those who hold or control capital, and workers directly linked to production.

The last dimension of the evolution of employment over these two decades consists of the rates of participation of the economically active population by sex and age groups. The pertinent data are found in Table 3.4. As Maria Helena F.T. Henriques observes in relation to the evolution of economically active men:

> "... For males the tendency corresponds to that historically observed in the societies of the developed capitalist world. That is, there is a clear withdrawal over time from economic participation for the two youngest age groups (10-14 and 15-19). On the other hand, the modal point of the curve

> is located at a younger age and the curve as a whole has become more concentrated. For ages greater than 50 years old, the phenomenon of withdrawal can also be observed, although on a lesser scale than at the lower limits of the distribution. The acceleration of urbanization in large part explains this occurrence."[5]

It is in the economic participation of women that the most remarkable changes have occurred during the twenty-year period considered here. During the 1960s there was a slight increase in the rates of activity in all age groups up to 29 years old (though the rate for the 15-19 age group declined slightly), with the largest increment in the rate of activity, almost 9 percent, occurring in the 20-24 age group. However, it was in the 1970s that the great increase in the economic participation of women occurred. In fact, the growth in the rates of activity can be seen in all age groups up to 69 years old. The most significant fact is that the age groups between 20 and 49 showed a growth that fluctuated between 10 percent and 14 percent. As Henriques observes:

> "... The expected bi-modal distribution that is common for the participation of women in capitalist societies does not occur in the Brazilian case. The present curve is higher and more concentrated than the previous ones and reflects an enormous increase in the economic activity of women during the last decade.[6]

This entrance *en masse* of women into the work force has meant that the female EAP as a proportion of the total EAP has grown from 17.9 percent in 1960 to 20.9 percent in 1970 and 27.5 percent in 1980. For these same years, the female share of the non-agricultural EAP has grown from 26.6 percent to 29.8 percent and 33.6 percent respectively.

TABLE 3.4

Specific Rates of Participation by Gender
and Age Groups, 1960-1980
(as percentage of age class)

Age Groups	Men 1960	Men 1970	Men 1980	Women 1960	Women 1970	Women 1980
10-14	26.28	19.16	19.95	5.61	6.36	8.37
15-19	81.09	62.19	64.92	25.74	24.45	31.36
20-24	90.77	88.65	90.50	19.84	28.67	38.50
25-29	98.55	94.28	96.34	22.00	22.77	36.32
30-34	98.47	96.91	95.92	17.19	21.16	35.14
35-39	95.80	95.38	94.50	16.65	20.39	34.20
40-44	97.21	93.92	90.50	16.83	20.28	31.70
45-49	94.77	92.33	85.00	16.16	18.67	28.50
50-54	94.39	87.80	84.00	15.12	16.52	24.50
55-59	89.94	82.61	77.00	13.76	14.19	18.90
60-64	95.14	73.54	64.90	14.40	11.37	13.50
65-69	62.89	62.71	51.50	6.33	8.77	13.00
70-74	48.05	47.05	36.50	5.50	7.50	4.90
75-79	33.00	30.00	21.50	5.00	4.50	2.50
80 +	11.00	11.00	8.50	2.10	1.80	1.00

Sources: Maria Helena F. da T. Henriques, *Considerações sobre a evolução da população economicamente ativa no Brasil: 1940-1970*, December 1979 mimeo, p. 9, Table 5; IBGE; and same source as Table 3.1.

What remains to be shown is a breakdown of occupations occupied by this contingent of women who have been incorporated into the work force. Table 3.5 presents the sectoral structure of employment for economically active women between 1960 and 1980.

The first finding is that the redistribution of women among the various sectors of activity closely corresponds to the transformations of the overall structure of employment. One of the most significant changes lies in the rapid decline of the relative share of women in the primary sector, which decreased from 30.1 percent in 1960 to 14.8 percent in 1980. In industrial activities, where there was a drop in the relative share of women in the 1960s (from 12.1 percent to 10.3 percent), the opposite phenomenon occurs in the following decade. The relative share of women increases 4.9 percent and in absolute terms the increase in the number of women employed in industry is related to the rejuvenation of employment in traditional industries (for example, the number of women in the apparel industry grew from 422,000 to 857,000), to the increase in the number of women employed as bureaucratic and administrative functionaries, and to a small increase of female employment in some modern industries, such as electronics.

The tertiary sector constitutes the principal source of employment for women, absorbing 57.8 percent of them in 1960, 69.3 percent in 1970 and 70 percent in 1980. Within the tertiary sector itself important modifications in the structure of female employment have taken place. In personal services, the sector that has the greatest proportion of women, a slight increase in the relative share occurred in the 1960s (from 36.3 percent to 38.8 percent) and a drop to 33.8 percent in 1980. In production services, the female share increased rapidly, especially in retail and wholesale trade, where it grew from 4.2 percent in 1960 to 10 percent in 1980. Equally rapid has been the growth of the relative share of women in collective consumption services, most notably in social services, where this participation increased from 10.4 percent in 1960 to 18.4 percent in 1980.

TABLE 3.5

Sector of Activity of Economically Active Females
Ten Years of Age or Older, 1960-1980

	1960		1970		1980	
	N	%	N	%	N	%
Agriculture, Vegetal Extraction and Fishing	1,228,340	30.1	1,257,659	20.4	1,732,961	14.8
Industrial Activities	493,986	12.1	653,892	10.3	1,789,025	15.2
Retail and Wholesale Trade	170,831	4.2	370,387	6.0	1,169,721	10.0
Personal Services	1,479,457	36.3	2,389,508	38.8	3,975,940	33.8
Transportation and Communications	41,805	1.0	61,735	1.0	144,710	1.2
Social Services	424,055	10.4	987,689	16.0	2,157,911	18.4
Public Administration	80,550	2.0	160,194	2.6	382,094	3.2
Other Activities	157,837	3.9	302,383	4.9	394,489	3.4
TOTAL	4,076,861	100.0	6,165,447	100.0	11,746,851	100.0

Source: FIBGE, Tabulações Avançadas do Censo Demográfico, 1980, I, Tomo 2.
Note: The total number of women in the EAP in 1980 excludes 292,078 who were looking for work.

Although there still exists a high degree of vertical and horizontal occupational segregation, the growing technical division of labor, through the generation of new occupational positions, has led to a better distribution of the female work force in the occupational structure and to a decline in the concentration of women in specific groups of occupations. It is sufficient to note here some of the tendencies in this direction. The relative share of the female EAP in administrative occupations increased from 8.2 percent in 1960 to 15.4 percent in 1980. It should be emphasized that this increase, both in relative and absolute terms, occurred principally in subordinate positions, that is, among bureaucratic and office functionaries. Within the technical and scientific occupations, the proportion of women in two sexually typed occupations, namely, elementary and secondary teachers and nurses, declined by 10 percent. At the same time, the number of women in more prestigious professions (such as medicine, law, higher education, engineering) increased from 19,000 in 1970 to 95,800 in 1980. There was also a decline in the proportion of women employed in the textile and apparel industries among those employed in industry and a decline in the proportion of domestic servants among the women employed in personal services. Clearly, women have not only tended to achieve a better distribution in the occupational structure, but have also been abandoning those sectors that absorb the least qualified and worst paid work force in order to enter in growing proportions into industry and modern services.

From these tendencies, it is plausible to suggest the possibility of a differentiation in female labor markets: while poorly educated women from the popular classes tend to concentrate in personal services and production line jobs, better educated middle class women gravitate toward production services and collective consumption services. This improvement in employment opportunities and the great increase in female employment stems from the rapid opening of jobs in the occupational structure and from the modernization of the Brazilian economy. These transformations have a positive side, but there is a less optimistic side as well. Due to income concentration and the resulting fall in the wages of heads of low-income families, it is quite likely that part of the incorporation of women into the labor market flows from the compelling necessity to supplement family budgets.

Reviewing the main changes in the employment structure, we have seen how employment in the primary sector of the economy has decreased rapidly at the same time that the employment in industry and in modern services has increased at a rapid pace. In addition, a tendency for the decline of the proportion of self-employed and unpaid workers has been shown. These tendencies have been interpreted as implying a qualitative improvement in the conditions of labor in developing countries to the extent that they represent a displacement of people from employment of low productivity and low pay to other, better paid and more productive jobs.[7]

In the Brazilian case, these positive implications of development have been neutralized, in large measure, by the concentration of income and by the state's inadequate provision of collective consumption goods and services that are required by a rapidly growing urban population.[8] Without even considering the effects of the serious economic crisis the country underwent from 1980-1984, it is enough to mention the ways in which living conditions of low-income urban strata were deteriorating *before* the crisis. The list includes an increase in infant mortality during a good part of the 1970s, a rapid increase in work-related accidents (both at work and on the way to work), a deterioration and insufficient growth of the urban transportation infrastructure, a growing housing shortage and the on-going problems of basic sanitation, the persistence of high student drop-out rates at the elementary school level and inadequacies in the medical and hospital care furnished by the social insurance system. Other examples could be added.

We want now to make some observations about the evolution of production and the minimum wage during the period of rapid economic growth starting in 1968, and about the process of income concentration between 1960 and 1980. The series of figures in Table 3.6 portray the evolution of the GDP per capita and the real minimum wage (calculated according to different deflators) between 1968 and 1980.

TABLE 3.6

GDP Per Capita and Real Minimum Wages, 1968-1980
(1970 = 100)

Year	GDP Per Capita(a)	Min. Wage São Paulo(b)	Min. Wage Rio de Janeiro(c)	Min. Wage by Basic Food Ration(d)
1968	88.5	101	105	111
1969	94.6	98	102	103
1970	100.0	100	100	100
1971	109.3	96	101	97
1972	118.3	94	104	102
1973	131.8	86	107	85
1974	140.8	78	102	78
1975	145.1	83	107	81
1976	155.3	83	105	79
1977	159.8	86	106	86
1978	163.4	88	108	82
1979	170.1	88	108	80
1980	179.0	90	111	77

Sources: (a) Anuário Estatístico do Brasil, FIBGE, 1980, p. 802; 1982, p. 802; (b) João L.M. Saboia, "A ração essencial e sua utilização como deflator do salário mínimo—1940/1981." Texto para Discussão no. 23, Instituto de Economia Industrial, Universidade Federal do Rio de Janeiro, 1983, Table I, p. 11. For São Paulo the minimum wage was deflated according to the DIEESE series; (c) Saboia, p. 11, Table 1. For Rio de Janeiro the minimum wage was deflated monthly by the Rio de Janeiro Cost of Living Index; (d) Saboia, p. 18, Table 8.

The strikingly dissimilar evolution of the GDP per capita and the minimum wage requires few comments. During the years of the economic "miracle" the GDP per capita grew 60 percent whereas the minimum wage lost ground according to the following three indices. While the per capita GDP doubled, even in the most optimistic hypothesis -- that of the index deflated by the cost of living in Rio de Janeiro -- the minimum wage grew only 5.7 percent. It should be noticed that the Rio de Janeiro cost of living index takes into account a wide range of family budgets, including families with a family income varying between 1 and 5.2 minimum wages. According to the DIEESE index number for São Paulo, which reflects the costs of living of families with a monthly income of up to three minimum wages, the real minimum wage suffered a loss of 11 percent during the same period. The third index number deflates the minimum wage by the cost of the essential ration or daily amount of food for adult workers, defined in Law 399 of 1938. Although it excludes other items of family expenses, it has the advantage of using the minimum wage legislation and the fact that food represents the biggest expenditure of workers receiving the minimum wage.[9] According to this index the minimum wage lost 30.6 percent of its real value between 1968 and 1980.

Economists disagree about the extent to which the minimum wage determines the remuneration of the labor force of the formal sector of the Brazilian economy. One of the most recent studies on this subject, based on the data from the construction industry for the period 1969/1979, showed that the wages of unskilled workers in this industry were practically tied to the level of the official minimum wage and that the wage differential between unskilled and skilled workers remained relatively constant during the period.[10] Evidence from this study suggests that the minimum wage policy had inhibiting effects on real wages not only of the less skilled workers but of the entire labor force.

Turning now to the income distribution data, these show the percentage share of income received by the EAP by selected percentile groups over time (Table 3.7).

TABLE 3.7

Percentage Share of Income by Selected Percentile Groups, 1960-1980

Percentile	1960	1970	1980
Poorest 50%	17.71	15.05	14.17
Richest 10%	39.66	46.47	47.81
Richest 1%	12.11	14.11	18.21

Source: Carlos G. Langoni, *Distribuição de renda e desenvolvimento econômico do Brasil* (Rio de Janeiro, 1973), Table 3.5, p. 64; Pedro Malan and Regis Bonelli, Chapter 1 in this volume.

It is well known that income concentration during the 1960s led to an extremely unequal pattern of distribution. A comparison of the 1970 and 1980 figures and a small increase in the Gini index calculated by different researchers seem to indicate a further worsening of the income distribution during the 1970s. However, sampling problems of the preliminary tabulations of the 1980 census and the different definitions of income in the 1970 and 1980 censuses prevented those who studied the problem from reaching precise conclusions about the trends of income distribution in this decade. But we can say that the impressive changes in the Brazilian economy observed in the 1970s coincided with a persistent and stable pattern of unequal income distribution.

Moreover, if this was the discernible trend in the income distribution for the whole EAP, it certainly was not the case of the EAP in agriculture. Despite the existence of the Land Statute (Estatuto da Terra) since the Castelo Branco government, the creation of FUNRURAL (a rural social insurance program) and the vigorous propaganda of the government about the distribution of land ownership titles, particularly in the Central-West region, the tendency in agriculture was for a rapid growth in mean income to occur, together with an increase in the inequality of income distribution. Between 1970 and 1980 the share of the poorest 50 percent of the EAP in agriculture declined from 22.2 percent to 17.6 percent of the income at the same time that the share of the richest 10 percent grew from 36.3 percent to 47.9 percent.[11]

Despite its rapid structural transformations and economic modernization, Brazil found itself with the dubious distinction of being the only country, among 32 researched, where the share of the national income of the richest 10 percent of families exceeded 50 percent.[12] It represents a case of income concentration greater than that recorded in South Korea, Indonesia and the Philippines, countries considered to be successful examples of conservative modernization. Many new jobs were created, but at a high social cost.

To conclude this section, some remarks are in order about a less talked-about feature of Brazilian society. We refer to the structure of racial inequalities in the country of "harmonious race relations." Due mostly to the repeated failure of the Brazilian census bureau (IBGE) to *collect and publish* data on race, it is practically impossible to grasp the evolution of the relative socioeconomic position of blacks (*pretos* and *pardos*) in the past few decades.

However, given the disproportionate concentration of blacks in agriculture and the lower urban occupational strata, it is quite possible that the small gains obtained by urban blacks since passing of the minimum wage legislation (1938) and the end of the Second World War were reversed after 1964. It is not difficult to suspect that Afro-Brazilians lost more ground than they gained during the Brazilian "miracle." As in all multiracial societies, racial ascription in Brazil plays a fundamental role in the social division of labor, the structuring of social opportunities and the distribution of material and symbolic rewards.

Access to educational opportunities is the first relevant dimension of racial inequalities to be considered. In 1980 blacks were almost two times more likely than whites to be illiterate (48 percent and 25 percent respectively). Moreover, the degree of inequality or exclusion experienced by blacks increases sharply when higher educational levels are taken into account. Also in 1980, whites had a 1.6 greater chance than blacks to complete between five and eight years of school; 2.5 more opportunities to complete between nine and eleven years of school, and a 6 times greater chance to finish twelve or more years of education.

As a result of limited access to formal education and racial discrimination in the labor market, the participation of blacks in the economic system is repeatedly characterized by their disproportionate concentration in sectors that absorb unskilled and underpaid labor. According to the 1976 National Household Survey (PNAD), blacks were concentrated mostly in agriculture, the construction industry, and services (mostly personal and domestic), the sectors where the unskilled and underpaid workers are to be found. These three sectors employed 68 percent of the economically active blacks and 52 percent of whites.

It is reasonable to expect that the gaps between whites and blacks in educational attainment and employment structure have a strong effect on the distribution of income. The 1980 Demographic Census indicates that among blacks with declared income, 48.2 percent received up to one minimum wage, while only 25.5 percent of whites were in the same low bracket. At the other end of the distribution, 15.3 percent of whites and only 3.9 percent of blacks received more than five times the minimum wage. The estimates based on both the 1976 PNAD and the 1980 census are that the mean income of economically active blacks is close to half that of whites.

Recent research on social mobility of whites and blacks suggests that this structure of racial inequality is not the exclusive result of a distant past -- the legacy of slavery. The causes of racial inequality operate in the present. Racism, through discriminatory practices and the cultural stereotyping of roles deemed "adequate" for blacks, perpetuates an unequal structure of social opportunity.[13]

As a result of discriminatory practices and the symbolic violence inherent to a racist culture, blacks have more limited educational opportunities than whites of the same social origin. In turn, the educational achievements of blacks are translated into smaller occupational and income gains than those of whites. This being so, it is very unlikely that the ideal of racial equality will be achieved through the market-like mechanism of individual social mobility. In terms of social inequities, this is the outcome reached by a society that proclaims formal equality of rights, and defines itself as a "racial democracy."

OCCUPATIONAL STRUCTURE AND SOCIAL MOBILITY

The extent to which the pattern of industrialization and of economic development affects the structure of employment is reflected in the distribution of chances for social mobility in Brazil. In other words, we ought to discuss the impact on the occupational structure of processes associated with urbanization and industrialization, such as the extension of capitalist relations into the countryside and the actions of large private or state oligopolistic corporations, with their dynamic poles located in export agriculture and the production of consumer durables. Here, the term "occupational structure" is employed in the sense of a *relationship* between various occupational strata, these strata being constituted as the real units of analysis. We are interested not so much in the individuals who make up these strata, but above all in patterns of interrelationships among these occupational subgroups. In this context our fundamental concern will be to assess how recent changes in the productive apparatus have affected the recruitment patterns of various social strata, which is to say, how they have shaped the current Brazilian occupational structure.

Some important questions on the effects of these structural changes come to mind. For example, how has the rapid urbanization of our society altered the occupational prospects of individuals of rural origin? Have they had broad access to all strata or have their chances for mobility been limited to some of these strata? How has the increasing bureaucratization of the Brazilian social structure been reflected in the recruitment for non-manual occupational groups? How does it compare to that of other societies?

The objective of this section is to try to respond to questions of this sort, taking advantage of information about Brazilian occupational mobility produced by the Pesquisa Nacional por Amostragem de Domicílio [National Household Survey, or PNAD] carried out by the Fundação IBGE in 1973.

The analysis of the patterns of mobility that we are going to carry out will be anchored in an occupational scale composed of ten strata, hierarchically ordered according to their socioeconomic position (consistent with the detailed occupational scale used in Silva,[14] and which can be described generically in the following way:

Stratum 1: Workers in farming and animal husbandry
Stratum 2: Manual workers in traditional industries and artisans
Stratum 3: Workers in domestic service and personal care
Stratum 4: Vendors and sales clerks
Stratum 5: Manual workers in modern industries
Stratum 6: Manual workers in transportation, communications and services in general
Stratum 7: Non-manual clerical workers
Stratum 8: Proprietors (small businesses) in commerce and services
Stratum 9: Proprietors (small holdings) in farming and animal husbandry
Stratum 10: Administrators, technical personnel, and liberal professionals

Some preliminary observations should be made with respect to this scale. In the first place, although the strata are hierarchically ordered in terms of their *average* socioeconomic position, there is sometimes a significant degree of variation within these strata. Consequently, there is a certain overlapping among them. For example, the high degree of overlap in the socioeconomic position of the occupations that make up strata 2 through 4 (workers in traditional industries, in domestic service, and vendors) is such that we cannot characterize movements among these strata as involving either "upward" or "downward" mobility. The overwhelming majority of these movements probably do not imply any relevant change in the socio-economic position of the individuals involved. A similar situation occurs with strata 5 and 6 (workers in modern industries and in services) and with strata 7 and 8 (non-manual clerical workers and small proprietors in commerce and services). Thus we can only distinguish six levels of unambiguously hierarchically ordered strata, a fact which will require certain qualifications when we deal with the direction and changes in occupational mobility in Brazil.

A second observation we would like to make has to do with the manual/non-manual distinction established between strata 6 and 7. It is necessary to keep in mind that on both sides of this line there are occupational categories that are in fact on the very edge of this line (*e.g.* typists), and it is ofen difficult to classify them in one or the other category reflecting that distinction. In these cases, the decisive factor for resolving the classificatory dilemma was frequently the occupational *site*. Office jobs, for example, were classified in the non-manual groups.

Changes in the structure of employment must have had a strong impact on patterns of social mobility in Brazil. In order to assess the strength of this impact we have used data derived from the 1973 PNAD survey.[15] From the sample of the PNAD-73, a subgroup was selected consisting of males between 20 and 64 years old, based on 83,891 returns (including cases lacking information).

PNAD data on the respondant's present occupation, his first job and his father's occupation when the respondant entered the labor market was matched to the ten occupational strata previously described. From this occupational scale three cross tabulations were constructed to characterize, respectively; total occupational mobility (*i.e.*, the occupation of the father *x* the present occupation of the respondant); intergenerational mobility in the strict sense (*i.e.*, the occupation of the father *x* the first occupation of the respondant); and intragenerational or "career" mobility (*i.e.*, the first occupation *x* the present occupation). These data are presented in Tables 3.8 through 3.10.

TABLE 3.8

Total Occupational Mobility, 1973

Occupation of Respondent's Father	Present Occupation of Respondent										
	1	2	3	4	5	6	7	8	9	10	
1	17,796	7,525	2,127	1,244	2,227	2,484	2,154	1,660	1,424	889	39,540
2	546	1,915	383	278	831	613	1	191	50	424	6,231
3	54	284	171	89	261	201	341	50	1	109	1,561
4	46	184	56	126	115	120	188	67	4	100	1,006
5	39	238	79	55	484	170	334	56	8	159	1,622
6	59	311	127	107	305	467	562	64	4	268	2,274
7	94	280	116	116	276	326	1,049	108	11	629	3,005
8	137	240	131	250	227	375	824	467	67	710	3,428
9	959	351	141	112	161	272	473	250	803	364	3,886
10	43	150	48	53	139	228	578	106	26	980	2,351
	19,773	11,478	3,379	2,430	5,026	5,256	7,503	3,019	2,398	4,642	64,904

Source: FIBGE, PNAD-73, *Tabulações especiais.*

TABLE 3.9

Intergenerational Occupational Mobility, by Respondent's First Occupation (1973)

Occupation of Respondent's Father	First Occupation of Respondent										
	1	2	3	4	5	6	7	8	9	10	
1	34,777	2,596	686	1,015	471	323	498	74	5	76	40,521
2	841	3,017	648	827	488	201	393	11	0	33	6,459
3	105	475	353	276	148	86	167	2	2	7	1,621
4	74	223	127	377	84	41	96	3	0	8	1,033
5	80	439	186	214	479	83	188	1	1	14	1,665
6	113	674	316	396	255	199	360	9	0	22	2,344
7	240	550	351	421	219	212	983	10	0	127	3,113
8	211	298	405	1,353	156	187	644	71	3	127	3,555
9	2899	198	87	185	73	73	300	46	23	80	3,964
10	68	371	236	285	183	204	864	17	3	278	2,509
	39,408	8,941	3,395	5,349	2,556	1,609	4,490	244	37	772	66,804

Source: Same as Table 3.8.

TABLE 3.10

Intergenerational Occupational Mobility, by Respondent's Present Occupation (1973)

First Occupation of Respondent	Present Occupation of Respondent (1973)										
	1	2	3	4	5	6	7	8	9	10	
1	20,926	7,985	2,282	1,182	1,993	2,438	1,869	1,675	2,310	737	43,397
2	862	4,217	674	440	1,445	1,358	1,441	418	91	566	11,512
3	89	566	746	224	443	492	1,138	194	19	632	4,543
4	205	831	351	969	564	764	1,498	780	84	793	6,839
5	62	273	86	86	1,490	457	432	102	10	315	3,293
6	67	193	75	69	214	685	353	87	18	331	2,092
7	37	115	100	104	182	406	3,036	185	45	1,780	5,990
8	9	24	11	21	6	28	50	122	17	42	330
9	1	0	1	0	0	3	3	2	33	3	46
10	2	7	3	9	6	40	148	38	7	737	997
	20,260	14,211	4,329	3,104	6,343	6,671	9,968	3,603	2,634	5,936	79,039

Source: Same as Table 3.8.

Let us first examine the data relating to total occupational mobility. The rows of Table 3.8 correspond to the ten categories of the variable "occupation of respondant's father." The columns represent the present occupation (that is, in November 1973) of the respondent. It is important to stress that the marginal totals of the rows do not represent the occupational distribution of a "generation" of fathers, but rather merely a *hypothetical* occupational distribution corresponding to the case where all the respondents belong to the same occupational strata as their respective fathers. The sample taken is a sample of "sons." For several reasons, it is inadvisable to make a rigid interpretation of mobility that treats the relationship between the occupations of fathers and sons as a demographic transformation consisting of a generation of fathers being replaced by a generation of sons, the most important reason being the existence of differential rates of reproduction across occupational strata.[16] To take the difference between the marginal totals of the rows and those of the columns as a "structural" change or mobility would be a dubious interpretation given that this difference reflects an amalgam of effects, only some of which can be adequately described as "structural." Although it is usual to refer to a "structural mobility" or "induced mobility," (usually represented by the difference in the marginal totals of the mobility table), it is important to keep in mind the precarious and specific character of the concept of "structural" in this context. Bearing these caveats in mind, we believe that the changes in occupational profiles over time constitute the main element in "structural mobility" as usually measured.

Examining total mobility, that is, the relationship between the occupation of the father and the present occupation of the respondent, the most notable fact is probably the great predominance of *upward* mobility. Almost half of the individuals are located above the main diagonal of Table 3.8, which means that they presently occupy positions socially superior to their fathers. Even when we define the occupational groups in a more strict manner, admitting only six hierarchical levels among them (as discussed above), the proportion of upwardly mobile individuals still amounts to approximately 46 percent of the cases in the sample. Individuals in the reverse situation, that is, in an inferior position to their fathers, constitute only about 13 percent of the sample.

No matter how we analyze occupational mobility in Brazil, the fact of its enormous extent leaps into view. For example, if we consider the outflows from various occupational groups, we find that 55 percent of the sons of rural workers are presently employed outside of agriculture, and of these mobile individuals of agricultural origin about 29 percent now find themselves in non-manual occupations. Another striking aspect of the outflows is the attraction exerted by non-manual clerical occupations (stratum 7) on urban manual strata, recruiting on the average 20 percent of the individuals from this social origin. Thus in Brazil, as in other capitalist societies, the lower stratum of the non-manual group seems to be an anchoring point for upwardly mobile individuals of working class origins. In a similar way, this stratum also appears to establish a clear boundary for the downwardly mobile sons of non-manual workers. Despite the clear existence of this barrier, less than half of the sons of liberal professionals (stratum 10) managed to maintain a position equivalent to their fathers, with almost 28 percent of them descending to the level of manual workers.

Turning now to examine the inflows into the various strata, we can evaluate the social composition of each. To begin with, one notes that *all* strata recruit workers from agricultural origins. This recruitment reaches a maximum among agricultural workers (90 percent), and declines sytematically (ignoring for the moment the strata of small proprietors) up to the top level of the occupational hierarchy. But even within this last stratum, the sons of agricultural workers still represent a large proportion, constituting almost one fifth of liberal professionals and administrators in 1980.

The very high level of internal recruitment of agricultural workers together with the high degree to which the current proprietors in agriculture are recruited from among the sons of agricultural workers indicates the isolation of the rural strata from the other strata in terms of their social composition. Without doubt, almost no one outside of agriculture becomes a worker or proprietor in this sector: about 95 percent of the workers and 98 percent of the proprietors come from families in these same strata. On the other hand, the fact that even the urban proprietors in commerce and services are drawn heavily from workers with agricultural origins (more than 63 percent of them have fathers in strata 1 and 9) indicates the precarious and modest nature of their advancement.

Thus, when all the inflows are examined, it becomes evident that the ruling classes in Brazil are recruited in large proportions from all strata of the occupational hierarchy. For example, 42 percent of the individuals currently at the top of the occupational hierarchy originated in the manual labor category. Social mobility in Brazil, therefore, turns out to be very high. Although movements of a short distance predominate, it frequently involves large shifts such as those just cited. It makes sense, then, to take a look at the causes of such extensive recruitment.

In analyzing these mobility patterns, rural-urban migration is particularly important. The centrality of migration is clear when we observe that 73 percent of the upwardly mobile individuals in Brazilian society were originally from the stratum of agricultural workers. As José Pastore observes,

> "... There clearly exists an intense movement at the base of the Brazilian social pyramid that, in turn, is associated with the transformations that have occurred in the agricultural labor market and with the intense negative flows of the last 50 years... Upward mobility in the 'middle class' strata has assumed smaller but not negligible proportions. Considering that the sons of the 'middle class' had much less social space to traverse, the mobility observed is quite significant for the three middle strata." [17]

TABLE 3.11

Distribution of Origin, Distribution of Destination, and Structural Mobility in 3X3 Tables of Occupational Mobility for Ten Countries: Adult Men

	Distribution of Origin			Distribution of Destination			Index of Structural Mobility
Country and Year	Rural	Manual	Non-manual	Rural	Manual	Non-manual	
Czechoslovakia, 1967	39.4	47.9	12.7	14.0	52.8	33.1	25.4
Hungary, 1973	49.9	40.4	9.7	26.7	52.9	20.4	23.2
Poland, 1972	54.8	36.7	8.5	28.7	51.6	19.7	26.1
United States, 1973	23.2	47.3	29.5	4.3	49.7	46.0	18.9
France, 1964	34.3	33.6	32.1	17.2	46.7	36.1	17.1
West Germany, 1969	35.6	25.0	39.4	20.7	31.9	47.4	14.9
Japan, 1965	48.0	22.6	29.4	19.4	35.6	45.0	28.6
Philippines, 1968	81.1	10.2	8.7	67.6	19.1	13.3	13.5
BRAZIL, 1973	60.9	19.6	19.5	30.5	42.5	27.0	30.4

Source: Albert A. Simkus, "Historical Changes in Occupational Inheritance Under Socialism," in R. Robinson, ed., *Research in Social Stratification and Mobility*, I (Greenwich, CT, 1981); and Table 3.8 for Brazilian data.

The assessment of the effects of structural changes is normally made through a index of dissimilarity between the sets of marginal totals of row and column.[18] Applying this index to our matrix of total mobility we see that the "structural" mobility reaches a level of 33.4 percent of the cases, representing 57 percent of all observed mobility. In other words, more than one third of the individuals experienced a process of occupational mobility that originated in changes in the economic and demographic structure in Brazilian society. The profound character of the "structural" changes in Brazil becomes clearer when this index is compared with similar indices for other countries. In order to do so, we aggregated the matrix of mobility from the following strata: "agricultural workers," "urban manual workers," and "non-manual workers." In the Brazilian case, this matrix should not do much violence to reality, since it appears to correspond to the basic cleavages of the class structure.[19] This aggregation reduces the index of structural mobility to the level of 30.4 percent, a value that can be compared to those of a group of modern societies, both capitalist and socialist (see Table 3.11).

Even so, the "induced" mobility in Brazil is clearly superior to all of the other countries examined, the closest figure being that obtained for Japan during the 1960s. For all countries the index of structural mobility reflects the difference in the proportion of workers employed in agriculture between the distributions of origin and of destination. Such is the change in the urban-rural profile experienced in recent years by Brazilian society, probably one of the most radical experiences yet observed in any society.

Another question that should be addressed concerns the effect of structural changes on circulatory mobility. How do changes in the occupational profile between the social origin and destination of individuals alter the patterns of mobility? Which routes of mobility are being choked, which opened up? To answer such questions, we need to estimate the pattern of circulatory mobility so that by comparison with the real patterns observed we can then infer the effects of the structural changes under review.

To estimate mobility "through exchanges" (*por trocas*), Pullum suggests an iterative method of proportional adjustment of the tables, usually associated with Deming and Stephan.[20] This technique permits the adjustment of the cells of a table in such a way that the marginals determined *a priori* are obtained, preserving all of the interactions shown in the original table.[21] Thus, if the distribution of destination is made equal to the distribution of origin in the total mobility table, we can answer the question: what would be the pattern of occupational mobility in the absence of "structural" change? The estimated matrix of mobility "through exchanges" that answers this quesion is presented in Table 3.12 and the comparison with the matrix of actual mobility (Table 3.8) will allow us to better assess the effect of structural changes on the pattern of mobility.

TABLE 3.12

Total Circulatory Mobility
(Adjusted by Dening-Stephan Method)

Occupation of Respondent's Father	Present Occupation of the Respondent									
	1	2	3	4	5	6	7	8	9	10
1	32,010	2,466	565	260	318	500	331	1,025	1,909	156
2	2,522	1,607	260	149	305	318	395	305	175	195
3	350	331	162	65	136	143	187	110	6	71
4	260	188	45	84	52	78	91	131	19	58
5	279	312	84	45	276	136	199	136	45	110
6	415	396	18	84	170	375	341	158	19	188
7	656	360	6	91	157	249	630	260	58	428
8	732	234	104	157	98	224	380	863	266	370
9	2,004	136	45	26	26	65	84	179	1,250	71
10	312	201	52	45	84	186	367	261	139	704

Source: Table 3.8.

TABLE 3.13

Effects of "Structural" Change on Mobility Factors

Occupation of Respondent's Father	Present Occupation of the Respondent									
	1	2	3	4	5	6	7	8	9	10
1	-0.44	2.05	2.79	3.82	5.95	3.96	5.48	0.62	-0.26	4.67
2	-0.78	0.19	0.47	0.88	1.71	0.93	1.52	-0.37	-0.71	1.21
3	-0.85	-0.19	0.06	0.35	0.94	0.39	0.81	-0.55	-0.79	0.58
4	-0.82	-0.04	0.20	0.53	1.20	0.57	1.05	-0.49	-0.76	0.79
5	-0.86	-0.23	-0.05	0.22	0.75	0.25	0.64	-0.59	-0.81	0.43
6	-0.86	-0.22	-0.03	0.23	0.77	0.27	0.66	-0.59	-0.81	0.45
7	-0.86	-0.21	-0.02	0.24	0.79	0.28	0.67	-0.58	-0.81	0.46
8	-0.81	0.03	0.27	0.62	1.33	0.67	1.18	-0.46	-0.75	0.90
9	-0.52	1.53	2.26	3.16	4.99	3.28	4.59	0.39	-0.36	3.89
10	-0.86	-0.25	-0.07	0.19	0.71	0.22	0.60	-0.60	-0.82	0.40
P(j)=	-0.50	0.84	1.17	1.42	2.10	1.31	1.50	-0.12	-0.38	0.97

Source: Tables 3.8 and 3.12.

As we saw previously, aggregate "structural" mobility is estimated through the index of dissimilarity between the marginal distributions of origin and destination from the matrix of mobility. However, we can estimate, for each occupational stratum, the relative change in that stratum:

$$P_{(j)} = \frac{F_j - P_j}{P_j}$$

where F_j and P_j are the bottom and right hand marginals, respectively, of the matrix of mobility. Negative values of $P_{(j)}$ indicate that the impact of "structural" changes acts in the direction of minimizing category "j" and in the same way positive values indicate an effect in the direction of broadening the relative share of category "j". For our occupational strata, the values of $P_{(j)}$ derived from the matrix of total mobility are listed in the last row of Table 3.13.

Three groups appear to have been affected by structural factors, in the direction of minimizing mobility: the two strata of petty proprietors and the stratum of rural workers. Along with the extensive rural-urban migration, an important component of this relative minimization (or better, social *disinheritance*) are the high birth rates in these strata. The existence of high reproduction rates combined with the modest size of most rural holdings means that these occupational groups serve as a demographic reserve for the other strata. The group of rural workers ends up showing a net disinheritance of 50 percent. In conjunction, the other strata experience positive impacts, with those relating to the strata of manual workers in modern industries and non-manual clerical workers being the most important. These show net gains of 210 percent and 150 percent respectively. We believe that the growth of these strata are explained by changes in agricultural production as discussed previously.

As for the effects of structural changes on each specific flow, we can measure them through the comparison between the flows estimated for mobility "through exchanges" and the actual flows observed. Thus, for each origin "i" and destination "j," the effect of structural factors on flows is:[22]

$$P_{ij} = \frac{M_{ij} - V_{ij}}{V_{ij}}$$

where M_{ij} are the flows in the matrix of total mobility (Table 3.8) and "ij" are the flows in mobility "through exchanges." The results of the calculation of all the effects of P_{ij} are presented in the cells of Table 3.12. The net losses of each stratum, summarized briefly above, order the various specific flows as follows:

1) The rural strata, both of workers and of proprietors all have negative inflows (columns 1 and 9), indicating a strong choking off of these flows. On the other hand, all the outflows of these strata area positive and high. Clearly, these are strata with a high level of social disinheritence. The effect of "structural" changes in this case is in the direction of restricting mobility toward these strata and expanding mobility out of them.

2) A parallel phenomenon occurs with the group of small urban proprietors. All the inflows are limited, with the exception of those originating from rural strata. At the same time, all the outflows are substantial, except those in a rural direction. That is, there is a strong disinheritence of this stratum in favor of other urban strata at the same time that access to it is blocked.

3) The process repeats itself for the strata of manual workers in traditional industries, of artisans and of workers in domestic service and personal care. The "structural" changes in this case act to increase both the capture of persons originating in the three strata mentioned above and the outflows to the remaining strata. The fact that these two

strata receive the most significant portion of the manual workers of rural origin (48 percent of the sons of migrating rural workers are currently found in these strata), suggests that they play a role as an inter-generational "way-station" on the road carrying the migrant and his sons to the modern social sectors.

4) Finally, the "structural" changes have the effect of increasing the mobility among the other strata, both in an upward and downward direction, therefore restricting the occupational inheritance in these occupational groups.

The breakdown into inter- and intragenerational mobility shows that the former in fact disguises two movements with distinctly different patterns. Within intergenerational mobility in the strict sense (Table 3.9), it is immobility that largely predominates, and even among the mobile downward mobility is greater than upward mobility: 61 percent of the individuals in the sample began their careers in the same occupational stratum held by their fathers at that point. Moreover, 24 percent of the cases observed entered the market in a position inferior to that occupied by their fathers. This predominance of downward mobility over upward mobility is not, however, very marked (a difference of approximately 8.5 percent), and the distance whether down or up is short. That is, there is a strong tendency for individuals to begin their careers in positions equal or similar (with a slight preponderance of lower positions) to those that their fathers occupied at that point.

The pattern of intragenerational mobility is quite another matter. Here upward mobility largely predominates, as more than half (58.3 percent) of the individuals in the sample experienced ascending careers. The proportion of individuals with descending careers is very low, less than 7 percent of the cases observed. Thus, while at the beginning of their careers people tend to reproduce the situation of their fathers, the majority experience an improvement with respect to the initial position. The predominance of upward mobility observed in the total mobility of individuals is, therefore, fundamentally a phenomenon that occurs during their careers in the labor market.

SUMMARY AND CONCLUSIONS

The last two decades mark the consolidation of capitalist society in Brazil. High rates of economic growth and rapid urbanization were linked to expanding industrial production. This contradicted certain pessimistic perspectives about the low capacity of the secondary secttor to absorb new and growing contingents of labor in countries on the capitalist periphery. The modern industrial sector in particular has shown an unexpected capacity to generate new jobs. Changes in the composition of the work force have followed two major lines of development. First, there has been a rapid expansion of capitalist labor relations, as indicated by the overall share of wage workers which grew rapidly. This was propelled in large measure by rapid industrial growth and by the urbanization of the occupational structure, along with a rapid relative decline of employeemnt in the primary sector, the traditional redoubt of the self-employed and of unpaid family workers.

Second, as a consequence of the expanding functions of the state, of the process of capital concentration and the strengthening of large private and state enterprises, there has been a very rapid growth in the group of non-proprietor administrators, whose proportional share almost tripled. In the same way, routine clerical occupations and technical and scientific occupations also expanded their share rapidly, more than doubling their relative number over the course of the two decades.

The consequences of these changes for the class structure is that workers engaged in simple commodity production and the self-employed tend to join the wage-labor pool. To this we can add, in keeping with the bureaucratization of labor, the growth of an increasingly differentiated layer of administrators and bureaucrats which is interposed between those who hold or control capital and workers directly linked with production.

One of the most important changes in the work force is the entrance *en masse* of women. Despite the persistence of occupational segregation based on gender, women have improved their distribution in the occupational structure, reduced their participation in the less-skilled job sectors, and have entered increasingly into the modern sectors of industry and services.

Rapid change in the direction of a more complex class structure is reflected in extreme social mobility. In fact, the occupational mobility induced by changes in the structure of employment (as well as demographic changes) has reached very high levels in Brazil. A comparison with other modern societies, although crude, makes us believe that the recent Brazilian experience is one of the most radical yet observed in any society. Meanwhile, a perverse process of income concentration, the inadequate provision of goods and services for collective consumption by the State, and the persistence of deep socioeconomic differences between black and white Brazilians represent the other side of the coin. If on the one hand the model of conservative modernization has profoundly modified the class structure, on the other hand it has given rise to a society marked by extremely pronounced levels of inequality. The economic crisis of the 1980-84 period certainly did nothing to improve the situation. The more evident and crude facts of these years were the deterioration of real wages in the formal labor market, and a substantial increase in the rates of unemployment and underemployment. Thus in 1983, out of 33,433,000 persons in the non-agricultural labor force, 2,307,000 were unemployed and 10,374,000 were underemployed.[23] Much has been written about the social and human costs of Brazil's modernization experience. The economic crisis of 1980-84 leads us to believe that these assessments could have been even more negative than they have tended to be. As for the post-1984 recovery, its effects on socity in terms of jobs created and jobs regained remains to be investigated.

NOTES

1. Paul I. Singer, "Força de trabalho e emprego no Brasil: 1920-1969," *Cadernos CEBRAP*, no. 3 (1971).

2. H.L. Browning and J. Singelman, "The Transformation of the U.S. Labor Force: The Interaction of Industry and Occupation," *Politics and Society*, 8:3-4 (1978), pp. 490-491.

3. Browning and Singelman, pp. 490-491.

4. P.I. Singer, pp. 61-62.

5. Maria Helena F.T. Henriques, "Projeções da população total segundo algumas alternativas de crescimento demográfico e projeções da população economicamente ativa segundo o nível atual do emprego," mimeo, 1983, p. 7.

6. M. Henriques, p. 11.

7. See, for example, Peter Gregory, "An Assesment of Employment conditions in Less Developed Countries," *Economic Development and Cultural Change*, 28:4 (1980), pp. 673-700.

8. For a conceptual and empirical analysis of social policies implemented during this phase of Brazilian development, see Wanderley Guilherme dos Santos, *Cidadania e justiça* (Rio de Janeiro, 1979), especially chapter 5.

9. João L.M. Saboia, "A ração essencial e sua utilização como deflator do salário mínimo - 1940/1981," Texto para Discussão No. 23, Instituto de Economia Industrial, Universidade Federal do Rio de Janeiro, 1983, p. 2.

10. Andres Drobny and John Wells, "Salário mínimo e distribuição de Renda no Brasil: uma análise do setor de construção civil," *Pesquisa e Planejamento Econômico*, 13:2 (1983).

11. David Denslow, Jr. and William G. Tyler, "Perspectivas sobre pobreza e desigualdade de renda no Brasil," *Pesquisa e planejamento econômico*, 13:3 (1983), p. 900.

12. World Bank, *Relatório sobre o desenvolvimento no mundo*, 1981. The data on Brazil refer to 1972. The table with the data is reproduced in Eduardo Suplicy, "A Concentração e o Presidente," *Folha de São Paulo* (June 6, 1982).

13. See Carlos A. Hasenbalg, "Race and Socioeconomic Inequalities in Brazil," in Pierre-Michel Fontaine (ed.), *Race, Class and Power in Brazil*, Center for Afro-American Studies, University of California, Los Angeles (Los Angeles, 1985), pp. 25-41; Nelson do Valle Silva, "Updating the Cost of Not Being White in Brazil," in Fontaine, pp. 42-55; also "Côr e o processo de realização sócio-econômica," *Dados* 24:3 (1981); and Lucia E. Garcia de Oliveira, Rosa M. Porcaro and Tereza Cristina N. Araujo Costa, *O lugar do negro na força de trabalho* (Rio de Janeiro, 1983).

14. Nelson do Valle Silva, "Posição social das ocupações," FIBGE, 1973 (mimeo).

15. The PNAD-73 consisted of a random sample, encompassing persons who live in private and collective housing facilities with the exception of members of the armed forces living in military quarters; the inmates, patients and members of institutions, such as sanatoria, religious cloisters and penitentiaries. The employees of these institutions and their families residing there are included in the survey. For a detailed description of the methodology of the PNAD, consult FIBGE, *Methodologia da pesquisa nacional por amostra de domicílios na decada de 70* (Rio de Janeiro, 1982).

16. O.D. Duncan, "Methodological Issues in the Analyses of Social Mobility," in Neil J. Smelser and Seymour M. Lipset (eds.), *Social Structure and Mobility in Economic Development* (Chicago, 1966); N.V. Silva, "As Duas Faces da Mobilidade," *DADOS*, no. 21 (1979).

17. J. Pastore, "Mobilidade social no Brasil," *O Estado de São Paulo* (24 September 1978).

18. J. Matras, "Differential Fertility, Intergenerational Mobility and Change in Occupational Distribution," *Population Studies*, no. 15 (November, 1961) pp. 187-197.

19. N.V. Silva, *op. cit.*, 1979, pp. 60-61.

20. T. Pullum, *Measuring Occupational Inheritance* (San Francisco, 1975); W.E. Deming, *Statistical Adjustment of Data* (New York, 1943).

21. F. Mosteller, "Association and Estimation in Contingency Tables," *American Journal of Sociology*, v. 63 (1958). pp. 1-28; S. Feinberg, "An Iterative Procedure for Estimation in Contingency Tables," *Annals of Mathematical Statistics*, v. 41 (1970), pp. 907-917.

22. T. Pullum, *op. cit.*; N.V. Silva, *op. cit.*

23. Underemployment is here defined as the sum of self-employed people without a legal labor contract earning up to two minimum wages, domestic employees, and those working without monetary remuneration.

PART TWO

Institutions and Organizations

4

Dilemmas of State-led Modernization in Brazil

Edson de Oliveira Nunes and Barbara Geddes

Two characteristics of the Brazilian techno-bureaucracy[1] strike the observer: its relative success in fostering economic growth during the past 30 years and its tendency to escape from political control.[2] These two characteristics have been compatible, perhaps even mutually reinforcing, during periods of economic expansion. During the recent recession, however, difficulties in exerting political control over state economic actors worsened the economic crisis. Economic planners found it hard to impose limits on spending and borrowing on state entities that would be consonant with a general program of austerity. Their difficulties revealed the practical urgency of establishing some means of controlling the behavior of these entities. Now, one of the central tasks facing the first elected government in more than twenty years is the need to assert democratic political control on what have become relatively autonomous segments of the state -- without undermining their economic effectiveness.

Reconciling political control with growth-inducing state intervention in the economy has been one of the central dilemmas associated with state-led industrialization in many nations. In Brazil, the roots of this dilemma lie in the institutional innovations devised during the thirties, forties and fifties to overcome the inadequacies of a state apparatus pervaded by clientelism. These innovations, which we label insulated bureaucracies, developed as a means of nurturing economic expertise and of shielding governmental economic decision makers from particularistic and partisan pressures. Insulation, however, has had the unforeseen consequence of removing critical parts of policy making from political control.

By referring to bureaucratic agencies as insulated, we do not imply that they are cut off from all outside influences or free from party politics. We mean, rather, that although information and resources flow between an insulated agency and its environment, the agency is able to maintain its organizational integrity and to pursue its own goals. It can enter into coalitions and cooperative relationships with other organizations, as, for example, some Brazilian agencies have with industrialists' associations. Insulation, however, enables the agency to limit the capacity of outside actors to define or subvert its goals. In practical terms, this means that an insulated agency must actually control the material resources that it formally has at its disposal. And it must be able to insure that its personnel are chosen on the basis of professional competence and commitment to agency goals. It is not that no one does favors for friends in an insulated agency, but only that the favors are not so pervasive that they interfere with the performance of the formal functions of the agency.

The insulated bureaucracy includes the part of the Brazilian state apparatus that has been especially responsible for implementing economic policies since the 1940s.[3] It includes some of the state enterprises, some state controlled banks such as the BNDES, the various policy-making councils, the Executive Groups -- in short, many, though certainly not all, of the state agencies outside the traditional federal bureaucracy.

The insulated bureaucracy, though guided by the executive, has been shielded from many of the political influences coming from both inside and outside of government. In response to Brazilian political circumstances between 1930 and 1960, elites committed to economic development came to believe that insulation was necessary in order to enable these agencies to plan and implement policies conducive to economic growth. In the long run, however, lack of accountability to the public and a considerable capacity to subvert the executive's own goals when they are inconsistent with specific agency or para-statal goals have been unintended consequences of bureaucratic insulation.

Insulated agencies have been effective in formulating and implementing economic policies. They have, however, impeded the development of a public domain in Brazil. The same characteristic that gave these agencies the leeway to base decisions on economic rather than other criteria, and thus to operate effectively in the economy -- their insulation from a wide range of outside political pressures -- made them difficult even for an authoritarian government to control. Moreover, their economic success, until recently at any rate, tended to legitimate the notion that government actors *need* not, and perhaps even *should* not, be publicly accountable.[4]

The importance of clientelism in Brazilian politics and government led to the perception by elites that economic policy-making agencies needed to be insulated from partisan pressures. Historically, clientelism has pervaded the Brazilian bureaucracy, as it has the bureaucracies of most other governments in the world. What distinguishes the Brazilian bureaucracy is not the pervasiveness of clientelism, but the effectiveness of attempts to insulate a few techno-bureaucratic agencies crucial to the economy *from* clientelism. The government bureaucracy in contemporary Brazil contains both clientelistic and insulated segments.

The existence of this segmented system can be traced to three historical developments, which will be discussed in greater detail below. First, during the Estado Novo (1937-1945), the Vargas administration centralized political and administrative resources, and began to exercise control over access to new economic opportunities, to such a degree that, by the end of the dictatorship, the bases for autonomous political organization had become extremely limited. As a result, the individuals and resources available to newly forming parties in 1945 came mostly from within the state apparatus itself. During the process of democratization, two of the three major new political parties grew out of the pre-existing Vargas political machine, using government resources and patronage to consolidate support. The third major party had to offer the same kinds of individual benefits to political supporters in order to compete for votes. In consequence, clientelism was never effectively challenged as the basis of the party system.

Second, attempts to secure bureaucratic competence by imposing a comprehensive civil service reform, though somewhat successful during the dictatorship, proved to be too fragile to survive the return to competitive politics. Because of the failure of bureaucratic reform, policy making by traditional bureaucrats as well as politicians continued to be heavily influenced by clientelistic considerations.

And third, given the failure of efforts to institute universalistic reform, executives bent on using the state apparatus to further development goals began experimenting with alternative ways of increasing administrative competence. In an effort to create enclaves in which economic decision criteria would outweigh partisan concerns, techno-bureaucratic agencies designed to promote and administer the process of economic modernization began to be created which were independent of both the traditional bureaucracy and the political parties.[5]

This segmentation of the political system into insulated and clientelistic spheres has had serious consequences for relationships between institutions and society. It has given rise to a policy-making procedure that is not subject to public scrutiny or control. This system was not invented by the post 1964 military government, but it achieved dominance as a result of military rule. Whether the system will be seriously modified by the current democratic government remains to be seen. (For analysis along these lines consult Chapter 7).

POSTWAR PARTIES AND POLITICS

The literature on the postwar Brazilian party system is abundant,[6] and we make no attempt to summarize it here. We do want, however, to emphasize the long-term consequences of one especially pervasive charateristic of the Brazilian party system: clientelism.

Clientelism is an informal system for controlling the flow of resources, in which individuals are organized in networks or pyramids based on personal relationships and generalized exchange.[7] The membership of a clientele network may or may not coincide with the membership of some formal organization, such as a bureaucratic agency or neighborhood association. Frequently, clientele networks compete with one another for control over the resources within a single organizational domain. Participation in clientelistic relationships is voluntary, but there may be serious economic and social disadvantages to non-participation. Clientele relationships cannot be formally regulated, though norms of reciprocity are enforced by group pressures. Hierarchy within the clientele network may initially be based on status or charisma, but must be consolidated through the distribution of resources. Jobs are one of the resources most commonly distributed through clientele channels in Brazil.

Virtually all experts agree that clientelism has been one of the most marked characteristics of Brazilian political parties. Clientelism tends to be seen, however, as a characteristic of the old republic, of the politics of *café-com-leite*, of *coronelismo*, in other words, as a characteristic of pre-modern Brazil. Those who examine postwar clientelism frequently see it as a survival of the past, a survival that was on the way to extinction in the polarized political milieu prior to 1964.[8]

Despite scholars' expectations, however, political clientelism has remained very much alive in the two most modern urban centers of the country, Rio de Janeiro and São Paulo. Those who have analyzed two of the more prominent manifestations of clientelism during military rule -- Malufism in São Paulo and the Chagas Freitas machine in Rio de Janeiro -- see it as a product of authoritarianism. The military dictatorship, in their view, suppressed the mechanisms that would have allowed the confrontation of interests to such an extent that the only political language still available was the grammar of clientelism. Clientelism is interpreted as functional for the authoritarian regime in that it prevented the appearance of the antagonisms that would have been expected if the political party system had been able to reflect the real cleavages in Brazilian society.[9]

These interpretations have some plausibility. Nevertheless, they are incapable of explaining the resilience of political clientelism in modern areas of Brazil before, during, and, as the victory of Jânio Quadros in the recent São Paulo mayoral election suggests, after authoritarianism. Clientelism flourished during the previous democratic period. It remained strong during the period of authoritarianism. It did not disappear as a result of industrialization. It shows no signs of weakening during the current democracy. How can such strength and permanence be explained?

The persistence and reinforcement of clientelism can be traced to the preemption of political and, to some extent, economic resources by the Vargas dictatorship, which limited the development of autonomous parties during democratization and shaped the emerging political leadership. The democracy that was established in 1945 was dominated by the same political actors who had held power during the preceding dictatorship.[10] Getúlio Vargas played the leading role in creating the two most important parties, the Partido Social Democrático (PSD) and the Partido Trabalhista Brasileiro (PTB). Both depended on Vargas supporters for leadership and on the pre-existing Vargas political machine for organization and resources. As one of the politicians active at the time notes:

> "... The coup of 1945 was a coup *sui generis* because power was not handed over either to the military or to the opposition.... The brief interregnum of *Poder Judiciario* did not dismantle the state political machines.... And with the election of Eurico Dutra, the PSD [the Vargas machine], by then upheld by democratic legitimacy, installed itself in power."[11]

The PSD remained the strongest party in Brazil from its creation until 1964. The support base of the PSD was constructed around state and municipal *interventores*, who had been appointed by Vargas. They drew on the resources available to state and municipal administrations.[12] As Martin Shefter has noted, parties which originate within the regime whose place they are going to take arise with a stock of government resources for patronage.[13] These resources can be manipulated by elites who must seek popular support in order to remain in power after the regime change. The PSD, as Shefter would predict, was able to use the resources of the state to attract and cement the loyalty of potential party members.

The PTB was also mobilized from within the Vargas apparatus. Forged from the *Queremista* movement, the orchestrated popular movement to elect Vargas as the first democratic president, it absorbed the populist side of *Varguismo* not represented in the PSD. The PTB was organized by allies of Vargas such as Alexandre Marcondes Filho, who, as Minister of Labor from November 1941 to October 1945, "consolidated the labor laws and helped to produce the mystique of *trabalhismo* ('laborism')," and Alberto Pasqualini, a long-time supporter of populist policies from Vargas' home state.[14] Early in its existence the PTB began to distribute state resources.[15] The patronage resources conceded to the PTB contributed to worker mobilization. In the early fifties, the PTB grew as a result of Vargas' candidacy for the presidency. Later, after Vargas' election, the Ministry of Labor distributed large amounts of government largesse in the form of jobs and transfer payments to consolidate support.

At the time of their formation, both the PSD and PTB had resources available for patronage. Party members recognized and accepted clientelistic exchange as legitimate and desirable for the party. The initial strategy of seeking support in exchange for patronage provided by the treasury of the government constituted the critical experience of these parties, an experience the parties have found it difficult to transcend, at least in the short space of a single generation.

The UDN (União Democrática Nacional), in contrast to the PSD and PTB, was created from a different political base. The UDN brought together those excluded from or opposed to the Vargas political machine: oligarchs displaced by the Revolution of 1930, former allies of Vargas who had come to oppose him, liberals with a strong regional identification, and leftists.[16] The UDN advocated combat against administrative corruption and the cultivation of universalistic individualism. It expressed a distaste for the paternalism of Vargas. The UDN officially favored legislation aimed at "moralizing" public administration. The platform of its Twelfth Party Convention, for example, called for continuing "the struggle against the forces that have been dominant for many years, of administrative corruption and compromise of the moral bases of public life."[17]

The moralistic discourse of the national leadership, however, was combined in practice with a local and regional strategy of electoral coalitions with the PTB and/or the PSD. The pressure on the UDN to form coalitions with the other parties, in spite of its principles, was great. UDN party leader Prado Kelly's argument for allying with the PTB for the 1958 gubernatorial election in the state of Rio de Janeiro illustrates the attitude of party activists:

> "... The UDN is tired of glorious defeats; now we need to make a deal in order to get into the Government and attend to the needs of our comrades in the interior," because at that time...to be a member of the UDN was not to have your daughter chosen as teacher, it was not to have the road that led to your fazenda maintained, it was really a tremendous persecution to be a member of the UDN.[18]

In fact, even at the national level, the UDN remained in opposition only a very short time. UDN members participated in the first PSD government elected after the dictatorship.

Subverted by the "realistic" logic of the party system, the UDN lost whatever potential it may have had to become a bastion of universalism. It ended up in the grasp of the same personalistic and clientelistic "realism" as the other large parties, even at the national level. At times the UDN frankly contradicted its anti-corruption rhetoric. For example, when a measure was introduced in Congress that proposed granting special licenses to buy imported cars for legislators, UDN deputies voted for it. The thesis defended by the "realist" Juraci Magalhães, that the UDN should approve the project "since it wouldn't make sense to benefit only the PSD," won out, and most of the Udenistas imported Cadillacs (and resold them at enormous profit).[19]

The UDN, as a party created outside of and separate from the previous regime, had the potential to become a spokesman for the universalistic modernization of the Brazilian polity. Not only did it initially lack resources for patronage, but also, substantial portions of its leadership disapproved of clientelism as a means of obtaining political support. Moreover, public opinion strongly favored reform to raise the level of honesty and competence among government officials.[20] As the above examples illustrate, however, this did not occur. As a result of opportunistic decisions by leaders faced with competition from other patronage-based parties, it ended up "framed"[21] by the logic of the party system. When it was able to win state or local elections in coalition with other parties, the UDN then tended to use the patronage to which it gained access as a way of solidifying its political base, as other parties did.

A party's initial strategy for gaining support has long-run consequences because it creates expectations among supporters that become difficult to ignore later. Once a strategy has been established, the relationships between party leaders and supporters tend to solidify and to define the on-going characteristics of the organization. The kinds of relationships that develop between leaders and supporters also depend on how rapidly the party comes to power. A party excluded from power for an extended period of time must find ways of consolidating support that do not depend on access to state resources. A party which becomes part of a governing coalition almost immediately, however, as the UDN did, will have the opportunity of distributing state-controlled benefits to supporters.

In summary, clientelism dominated the organization of the three major political parties of Brazil between 1945 and 1964. The PTB and PSD grew out of the Vargas political machine and government patronage. The UDN, in contrast, initially could have institutionalized itself as a constituency for universalism. It succumbed to the temptation of opportunistic coalitions with other parties, however. These coalitions brought it to state and local office before any constituency for universalism had been consolidated. The resulting pressure to use patronage to build support and reward followers as its coalition partners were doing eroded whatever commitment to universalism had ever existed. Thus, despite moralistic rhetoric and a high level of public indignation about corruption, incompetence, and patronage, all the major parties contributed to their persistence.

Politics itself seemed to many to be inseparable from clientelism and corruption. Clientelism strengthened the party system, but at the same time decreased the effectiveness of party government. Clientelism strengthened party loyalties and contributed to the stability of the party system since, given the interpenetration between traditional bureaucratic agencies and the parties, the parties always had access to resources to exchange for support. Given the parties' need to maintain exchange relationships as the basis of support, however, they were unable to make decisions that would deal effectively with the crucial area of basic economic policy. This inability to provide economic leadership created a space in which the executive was able to maneuver autonomously.

Up to this point, we have painted an oversimplified picture of clientelistic parties. We do not mean to suggest that clientelistic concerns were the only motives for political activity during this period. Factions of the PTB were genuinely committed to left-wing goals and engaged in more ideologically oriented campaigns.[22] The UDN also included factions with serious right-wing and liberal ideological commitments.[23] Our point is that ideological politics and clientelistic, pork-barrel politics are not mutually exclusive. Both ideological and "physiological"[24] parties used patronage as a means of party building.[25]

CIRCUMVENTING POLITICAL CLIENTELISM

Serious efforts to insulate the bureaucratic agencies crucial to economic development from political clientelism began during the thirties. Early reformers focused their efforts on removing bureaucratic jobs from the category of political resources in order to increase levels of bureaucratic competence. Meritocratic hiring practices were instituted at the Bank of Brazil.[26] After the imposition of the dictatorship, the DASP (Departamento Administrativo de Serviço Público) sought to build an elite civil service by requiring competitive entrance exams for permanent functionaries and by differentiating these career public servants from other, less qualified public employees. The DASP was able to impose some changes on reluctant government agencies during the Vargas dictatorship. The DASP was a major political actor in its own right during the dictatorship, continually expanding its domain at the expense of other bureaucratic agencies. It was one of the most important spokesmen for the more right-wing, technocratically oriented strand of Varguismo. Daspians' commitment to efficiency and expertise outweighed their commitment to participation. Their authoritarian methods created a great deal of hostility, however. Many of the procedures the DASP had initiated were discontinued after the return to democracy. It lost most of its policing power at that time.[27]

Though the importance of the DASP as an innovating organization decreased markedly after the fall of the dictatorship, the people it had recruited and trained remained. They continued to be among the most effective public servants in Brazil. Moreover, they continued to exert considerable influence on policy from within government, especially from their base at the Fundação Getúlio Vargas. They tended to espouse technocratic, efficient, "non-political" solutions to Brazil's economic problems and to favor the creation of agencies insulated from the more traditional parts of government as a means of carrying out such solutions.

After the return to democracy in 1946, development-oriented elites, including those who had served in the DASP, faced a party system based on clientelism and a bureaucracy which had apparently successfully resisted universalistic reform efforts. These elites believed economic modernization to be impossible unless the bureaucratic agencies planning and implementing economic policies were staffed on the basis of competence rather than political connections. Their solution to the dilemma posed by the perceived incompatibility between clientelism and competence was an attempt to create economic policy-making agencies insulated from both the traditional bureaucracy and the parties. Their goals included stable economic policy, not subject to frequent political disruptions, and the protection of expertise. For both these purposes, they believed appointments to these agencies had to be removed from the spoils system.

Perhaps the first agency whose creators aimed self-consciously at creating an agency with autonomy and wide discretion was SUMOC (Superintendência de Moeda e Crédito), the Brazilian monetary authority.[28] It was created by Decree-Law 7293 on February 2, 1945, when it had become clear that the dictatorship would soon end and institutions capable of operating in a democratic context would be needed. SUMOC was in some respects patterned after the Federal Reserve Bank of the United States, whose autonomy from American political pressures was much admired by Octávio Bulhões, the principal architect of SUMOC. The autonomy and the power of SUMOC waxed and waned during succeeding years, depending primarily on whether it was supported by the president in office at the time. The general trend, however, was in the direction of acquiring more discretion over a broader area of policy as it developed more expertise. The economic ideology of SUMOC was relatively orthodox, tending to favor liberalization of trade. It maintained close ties with the IMF.[29] The establishment and evolution of the Brazilian National Development Bank, now called BNDES (Banco Nacional de Desenvolvimento Econômico e Social), followed much the same pattern, although its economic ideology differed from that of SUMOC.

During the late forties and early fifties, these and other more or less insulated agencies maintained themselves as enclaves of expertise and bastions of sets of values that distinguished them from the rest of the political and administrative system. They shared a commitment to efficiency and national economic development, and they shared a degree of hostility toward distributionist politics as usual. They differed, however, with regard to the specific economic ideology espoused, some taking a more orthodox, internationalist view and others a more nationalist position. These agencies affected policy decisions more at some times than at others. Their effectiveness could be undermined by a lack of executive support; by the president's use of leadership positions in the agencies as political rewards; by the withholding of funds, either by Congress or the Ministry of Finance. The agencies survived, however, frequently seeing themselves as islands of rationality in a sea of political deals and disorder. In effect, defending themselves against political interference constituted the critical experience of these agencies.

SYNCRETISM DURING THE KUBITSCHEK PERIOD: CLIENTELISM AND BUREAUCRATIC INSULATION

When Juscelino Kubitschek came to power in 1956, he used the pre-existing more or less insulated agencies, and created new ones, to plan and carry out the goals of the *Plano de Metas* (Target Plan). Staff members of the National Development Bank formulated the Plan during Kubitschek's presidential campaign.[30] The Development Bank and SUMOC both played crucial roles in carrying it out. Kubitschek took advantage of a favorable international economic situation, widespread domestic support for developmental nationalism, and the availability of expertise in the insulated agencies to nearly double Brazil's industrial output in a five year period.

Since the party system and the traditional bureaucracy did not seem either willing or able to carry out a concerted strategy of national development, Kubitschek relied on the insulated agencies to administer development policies. The insulated segment of the bureaucracy created incentives for the import of capital and designed fiscal measures to enlarge the state's investment capacity. Increased foreign investment and public expenditure furnished the means for supporting development based on a syncretic political model. This syncretism entailed maintaining clientelism in certain arenas of policy making while insulating others to allow them to function separately from the traditional political system.

Kubitschek's extensive use of insulated state agencies was a response to the dilemma created by the imperative of state involvement in economic development, coupled with an inability or unwillingness to reform the traditional state apparatus so that it would be able to carry out the development function. A contradiction was widely perceived by members of the elite, most importantly by Kubitschek himself, between the need for a state contribution to economic development and the capacity of the state, as it was then constituted, to make that contribution. A solution to that contradiction was sought and found, at least temporarily, in the Executive Groups and other insulated agencies.

The agencies in charge of economic development needed two resources in order to carry out their plans effectively: competent personnel and sufficient capital. Kubitschek devised ways of providing both. He used executive privilege to staff the insulated bureaucracy without going through any formal procedure whatsoever. In part, by borrowing the most competent personnel from the rest of the bureaucracy,[31] he bypassed not only the traditional bureaucracy but also whatever universalistic procedures existed. Celso Lafer notes that:

> "... If the Kubitschek government...is examined, one arrives at the conclusion that the Target Plan could be implemented...thanks to the use the Government made of organs such as the BNDE, the Bank of Brazil, and SUMOC -- where the merit system had not been diluted -- or the new organs such as, for example,

> the Executive Groups, to which was funneled, through requisitions, all the competence available in the public service. These organs, that together became a *parallel administration*, were successful....[32]

The Kubitschek government created special flexible administrative instruments to implement the Plano de Metas. Financial resources not subject to Congressional budget cuts were granted to quasi-autarchic governmental agencies charged with achieving the goals of the Plan.[33] Goals that depended on private sector effort were supported by a combination of several stimuli and subsidies under the coordination of the Executive Groups. These groups analyzed projects, made decisions, and provided rapid financing. They were composed of representatives of several governmental agencies and of private interests.[34]

Before the establishment of the Executive Groups, an industrial project would have had to travel through bureaucratic channels in one agency after another, a time-consuming procedure. A proposal for a new industrial plant had to be analyzed by CACEX (the foreign trade department of the Bank of Brazil) to verify the (non)existence of similar products already produced domestically; then the Ministry of War assessed the implications of the project for national security; finally, the Foreign Exchange Section of the Bank of Brazil ascertained whether foreign exchange was available and what was most necessary, given the nature of the project.[35] In addition to the long time spent in the bureaucratic morass, projects were not examined as a whole by the agencies interested in their execution. Each agency judged independently the elements of the project within its purview, which created multiple veto points. The selection of projects to support was thus problematic because each agency used different criteria to assess them. The absence of a single, overall perspective within the agencies made carrying out a national plan of industrial development extremely difficult.

By creating these Executive Groups, the Kubitschek administration was able to bypass both the party system and the traditional bureaucracy, and to escape the logic of clientelism. The escape from the traditional political system created a segment of the bureaucracy insulated from clientelistic demands, but permeable to the penetration of some industrial interests.

The Executive Groups were effective, as a look at the performance of one of them illustrates. GEICON (Executive Group for the Naval Construction Industry) was created by presidential decree on June 13, 1958, after Congress had approved Law 3381 on April 24, 1958, creating the Merchant Marine Fund. Beginning on July 11 of the same year, GEICON passed resolutions establishing norms for the nationalization of naval construction, procedures for the organization of shipyard projects, guidelines for encouraging naval construction, and rules for the concession of exchange subsidies for importing equipment needed for naval construction. Within a year, GEICON had approved ten major projects.[36] By the early 1980s, Brazil had one of the world's largest shipbuilding industries.[37] Such speed in approving and carrying out development projects was unprecedented in Brazil.

As a comparison between the Executive Groups and, for example, SUMOC suggests, the insulated agencies differed from one another in some ways. Some were more thoroughly insulated from interest group pressures than others. The Executive Groups, at one end of the continuum, included representatives of the domestic private sector and were designed to coordinate the interests of the government with the interests of designated private actors in order to elicit their cooperation. Thus, while participants report that government representatives dominated the Groups, domestic private interests were certainly represented. SUMOC, in contrast, was much less open to domestic private interests. Insulated agencies also differed from each other with regard to economic ideology. The National Development Bank espoused a more nationalist development strategy than did SUMOC. The Development Bank maintained close ties with ECLA and advocated extensive government intervention in the economy. SUMOC, as noted above, had more experience with

North American economists and economic institutions, and it favored a more liberal trade policy. Notwithstanding these variations, however, all the agencies were insulated from pork-barrel politics.

As a result of the effort to insulate techno-bureaucratic agencies from political clientelism, the administration of economic policies, as well as strategic decisions, came to be made outside the representative organs of the political system.

Bureaucratic insulation and clientelism were not new to the Brazilian political system in 1956. Consciousness that the traditional base of the Brazilian polity was impeding economic development had begun to spread in the twenties. During the Vargas period, attempts were made to create institutions capable of carrying out economic policies that would transcend the clientelistic and distributionist character of the Old Republic. The creation of state enterprises was part of that effort, in that they were created as entities separate from the traditional bureaucracy, though many did not remain insulated in practice. Such attempts were, for the most part, undermined by the traditionalism still dominant in the state apparatus. Only during the Kubitschek government were mechanisms successfully created that secured the techno-bureaucratic agencies' independence from the traditional political and administrative system.

None of the conditions that contributed to the success of the Target Plan were unique to the Kubitschek period. But Kubitschek made use of them in innovative ways. Most of the agencies that played an important role in carrying out the Target Plan had existed prior to Kubitschek's election. Kubitschek's contribution lay in creating the Executive Groups to coordinate the activities of the several agencies involved in each project; assuring secure, on-going financing for projects by setting up funds over which Congress and the Ministry of Finance had no control; and using his discretion over hiring to concentrate the ablest personnel available in the agencies critical to the success of the Plan. Thus, Kubitschek secured for the agencies involved the human and material resources adequate to the task of implementing the Target Plan. These resources could only be secured by more thoroughly insulating the agencies involved in implementing the Target Plan from the party system and the traditional bureaucracy.

Though relying on insulated agencies to carry out development tasks, however, Kubitschek used traditional job politics on a massive scale to consolidate political support. While he protected the insulated agencies and guaranteed them access to expertise and funds, Kubitschek managed the rest of the political system in a way that reduced potential challenges to developmentalist goals and his way of pursuing them. Many of the patronage appointments made during the Kubitscheck period went to his PTB supporters. Kubitschek is credited with having made 7,000 political appointments during his first year in office. Most of these appointments were made by João Goulart in the Ministries of Labor and Agriculture and their subsidiaries, especially the Social Security Institutes.[38] Kubitschek also annulled all appointments to non-classified positions and all acts granting permanent status to interim appointees going back to May 1952. The dismissals that resulted permitted Kubitschek's government to hire even more of its own supporters.[39]

This continuation of political clientelism and its extension to new participants in the political game reinforced the traditional Brazilian practice of seeking individual improvement through personal connections with the politically powerful. Group-based political activities, which would have entailed the formulation and articulation of policy suggestions beneficial to particular classes or interest groups, followed by organizations to make demands on political leaders for the enactment of such policies, remained relatively unimportant. Instead, political action tended to be individualistic and focused at the implementation stage of policy making -- to be dominated by petitions for exceptions, requests to be included in government programs, and demands for jobs. Though a case could have been made for opposition to the Kubitschek strategy of support for industrialization at the expense of agriculture, or to his lack of concern with broad distributive issues, opposition simply did not coalesce.

Thus, clientelism helped solidify Kubitschek's political base in two ways. First, it coopted individuals into the state apparatus, giving them a small share in the benefits of occupying government. Second, its prevalence tended to inhibit the development of class or interest-based opposition.

SYNCRETISM DURING THE KUBITSCHEK PERIOD: NATIONALISM AND INCREASED FOREIGN INVESTMENT

The Second World War accentuated Brazil's sense of economic vulnerability. The scarcity of imported manufactured products during the war created uncertainty about the future and once again raised discussions about the need to industrialize the country. A few years later, the Korean War, which many expected to become a new world war, intensified anxiety about the nation's future.[40] In consequence, during the fifties the consciousness of economic backwardness and of the need to alter the economic course of the country reached a critical mass.[41] Supporters of national developmentalism could by that time be identified in the military, in professional groups, in sectors of the state bureaucracy, in industry, and in the urban middle class.

The consensus favoring national developmentalism during Kubitschek's presidency continued the nationalist trend long evident in Brazil.[42] Despite consensus with regard to the goal of development, however, opinions were divided about which particular development strategy to pursue. The group centered at SUMOC favored trade liberalization, encouraging foreign investment, and limiting state intervention in the economy. Others, including Celso Furtado and some of the economists at the National Development Bank, favored state intervention, tougher controls on foreign capital, and encouragement of domestic industry. During the Kubitschek administration, an uneasy amalgam of the two conflicting points of view informed policy.

In 1955 SUMOC Instruction 113 initiated a policy designed to attract foreign manufacturing investment into priority sectors of the Brazilian economy. It contained attractive provisions concerning both initial investment and profit remission. The *initial* policy change embodied in Instruction 113 was possible because SUMOC decisions did not require legislative approval and because it corresponded to the policy preferences of the president at the time, João Café Filho, his Minister of Finance, Eugênio Gudin, and the head of SUMOC, Octávio Bulhões. Gudin was an orthodox economist of great personal and professional prestige and a staunch ally of Bulhões. Café Filho was a member of a relatively minor political party who became president as a result of Vargas' suicide, and his economic views were rather orthodox. Perhaps more important, he and his party had no serious future political aspirations, and thus his policy choices were relatively unconstrained by concern for public opinion.

Café Filho and Gudin continued in office for less than a year after Instruction 113 was issued, but the policy, somewhat modified, continued in effect until 1962. Kubitschek did not believe that the goals of the Target Plan could be achieved without foreign participation. During the Kubitschek period, the image of foreign investment changed.[43] Under his leadership, foreign investment in manufacturing came to be perceived as legitimate in that it contributed to national economic development. It was seen as a means of increasing needed imports, especially capital goods and technology, without having to expend foreign exchange. This view of foreign investment in manufacturing, espoused by Kubitschek and his economic advisors, was not seriously challenged in the press or elite public opinion during the first Kubitschek years, even though economic nationalism with regard to other issues continued to be widespread.

Nor was the policy of encouraging foreign investment in manufacturing effectively challenged by domestic industrialists. Most opposition by industrialists took the form of personal efforts to influence SUMOC and members of the Executive. Industrialists' efforts were half-hearted and rarely successful. The belief that foreign investment would contribute to development had become so pervasive within elite opinion that domestic industrialists felt that they were expressing egoistic, personal claims in opposition to the overriding national interest in development.[44] No alternative policy was articulated in a way that could mobilize widespread support.

To sum up the Kubitschek period, then, the president and his advisors were relatively unconstrained in the pursuit of their economic preferences. They had successfully mobilized a consensus around a particular development strategy that rendered opposition by domestic industrialists suspect and morally difficult to defend. By permitting the numerically largest portion of the bureaucracy to continue operating in its customary clientelistic way, they reinforced customary personalistic political activities and reduced the probability that serious class or interest group-based challenges to policies would arise. At the same time, though, Kubitschek insulated the agencies crucial to the implementation of his development goals from those same clientelistic pressures in order to insure their competence and to secure steady and adequate investment for economic projects.

The stability of the Kubitschek period depended on the simultaneous operation of both the traditional political system and the insulated bureaucracy. The traditional system of exchanging support for benefits contributed directly to political stability while the insulated segment of the bureaucracy made possible rapid economic growth, which also contributed to the popularity and stability of the Kubitschek government. However, the simultaneous existence of these two segments of government depended on an expanding economy's ability to provide resources to carry out the development policies while at the same time continuing to support clientelistic networks through patronage. Such a system is extremely complex and extremely expensive. It is complex because it requires the organizational capacity to communicate in an effective manner in two conflicting political grammars. That is, it must be able to communicate with groups and social forces with very different interests that act according to different, and frequently contradictory, logics. It is expensive because maintaining the clientele system frequently involves consuming public resources in ways that have a low economic rate of return, even though they may bring social benefits and certainly bring electoral benefits. At the same time, the rapid and concentrated investment in gigantic infrastructural projects demanded major public expenditures.

THE DISINTEGRATION OF SYNCRETISM

The disintegration of Kubitschek's syncretic solution to the problem of how to foster economic development in Brazil's political and ideological context contributed to the economic and political chaos that led to the military coup in 1964. The severe economic difficulties under which Goulart labored -- rapidly mounting inflation, a constricting balance of payments, and an overwhelming debt -- have been dealt with elsewhere.[45] For our purposes, the important point to make is that Goulart no longer had the economic leeway to maintain both the traditional bureaucracy and a slew of expensive development projects.

Besides the economic crisis, two additional factors contributed to Goulart's loss of political support. In the first place, the uneasy ideological amalgam of nationalism and reliance on foreign investment broke down. The Kubitschek development strategy began to be criticized, especially for its reliance on foreign capital and its lack of concern over distribution.[46] In keeping with the change in public opinion, Congress passed a law limiting profit remissions. Goulart attempted to change the distribution of political influence and threatened to change the distribution of income.[47] Together, these actual and threatened changes generated serious opposition to Goulart and further limited his ability to maneuver politically.

In the second place, the amalgam of clientelism and bureaucratic insulation began to disintegrate as Goulart, in an effort to consolidate political support, attempted to return previously insulated sectors of the bureaucracy to the realm of clientelism and cronyism.[48] The resulting decline in the effectiveness of previously insulated agencies had negative consequences for the already deteriorating economy. Perhaps even more important, it galvanized support for the military coup among some of the most important economists in the country and among other elites committed to development.

The agencies most visibly affected by Goulart's attempt to consolidate political support through appointments to previously insulated sectors of the techno-bureaucracy included the National Development Bank and Petrobrás, the state oil monopoly. These two cases involve different kinds of political interference. However, in each case the consequences were the same: first, a fall in performance as competence in the agency declined and as political decision criteria superseded economic decision criteria; and, second, the attempt by members of the agency committed to its formal goals to defend its boundaries, carry out its allotted tasks, and rally public support against political incursions.

At the Development Bank, political intervention took the form of appointing administrators who were untrained in economics and accessible to political pressures. At the beginning of his term Goulart appointed Leocádio de Almeida Antunes concurently to the two most important leadership positions in the Bank, president and superintendent. Antunes was a Labor Party representative and crony of Goulart's with no experience in economics or planning. The performance of the Bank suffered during this period, as did its reputation for integrity. Loans promised to major state-owned manufacturing enterprises were delayed, causing them serious financial embarrassment. The technical staff of the Bank was hostile to Antunes, but their ability to maintain professional standards without support from the executive was limited.[49]

In 1963 Goulart attempted to pay a political debt to his close friend Lomanto Júnior, governor of Bahia, by allowing him to name the next president of the Development Bank. During his campaign for governor, Lomanto had attacked the Bank for channeling too few resources to Bahia, and had promised to secure more funds if elected. Lomanto's choice to be president of the Bank was his brother-in-law Lelivaldo de Brito, a man who had no training or experience in banking. There followed a series of maneuvers and negotiations involving Goulart, Lomanto, two different finance ministers, and the Senate, at the end of which the Senate refused to ratify Brito's nomination.[50] In this case, the Bank, threatened with having an inexperienced person foisted onto it, who was in addition publicly committed to undercutting the economic criteria used to evaluate loan requests in order to benefit his region, was able to mobilize opposition to the appointment in Congress and in the press. Bank employees carried out a successful publicity and lobbying campaign against the Brito nomination, mobilizing hostility toward Goulart in the process.

Goulart's intervention at Petrobrás took the form of greatly increasing the decision making power of the Oil Workers' Union. The union's concern centered on the welfare of its members and allies inside and outside the enterprise, not the economic performance of Petrobrás. The union ended up being able to dictate policies to the administration of Petrobrás. The management of Petrobrás became increasingly disorganized, and production fell as a result of internal disorganization and the serious downturn in the economy as a whole. Petrobrás had four presidents during Goulart's term, only one of whom lasted more than six months.[51] It lost technical and managerial personnel who were dissatisfied with low pay and frustrated by the general mismanagement. Enterprise funds were diverted into the coffers of the PTB, which was closely allied with the union.[52] Getúlio Carvalho sums up the situation at Petrobrás as follows:

> "... The institutional objectives of the enterprise were damaged and seriously distorted as a result of the search for political support from the unions.... The central concern of [the group with decision making power] revolved around the possible benefits for its members, relegating to second place the economic goals of the state enterprise."[53]

As a result, the technicians at Petrobrás became increasingly alienated. Scandals and corruption reported in the press led to a public outcry against the union and Goulart. Most important, the military, with a long time national security concern about petroleum supply, was alarmed by the deteriorating performance of Petrobrás.

These two agencies had been known for competence and professionalism before Goulart took office. Both had been insulated from clientelistic pressures during periods of their existence. In both, performance and morale declined when their insulation from individuals and groups bent on using their resources for partisan purposes eroded. Dismayed by the agency's inability to maintain its organizational integrity, some individuals in each responded by supporting the military coup.

THE CONSEQUENCES OF BUREAUCRATIC INSULATION

Operating with a world view dichotomized along the dimension of tradition versus modernity, the creators of the insulated bureaucracy sought to create in Brazil a modern society that could escape the constraints of traditionalism. The vision of modern Brazil espoused by the Tenentes in the twenties, by the UDN in the forties, and by the military and groups of technocrats in the fifties involved the creation of a public domain based on impersonal procedures, as well as industrialization. Many of these modernizers, however, came to see representative institutions such as parties and Congress as obstacles to the creation of a modern order since their pervasive clientelism perpetuated the personalistic, private basis of the traditional political system while at the same time diverting resources away from investments needed for industrialization.

Roberto Campos, for example, has argued that the legislative process of bargaining and forming consensus itself obstructed progress. Congressmen, he maintained, because of their sensitivity to the immediate demands of their clienteles, exerted pressure in favor of premature and unrealistic assistence schemes and regional projects of low productivity which reduced the rate of capital accumulation and the overall efficacy of investments.[54] According to Campos, before 1964 the Congress:

"... had been transformed into an engine of inflation by multiplying budget expenditures, and into a cause of investment distortion capable of destroying the coherence and equilibrium of plans and programs through its hypersensitivity to regional pressures.[55]

Bureaucratic insulation was justified by this sort of rationale during the fifties. The insulated bureaucracy's critical experience was one of escape from political intervention, in search of efficiency not enervated by clientelism. This escapism characterized the "pockets of efficiency" from the beginning and was crystallized in the early experiences of the insulated agencies. Insulation was taken to extremes by Campos himself and other technocrats who, coming from the experiences of planning and industrialization since the forties, collaborated with the military government after 1964. The influence of individuals associated with one of the insulated agencies, SUMOC, became decisive after the military came to power. They designed the severe stabilization measures imposed by the military, which included large reductions in real wages and which caused a wave of bankruptcies among domestic manufacturers.

Much of the military's policy toward the bureaucracy can be interpreted as a generalization of earlier experiences with insulated agencies, as an attempt to insulate the entire bureaucracy from popular, political, and personalistic pressures. The proliferation of state enterprises and other decentralized agencies during military rule was a continuation of the early strategy for end-running the traditional federal bureaucracy. Authoritarianism, repression of the unions, and destruction of the old political parties severely restricted the ability of organized interest groups to press demands through bureaucratic or party channels.

Initially, the military succeeded in reducing the exchange of jobs and other favors for political support. They also tried, especially during the early years, to reduce the numbers of redundant federal employees and to eliminate corruption. Putting a branch of the National Information Service (SNI) in each bureaucratic agency was an attempt to enforce ideological orthodoxy and prevent personal corruption. The organization and function of these SNI branches bring to mind the DASP's enforcing agencies, the *Comissões de Eficiência*, in each ministry. These efforts achieved very limited results, and most bureaucratic agencies continued to operate more or less as usual.

When the *abertura* forced the military itself to compete for political support, they, like any other electoral competitor, distributed jobs in state agencies to loyal supporters. As recent audits of the Brazilian Coffee Institute, the Institute for Sugar and Alcohol, and Embratur, the state agency in charge of tourism, show, the lack of public scrutiny during authoritarian rule increased the opportunities for corruption. The audit claims that Embratur hired many employees during the year prior to the presidential election in return for favors, and that only 900 of the Coffee Institute's 7,672 employees perform "a useful daily function."[56]

The insulated bureaucracy has thus come to share certain features typical of clientelistic agencies. Bureaucratic insulation permits the privatization of public resources which can then be used to generate political support or improve the welfare of agency or parastatal employees. Agencies lacking public accountability can use resources allotted for economic tasks instead to hire additional employees, to pay employees exceptionally well, and to offer them fringe benefits not available to ordinary citizens, such as special pension and health plans, financing for buying houses, salary bonuses, and so on.[57] The same insulation which shields agencies from partisan pressures also shields them from the public scrutiny which would limit the misuse of funds within agencies.

In sum, the military's attempt to insulate the entire government, though only partially successful, reduced still further the accountability of government bureaucracies. Modernizing groups, such as the technocrats in Brazil, are frequently assumed to be carriers of modern and universalistic values. And, in fact, the values they hold as individuals are undoubtedly modern. Nevertheless, their activities have not led to the creation of a modern order in the sense of a *public domain*, in which impersonal procedures allow citizens to scrutinize and influence government decisions without conferring on individuals particularistic rights of access to officials or to benefits. Instead, "modernizers" have contributed to maintaining unaltered the bases of "regulated citizenship"[58] of the Old Republic. Occupying the vacuum left by clientelism, some segments of the bureaucracy efficiently administered the economy, but the bureaucracy as a whole avoided becoming responsible and accountable to the citizens. The "bureaucratic rings"[59] linking bureaucrats with modern sectors of the industrial bourgeoisie may have intensified, but the insulated bureaucracy became as remote from the *res-pública* as the clientelism of the political parties had been during its heyday.

As a result, the traditional order has "framed" the modern order in the sense that reliance on politically insulated agencies to make vital policy decisions has perpetuated and reinforced traditional concepts of citizenship, participation, and the public domain. The decentralized state apparatus has ended up enjoying sufficient autonomy to enable it to get around many attempts at public control over its activities and has begun independently reproducing itself through the creation and acquisition of subsidiaries.[60] At the present moment, the question of public control over the insulated bureaucracy still has not been settled.

CONCLUSION: A NEW CYCLE

As Brazil has moved from abertura to democracy, a number of challenges resulting from the state-led modernization strategy of the past face political leaders. If effective forms of popular participation are to be found, they must include input into economic policy decisions. At the same time, though, state intervention in the economy is so extensive that any political intervention that results in mismanagement or serious inefficiency will be economically disastrous. To make matters worse, the environment of scarcity in which Brazilian policy makers must now operate, in contrast to the easy economic environment of the early

Kubitschek years, reduces the range of solutions available and makes every decision with distributive consequences more difficult.

The Sarney administration stands committed to increasing the accountability and responsiveness of the Brazilian government to its citizens. Yet it confronts the same dilemma faced by earlier democratic governments: an apparently unresolvable conflict over the allocation of jobs and other resources between party activists and Congressmen, on the one hand, whose allocation criteria reflect the priority they give to winning the next election, and administrators, especially in the Ministries of Planning and Finance, on the other, whose allocation criteria reflect a much greater concern for long-term growth.

Congress and the parties continue to be responsive to regional and particularistic demands and, in consequence, have been unable to take national policy initiatives. In their concern about re-election and their responsiveness to constituency interests, Brazilian legislators resemble their counterparts in other democracies. For several reasons, however, the common Congressional practice of exchanging favors for support seems more potentially damaging to the economy in Brazil than elsewhere. First, the Brazilian government intervenes quite extensively in the economy so that opportunities for introducing incompetence or corruption into the economic system are very numerous. Moreover, the agencies that implement economic policy tend to be fluid and flexible, which, while conferring obvious advantages for responding to changing circumstances, also makes them more easy to penetrate than a fully institutionalized arrangement would be. Second, as a result of years of gerrymandering by the military, the more backward and traditional areas of Brazil -- which gave the military its firmest base of support -- are overrepresented in Congress. Thus, although responsiveness to constituency interests in the industrializing parts of the country might lead to little conflict over whether to use resources for patronage or growth-inducing investment, constituency interests in the backward areas tend to be more particularistic and more distributionist. Finally,

Brazilian political culture, especially in the less developed parts of the country, encourages reliance on personal connections and favors over impersonal procedures, and places few restraints on the kinds of favors that might legitimately be asked for or granted.

In this context, technocrats in the Ministries of Finance and Planning -- in spite of the genuine commitment they feel toward participatory democracy -- continue to develop economic policy in virtual secrecy, with little input from elected officials, just as other technocrats did under the military. Both the Cruzado Plan[61] announced in February 1986 and the Plan of National Goals announced in July were developed in secrecy by a team of young economists and other technocrats in the Ministries of Finance and Planning. Members of Congress and party leaders had no direct influence on the content of either package and, in fact, were kept ignorant of their content in order to prevent them from mounting opposition to particular elements of the policy packages or insisting on exceptions for particular constituents. The policy packages were enacted as Decree Laws by the executive rather than being voted in Congress.

The problem which originally led to the creation of insulated agencies -- the dissipation of resources through patronage -- also remains severe. The Brazilian bureaucracy, like many others, is frequently described as bloated and overstaffed. The economic teams within the Sarney administration advocate reducing the number of redundant employees in order to reallocate the income now going to salaries to more productive uses. They have been opposed, however, by the Ministry in charge of bureaucratic reform, which has come to represent the interests of civil servants, and by the parties, which still view jobs as one of the most important forms of patronage. President Sarney, pressured by party and electoral concerns on the one side and by the need for policies that will contribute to growth on the other, favors reducing the public work force if it can be done without firing anyone.

Given these conflicting goals, the government is now trying to reduce the numbers of state employees by giving them incentives to find jobs in the private sector. Early retirement is being encouraged, and some government workers have been laid off with full pay, which at least saves the government money in electricity and phone bills, xeroxing, and office supplies. These efforts can be expected to have some success since the private sector is growing rapidly enough to absorb some new employees. Furthermore, these measures should not cost the government the votes of disgruntled or threatened civil servants. It is hard to believe, however, that they will greatly decrease the burden of salaries on the public budget.

Jose Sarney appears to be trying, though perhaps not consciously, to follow the Kubitschek strategy of combining clientelism in most of the bureaucracy with the insulation of the most essential economic policy-making organs. The balance between clientelism and bureaucratic insulation during the Kubitschek period depended on the president's extraordinary political capacity and on the propitious economic circumstances discussed above. The precarious institutionalization of this amalgam made the system dependent on circumstantial factors such as the political ability and preferences of the president and the state of the international economy. If a balance, even though precarious, between a certain amount of public control exercised by the legislature and a degree of autonomy practiced by the insulated bureaucracy was possible thanks to the Kubitschek administration, the same cannot be said of the Goulart government, much less the military governments after 1964. Is it possible that Sarney, who began his administration with an extremely fragile political base and faces a much more hostile international economy than did Kubitschek, will be capable of following a similar syncretic strategy?

To the surpise of most observers, Sarney may turn out to possess sufficient political sagacity and economic leeway to manage such a dualistic system. On the economic side, the much criticized policies of the military during the years since the miracle began to fade bequeathed to Sarney a large positive balance of payments and a highly developed industrial infrastructure, though at great social cost. The fall in the price of imported oil and the discovery of new off-shore oil reserves also contribute to leeway in the balance of payments. Sarney's most serious economic problem is the debt, which imposes severe limits on economic policy options. Even so, the international economy has had its silver lining: expanding markets for Brazilian exports. All in all, though the economic situation Sarney confronts is far more difficult than that faced by Kubitschek, some leeway exists, and the success of the Cruzado Plan so far suggests that the Sarney administration may be able to make the most of it.

On the political side, the ingredients for an amalgam are all in place: a president whose closest advisors are members of his family and old friends; a Congress, parties and large parts of the bureaucracy dominated by clientelism; and an insulated sector of the administration which makes the most important economic decisions. The balance among these forces is certainly precarious, and it is impossible to tell at the moment whether Sarney will be able to continue managing it. He has not done badly so far, however. Whether the amalgam can be institutionalized in some fashion that will spare Brazilians future swings between repressive authoritarian experiments in total insulation and almost equally disastrous experiments with unfettered clientelism remains to be seen.

NOTES

1. We use the term techno-bureaucratic to distinguish those agencies whose performance depends on technical expertise from the rest of the bureaucracy.

2. We would like to thank the other participants at the conferences in Nova Friburgo, Brazil, and Berkeley, California, for their helpful comments and criticism of earlier drafts of this paper. We are of course responsible for whatever errors of fact and interpretation remain.

3. Though an integrated industrialization policy only took shape in Brazil during the 1950s, some government agencies that aimed to improve Brazil's economic standing had existed for decades. On the relationship between government policies and early industrialization, see Pedro S. Malan *et. al.*, *Política econômica externa e industrialização no Brasil (1937/52)*, Relatório de Pesquisa no. 36 (Rio de Janiero: Instituto de Planejamento Econômico e Social/Instituto de Pesquisas, 1977); Albert Fishlow, "Foreign Trade Regimes and Economic Development: Brazil," forthcoming as Volume 10 of the Special Conference Series on Foreign Trade Regimes and Economic Development, National Bureau of Economic Research/USAID; Regis Bonelli and Ricardo Tolipan, "Industrial Policies in Brazil: A Summary of Two Decades," (Rio de Janeiro: IPEA xerox, no date); and Eli Diniz, *Empresariado, estado, e capitalismo no Brasil* (Rio de Janeiro, 1978).

4. In a 1972 survey, for example, 74 percent of respondents who expressed an opinion agreed that, "the people know what is best for themselves, but not what is best for Brazil." An even larger number, 84 percent, agreed that "if the government paid too much attention to what the people want, the country would end up in a mess." These data are drawn from the survey "Representation and Development in Brazil, 1972-1973," conducted by the Instituto Universitário de Pesquisas do Rio de Janeiro and the University of Michigan. The data are available from the Inter-University Consortium for Political and Social Research at the University of Michigan.

5. These political and administrative developments were, of course, affected by developments in the international economy, though we will not discuss these developments here. On these issues, see, in addition to the items cited in Note 1 above, Carlos Lessa, "Quinze anos de política econômica," in *Cadernos do Instituto de Filosofia e Ciências Humanas*, UNICAMP, 1975 (published by ECLA in English as "Fifteen Years of Economic Policy in Brazil," *Bulletin for Latin*

America, IX:2 [November 1964] 153-214); Francisco de Oliveira, *A economia da dependência imperfeita* (Rio de Janeiro, 1977); Carlos Estebam Martins, ed., *Estado e capitalismo no Brasil* (São Paulo, 1977); Maria da Conceição Tavares, *Da substituição de importações ao capital financeiro* (Rio de Janeiro, 1972); Tavares, "Acumulação de capital e industrialização no Brasil," Tese de Livre Docência, FEA, UFRJ, 1974; Carlos Von Doellinger, "Política, política econômica e capital extrangeiro no Brasil: as décadas de 30, 40, 50," *Revista Brasileira de Mercado de Capitais*, 3:8 (May-August 1977). Our focus on the political causes and consequences of the institutional context within which policies were made does not imply that we think either the economic challenges facing Brazil or the content of the economic policies designed to meet those challenges were unimportant. But we do believe that understanding would be incomplete without attention to the political and administrative aspects of economic policy making.

6. A very incomplete list includes Thomas Skidmore, *De Getúlio a Castelo* (Rio de Janeiro, 1969); Olavo Brasil de Lima Junior, *Partidos políticos brasileiros* (Rio de Janeiro, 1983); Wanderley Guilherme dos Santos, "The Calculus of Conflict: Impasse in Brazilian Politics and the Crisis of 1964," Ph.D. dissertation, Stanford, 1979; Maria do Carmo Campello de Souza, *Estado e partidos políticos no Brasil* (São Paulo, 1976); Maria Victoria Mesquita Benevides, *A UDN e o Udenismo* (Rio de Janeiro, 1981); Lucia Lippi de Oliveira, "O partido Social Democrático," Masters Thesis, IUPERJ, Rio de Janeiro, 1973; Helio Jaguaribe, "Política de clientela e política ideológica," *Digesto Econômico*, 6:68 (1950); Bolivar Lamounier and Maria D'Alva G. Kinzo, "Partidos políticos, representação e processo eleitoral no Brasil, 1945-1978," *Dados*, no. 19 (1978).

7. "Generalized" exchange is a term used by anthropologists to distinguish structured systems of exchange which are based on an obligation to reciprocate in the absence of contracts from systems of "specific" exchange characteristic of

capitalist market economies. See S. N. Eisenstadt and L. Roniger, "Patron-Client Relations as a Model of Structuring Social Exchange," *Comparative Studies in Society and History*, 22:1 (1980) 42-77; Luigi Graziano, "Introduction," *International Political Science Review* IV:4 (1983) 429-430.

8. See, for example, Hélio Jaguaribe, "As eleições de 1962," *Tempo Brasileiro*, no. 2 (1962) p. 12.

9. Eli Diniz, "Clientelismo Urbano," *Novos Estudos Cebrap*, 1:4 (1982); see also, Diniz, *Voto e máquina política: patronagem e clientelismo no Rio de Janeiro* (Rio de Janeiro, 1982); J. A. G. Albuquerque, "Pra não dizer que não falei de rosas," *Novos Estudos CEBRAP*, 1:4 (1982).

10. Olavo Brasil de Lima, "Electoral Participation in Brazil 1945-1978: The Legislature, the Party Systems and Electoral Turnout," *Luso-Brazilian Review*, 20:1 (1983) 65-92.

11. Oswaldo Trigueiro, UDN governor of Paraiba, 1947, interview cited by M. Benevides in *A UDN e Udenismo*, p. 58. This and all other translations from Portuguese were done by the authors. For other analyses of the transition, see M. C. Campello de Souza, *Estado e partidos políticos*; Glaúcio Ary Dillon Soares, *Sociedade e política no Brasil* (São Paulo, 1973), Ch. IV; and Skidmore, *De Getúlio a Castelo*, p. 80.

12. L. Lippi de Oliveira, "O partido Social Democrático."

13. "Patronage and Its Opponents," xerox, Conference on the Scope and Practice of Social Science History, Madison, 1976.

14. Thomas Skidmore, *Politics in Brazil, 1930-1964: An Experiment in Democracy* (London, 1967) pp. 57, 357.

15. Fernando Henrique Cardoso discusses the PTB's control of government agencies in São Paulo in "Partidos

políticos," in Paul Singer and Vinicius Caldeira Brant, eds., *São Paulo: o povo em movimento* (Petrópolis, 1980), especially pp. 179-180.

16. M. Benevides, *A UDN e o Udenismo*, p.29; see also, Fernando Henrique Cardoso, "Partidos e deputados em São Paulo," in Bolivar Lamounier and F.H. Cardoso, eds., *Os partidos e os eleições no Brasil*, (Rio de Janeiro, 1978) for a discussion of the UDN in São Paulo.

17. Cited in Magalhães Pinto, "Relatório político do Presidente Magalhães Pinto," manuscript, 1960. For the perspective of a UDN politician and journalist whose intransigent opposition to Vargas and his heirs frequently took the form of campaigns against corruption, see Carlos Lacerda, *Depoimento* (Rio de Janeiro, 1978).

18. Recollected by Saramago Pinheiro, Deputy, and founder of the UDN in the State of Rio de Janeiro, interviewed by Márcia Silveira, November 11, 1979.

19. M. Benevides, *A UDN e o Udenismo*, p. 269. Quotes are from the Archives of the UDN.

20. See Barbara Geddes, "Economic Development as a Collective Action Problem: Individual Interests and Innovation in Brazil," Ph.D. dissertation, University of California, Berkeley, 1986, especially pp. 153-164, for a discussion of public attitudes toward administrative reform and citations to survey evidence.

21. Erving Goffman uses "framed" to convey the idea that individual behavior and group action are constrained by the institutional setting in which they occur. *Frame Analysis* (New York, 1974).

22. F.H. Cardoso, "Partidos políticos," pp. 183-187; O. Lima, "Electoral Participation," p. 77; David Fleischer, "The Role of the National Legislature in the Organization of

Political Parties in Brazil," presented at the APSA meeting, Washington, D.C., 1979; and Robert Wesson and David Fleischer, *Brazil in Transition* (New York, 1983), pp. 91-120.

23. G. Soares, *Sociedade e política...*, p. 65.

24. Physiological is the literal translation of the Brazilian term *fisiológico*, which is used to describe party members concerned only about benefits and not at all about ideological matters.

25. F.H. Cardoso, "Partidos políticos," pp. 179-187.

26. Celso Lafer, "The Planning Process and the Political System in Brazil: A Study of Kubitschek's Target Plan -- 1956-1961," Ph.D. dissertation, Cornell University, 1970, pp. 151-152.

27. For exhaustive treatments of the DASP, see Gilbert B. Siegel, "The Vicissitudes of Governmental Reform in Brazil: A Study of the DASP," Ph.D. dissertation, University of Southern California, 1966; Beatriz Wahrlich, *Administração de pessoal: principios e técnicas*, Fundação Getúlio Vargas (Rio de Janeiro, 1964); Lawrence Graham, *Civil Service Reform in Brazil: Principles vs. Practice*, (Austin, 1968).

28. Pedro A. C. Lago, "A SUMOC como embrião do Banco Central: sua influência na condução da política econômica, 1945/65," Masters Thesis, Department of Economics, Pontífica Universidade Católica, Rio de Janeiro, 1982, p.8, based on depositions by Eugenio Gudin and Casimiro Ribeiro.

29. P. Lago, *op. cit.*, pp. 8-131.

30. Rogerio Feital S. Pinto, *The Political Ecology of the Brazilian National Bank for Development*, Organization of American States (Washington, D.C., 1969), pp. 46-47; Lafer, p. 53. Former directors of the National Development Bank interviewed by Pinto reported that the Target Plan was

prepared by members of the Bank staff, under the direction of Roberto Campos, then superintendent of the Bank, and, according to Lafer, Lucas Lopes. The Target Plan benefited from the earlier work of the *Comissão Mista, Brasil-EUA*, the Abbink Mission, the *Assessoria Econômica* of the second Vargas administration, and the CEPAL-BNDE group. Without this accumulation of knowledge about the Brazilian economy during the preceding ten years, the Target Plan would not have been possible.

31. C. Lafer, "The Planning Process," pp. 151-152.

32. C. Lafer, *O sistema político brasileiro* (São Paulo, 1975), p. 67.

33. For details about the funds and surtaxes set up or reorganized to provide resources for the Target Plan, see Lafer, "The Planning Process," pp. 116-125.

34. For a thorough discussion of the Executive Groups, see Lafer, "The Planning Process," especially pp. 165-210. See also, Maria Victoria Mesquita Benevides, *O governo Kubitschek* (Rio de Janeiro, 1981) pp. 229-230.

35. Paulo Roberto Motta, *O Grupo Executivo como instrumento administrativo de implementação econômica*, Fundação Getúlio Vargas/EIAP, Monografia no. 19 (Rio de Janeiro, 1968).

36. "Análises e perspectivas da indústria naval," Arquivo do Sindicato da Indústria Naval (SINAVAL), June 1964; "Grupo Executivo da Indústria da Construção Naval, um plano em marcha," Serviço de Documentação, Comissão de Marinha Mercante, no. 22 (1958); *Síntese cronológica*, Presidência da República (Rio de Janeiro: 1959), pp. 83-84.

37. Bernard Rosen, *The Industrial Connection: Achievement and the Family in Developing Societies* (New York, 1982).

38. Carlos Verissimo do Amaral, "As controvertidas nomeações para a previdência social em 1963: estudo de um caso," in Amaral and Kleber Nascimento, *Política e administração de pessoal: estudos de dois casos*, in *Cadernos de Administração Pública*, no. 60 (Rio de Janeiro, 1966) pp. 17-19; Gilbert Siegel, "Administration, Values and the Merit System in Brazil, in Robert Daland, ed., *Perspectives of Brazilian Public Administration*, v. I, *The Comparative Series in Brazilian Public Administration* Los Angeles: University of Southern California and the Fundação Getúlio Vargas, Escola Brasileira de Administração Pública (1963) p. 7.

39. L. Graham, *Civil Service Reform...*, pp. 147-148.

40. See the interview with Walter Moreira Salles in *Isto E*, 5: 258 (December 2, 1981), p. 91, for a description of the atmosphere in Brazil just prior to the Korean War. See also José Serra, "Cíclos e mudanças estruturais na economia brasileira do pós-guerra," in R. Coutinho and L.G.M. Belluzzo, eds., *Desenvolvimento capitalista no Brasil* (São Paulo, 1982), p. 74. Documentation of the North American government's efforts to involve Brazil in the Korean War can be found in the Getúlio Vargas Archive, housed at CPDOC in Rio de Janeiro.

41. With respect to the importance of the consciousness of economic backwardness for the process of development, the classic reference is Alexander Gerschenkron, *Economic Backwardness in Historical Perspective* (Cambridge, Mass., 1962). In the Latin American context, with numerous references to Brazil, see Albert Hirschman, *A Bias for Hope* (New Haven: Yale University Press, 1971). See also the review by Caio Navarro de Toledo, *ISEB: Fábrica de ideologias* (São Paulo, 1977); Gabriel Cohn, *Petróleo e nacionalismo* (São Paulo, 1968). A version written in the heat of events is Hélio Jaguaribe, *O nacionalismo na atualidade brasileira* (Rio de Janeiro, 1958). The many "nationalisms" of the 1920's and 1930's are discussed in Mónica Pimenta Velloso, *O mito da originalidade brasileira*, (Rio de Janeiro, 1985).

42. Miriam Limoeiro Cardoso, *Ideologia do desenvolvimento: Brasil, JK-JQ* (Rio de Janeiro, 1977), especially chapters 10-11.

43. On April 6, 1958, the *New York Herald Tribune* published a poll showing that only 14 percent of Brazilians surveyed believed foreign investment to be "bad" for the country. This was the lowest percentage in any of the twelve countries included in the survey. Lincoln Gordon quotes a corporate executive as saying that "it was not Instruction 113 that made us decide to go into Brazil, but the investment climate that it represented." *United States Manufacturing Investment in Brazil* (Boston, 1962), p. 33.

44. Nathaniel Leff, *Economic Policy-Making and Development in Brazil, 1947-1964* (New York, 1968), pp. 59-66, based on interviews with industrialists and government economic bureaucrats.

45. See especially Michael Wallerstein, "The Collapse of Democracy in Brazil: Its Economic Determinants," *Latin American Research Review*, XV:3 (1980) 3-40. For discussions of the relationship between the kind of crisis that faced Goulart and characteristics of the import substitution model of development followed by Brazil, see Albert Fishlow, "Origins and Consequences of Import Substitution in Brazil," in Luis DiMarco, ed., *International Economics and Development* (New York, 1971); and Albert Hirschman, "The Political Economy of Import Substitution Industrialization in Latin America," in his *Bias for Hope*.

46. See, for example, N. Leff, pp. 132-153; Skidmore, *Politics in Brazil* pp. 179-284; Navarro de Toledo, *ISEB: Fábrica de Ideologias*; Rene Dreifuss, *1964: A conquista do estado: acão política, poder e golpe de classe* (Petrópolis, 1981).

47. Wallerstein shows that little if any change in the ratio of profits to wages actually occurred during the Goulart period, *op. cit.*, pp. 15-24.

48. W. Dos Santos offers quantitative evidence of this trend in "The Calculus of Conflict," pp. 214-220.

49. R. Pinto, *op. cit.*, pp. 56-57.

50. *Ibid*, pp. 57-58.

51. Getúlio Carvalho, *Petrobrás: do monopólio aos contratos de risco* (Rio de Janeiro, 1967), p. 166.

52. *Ibid*, pp. 127-150.

53. *Ibid*, p. 150.

54. Roberto Campos, "O poder legislativo e o desenvolvimento," in Cândido Mendes, ed., *O legislativo e a tecnocrácia* (Rio de Janeiro, 1975), p. 36. Campos was one of the technocrats most representative of the planning and insulation effort in the Brazilian bureaucracy. He has served in a number of posts, practically without interruption since the forties. Campos was secretary of the Brazilian delegation to the Bretton Woods Conference. He was economic advisor at the United Nations during the Dutra government, returning to Brazil to work on the Comissão Mista Brasil-EUA. When the BNDE was created in 1952, Campos became a director, later superintendent and, finally, under Kubitschek, its president. He was an advisor to President Quadros, and was ambassador to the United States under Goulart until he renounced the post in 1963 because of disagreements over Goulart's policies. After the coup in 1964, he was named Minister of Planning. The details of Campos' career are in Robert Daland, *Development Politics and Administration* (Chapel Hill, 1967), p. 33.

55. R. Campos, "O poder legislativo," p. 35.

56. See *Latin American Monitor* 2:7 (September 1985), pp. 205, 211, for a summary of the findings of the auditors and citations.

57. For a discussion of "regulated citizenship" in Brazil, see Wanderley Guilherme dos Santos, *Cidadania e justiça* (Rio de Janeiro, 1979); see also W. G. dos Santos, "Em defesa do laissez-faire" and Bolivar Lamounier, "Representação política: a importância de certos formalismos," both papers presented at the Seminar on Law, Citizenship, and Participation, sponsored by the Ordem dos Advogados do Brasil and the Associação Nacional de Pós-Graduação e Pesquisas em Ciências Sociais, São Paulo, 1979.

58. See, for example, Marcos de Sá Correa, *Veja*, May 12, 1983, who reports on the exclusive privileges of functionaries in public enterprises. Dealing with attempts to control the parastatals in light of negotiations with the IMF, *Veja* reports:

> Through the years the [state] enterprises, with the extra zero added as always when public money is involved, came to pay more than their employees of the monthly contributions to the [pension and social welfare] funds, in contrast to what happened to common mortals.... Now [the package negotiated with the IMF] wants to make the system uniform in such a way that the beneficiary will always pay the larger share of the contribution. At Petrobrás and the Bank of Brazil presently... the enterprise pays two thirds of the contribution. [The IMF] also wants to establish once again that the number of salary-months does not exceed thirteen, and they intend to prohibit the distribution of profits that are simply the result of the monetary correction of assets. Last year, Banerj suffered a financial loss, revalued its assets, generated an apparent profit, and divided it among its employees....

> With regard to the parastatals, ultimately the measures [proposed] will fall into the same vacuum into which all earlier attempts to get rid of special benefits and control salaries have fallen -- because of the simple fact that the implementors of the control laws will be, almost always, persons who benefit from the anomalies that the laws are intended to combat.

59. Fernando Henrique Cardoso develops the notion of "bureaucratic rings" in *Autoritarismo e democratização* (Rio de Janeiro, 1975).

60. Data on the number of state enterprises and their size can be found in Presidência da República: Secretaria de Planejamento-SEPLAN, Secretaria de Controle de Empresas Estatais, *Relatório*, 1981, and *Cadastro das Empresas Estatais*, 1980.

61. For summaries of the Cruzado Plan, see *Latin America Regional Report: Brazil* (March 14, 1986), p. 3; and *Latin American Monitor: Mexico and Brazil*, 3:2 (March 1986). For the economic theory and arguments that support the Plan, see Persio Arida *et. al.*, *Inflação zero -- Brasil, Argentina, Israel* (Rio de Janeiro, 1986); and Francisco Lopes, *O choque heterodoxo: combate a inflação e reforma monetária* (Rio de Janeiro, 1986.)

5

Novo Sindicalismo and Politics in Brazil

Maria Hermínia Tavares de Almeida

During the long transition from authoritarian rule to democratic politics in Brazil, a variety of new collective actors emerged on the political scene. Among them was the new union movement (*novo sindicalismo*), which represented a radical challenge to a state labor relations system that had since the 1940s demonstrated remarkable flexibility and adaptability. Brazil has a longstanding and highly complex set of institutions designed to control labor relations which are corporatist, undemocratic, subordinated to and part of the state apparatus. In the face of demands for union autonomy, freedom to organize, shop floor democracy and a decentralization of collective bargaining processes, these institutions stood their ground and blunted the effectiveness of the new unionism. Thus in the waning years of the military regime, novo sindicalismo had not yet effected a radical transformation of Brazil's system of labor relations. However, on its own turf in the automotive and engineering industries dominated by modern corporations, it successfully legitimized new demands, bargaining practices and forms of shop floor organization. These demands converged with broader demands for the recognition of working class citizenship within a liberalizing Brazilian polity. And while struggling against the authoritarian order the movement progressively expanded its scope to become the dominant force in the labor movement as a whole, and spawned the Partido Trabalhista (PT).

Until recently the Brazilian labor relations system permitted the existence and growth of state regulation and intervention in production activities, as well as modes of free, direct, and decentralized bargaining. As a result, labor relations reflected a mixture of conservatism and change. Changes were evident in the projection of labor beyond the sphere of strictly union activity, and into the national political arena with an alternative political party based on the anti-populist objectives of autonomous working people. However, conservatism was maintained by the state institutions that hindered the development of a fully autonomous labor movement. Only recently has the labor movement as a whole begun to emerge from the embrace of these old institutions, largely as a result of the formation of a new labor confederation, the Central Unica de Trabalhadores, in 1983.

This chapter traces the trajectory followed by novo sindicalismo as a union movement to its role in partisan politics. It is not intended to present an exhaustive reconstruction of recent Brazilian labor movement issues and trends. Its purpose is limited to describing and explaining the shift in orientation on behalf of movement leaders, from concern with specific authoritarian labor policies and corporatist labor institutions at the beginning, to a confrontation with the authoritarian regime itself, resulting in the attempt to organize a "new kind of party," a worker's party. The analysis shows how early demands for freedom and autonomy fostered by leaders acquired different meanings in changing circumstances, and came to embody new and different attitudes towards political participation and party politics more generally. In the final section I summarize the major dilemmas facing the movement and the PT today.

FROM UNION REFORM TO PARTY BUILDING

The Worker's Party (PT) was officially launched on February 10, 1980 at a São Paulo rally attended by delegates from all parts of Brazil. The founding group included academics, activists working with grassroots community groups linked to the Catholic Church (CEBs), and members of various Trotskyite or Trotskyist-oriented groups, all under the leadership of a nucleus of labor leaders. It had taken almost a decade to organize the party, to shift from protest against authoritarian labor policies to creating an opposition party. This period can be divided into several distinct phases.

The movement was born from the experience of workers in the automotive industry, organized by the Sindicato dos Metalúrgicos of São Bernardo do Campo (São Paulo),[1] and from 1970 to 1976 went through what might be termed its gestational phase. Originating in the context of large scale, mass production factories, the early movement responded to a specific set of social and economic circumstances. In this period, Brazil's economy was expanding vigorously. Data from Table 5.1 reveal the impact of this economic expansion on Brazil's occupational structure. Between 1960 and 1980 almost five million new jobs were created, an increase of nearly 350 percent in the manufacturing industries.

In their chapter in this volume, Hasenbalg and do Valle Silva calculate that in 1970, 28 percent of all manual workers in the manufacturing sector (some 1.2 million persons) were employed by modern high-productivity enterprises, led by the durable consumer goods, capital goods, and intermediate goods sectors.[2] In 1980, the number of persons employed in these sectors more than doubled (nearly 2.5 million), comprising some 34 percent of all manual laborers working in industrial manufacturing.

This dynamic economic growth took place when the the power of the authoritarian regime was at its height. Military governments promoted wage constraints, banned free collective bargaining, abetted employers in implementing harshly repressive personnel policies, clamped down on aggressive union activity, and reduced political life inside unions to quasi-ritualitualistic participation in highly controlled and non-competitive elections.

As a consequence of economic growth and policies which squeezed wages, income distribution was unequal and regressive. The real minimum wage, which regulates the pay of unskilled industrial workers, slumped from 1964 until 1974, and then began a modest recovery. But even when wages did improve, higher paid workers benefitted more than lower paid employees. Studies of the manufacturing industry of São Paulo have shown that from 1969 to 1975, the wages of unskilled workers increased 16 percent, while wages of manual semi-skilled workers increased 35 percent, those of middle level office employees 42 percent, and high wage-earners 63 percent.[3]

TABLE 5.1

Rates of Growth in Employment by 10-Year Periods
(in percent)

Sectors	1950-60	1960-70	1970-80
Primary	1.82	0.64	0.02
Secondary	1.93	6.06	7.26
Manufacturing	1.98	5.19	7.78
Construction	2.94	8.21	6.24
Other Industrial	(1.34)	5.01	7.14
Tertiary	5.43	4.02	6.00
Distribution	4.50	3.35	5.67
Service	5.45	2.62	6.09
Public Adminis.	4.88	6.22	6.11
Other	13.50	7.08	6.40

Source: FIBGE: Tabulações avançadas do censo demográfico de 1980, in Vilmar Faria, "Desenvolvimento, urbanização e mudanças na estrutura de emprego: a experiência brasileira dos últimos trinta anos"; B. Sorj, and M.H. Tavares de Almeida, (eds.), *Sociedade e política no Brasil pos-64* (São Paulo, 1983), pp. 146, 151.
Note: Data on the distribution of the economically active population among various economic sectors in the period 1960-1980 are found in Table 3.2 in this volume.

Despite repression in large modern factories, workers resisted from time to time with spontaneous slow-downs and, occasionally, strikes by particular shops, where most workers were highly skilled. The early 1970s saw the first work stoppages in the toolrooms of a number of auto giants, as protests against an excessive amount of compulsory overtime.[4] Despite very tight political constraints, new union leaders arose who came to be known as *autênticos*.

But because they were held in check by coercive legislation that the government strictly enforced, the unions were obliged to limit their actions to sending petitions, making speeches and holding congresses in 1974 and 1976. These early critiques of the wage and labor-relations policies of the authoritarian regime were colored by the perspectives of those working in modern industries. Demands were made and justified in terms of labor conditions in large plants equipped with the latest technology. These were: the repeal of policies tying wage hikes to productivity in a given branch of industry; free, direct, decentralized bargaining; the right to organize on the shop floor; and freedom and autonomy of labor unions. Such were the main demands of the São Bernardo metalworkers in the early seventies. These demands sprang from conditions in a heavy industrial setting, but they would soon spread to other sectors as well.

The First Congress of Metalworkers of São Bernardo do Campo and Diadema (1974) analyzed this situation very well:

> "... We all know that the major companies in our industry are part of the most modernized sector of our economy. We are familiar with their characteristics and with the implications of their being multinationals. We acknowledge the fact that they have made a valuable contribution by increasing the number of jobs on the labor market, and we recognize as well that workers in the auto and similar industries get higher nominal monthly rates of pay than do workers in other industries. Nevertheless, we are fully aware that it is the high productivitiy of our work that has given these companies the chance to achieve

> the highest growth rates.... We are also perfectly aware of the fact that our much-publicized 'higher than average' wages are only apparently so, if compared with those earned by workers in plants of the same companies in other countries, and when seen in terms of our productivity. It is a fact that these companies do give some extra 'perks' to a small number of very highly skilled employees, but the rest of the workforce, *i.e.* the overwhelming majority, is treated exactly like workers in traditional businesses, under cover of legislation that, in our opinion, is totally unsuited to present-day conditions. The high turnover of the labor force, used by the employers as a way around the compulsory wage hikes for senior employees; the extension of the working day, with the maximum exploitation of the worker's capacity; the deliberate wage squeeze, a practice adopted as a coordinated policy by the personnel departments of the major industrial firms; the open repression of union activities and union organization -- these are merely a few of the problems now faced by our class."[5]

At this first stage the unionists were avowedly nonpolitical. Leaders justified this stance in terms of their past experience and current circumstances. Labor's participation in politics during the populist period after 1945 was condemned for exposing workers to political manipulation by political elites. Nevertheless, criticism was not limited to the specific ways in which old-line populist unionism took part in the political arena. Past experience was generalized to condemn any form whatsoever of politicizing the unions, something now considered an illegitimate use of worker's organizations. Since politics was equated with manipulation, they argued, authentic unionism must therefore keep its distance while building itself as a militant and strong representative of workers against business in the collective bargaining process.

Thus union autonomy, the slogan that defined the new unionism, initially had a double meaning. On the one hand, it implied the independence of the labor union organizations from the state, which had previously subordinated and controlled them. On the other hand, it meant keeping out of the political sphere, in which workers had traditionally been assigned a subordinate role.

To be sure, this distrustful abstention from participation in politics undoubtedly reflected the experience of exclusion from citizenship under the authoritarian regime. This was indeed a feeling shared by large segments of the population in the early 1970s. Brazilian society as a whole was enveloped by political apathy, and by the privatization of everyday life. The 1970 cogressional elections provided an accurate picture of this climate.[6]

But this non-political attitude could not actually be put into practice without contradiction and ambiguities in a society where the public and private spheres were entangled, and where the state played such an important role in the development, regulation and functioning of the market. State interference in labor relations -- which the post-1964 authoritarian state had only exacerbated -- ended up transforming the government into labor's number one adversary. The state itself thus became a target for criticism and demands.

At the same time, since Brazilian authoritarianism after 1964 had not dispensed with elections or parties, both could occasionally be used as instruments for voicing discontent. The tendency of working people to vote for the regime's only legally recognized opposition party, the Movimento Democrâtico Brasileiro (MDB), was recognized by the emerging union leadership. This was especially so in 1974, when the elections took on the character of a plebiscite to judge both government and regime, and the vote went heavily against both.[7]

In this context, relations between the new unionists and the MDB were characterized by ambiguity, but became less so by the time political parties were reorganized in 1979. The president of the São Bernardo Metalworkers union who had been the first to articulate the demands of the new union movement, for example, abandoned his intransigent defense of non-political union activism to become a member of the MDB and, later, a city councilor. Attributing significance to elections and to the opposition party (the MDB) as vehicles for protest became more and more meaningful as the political liberalization process (known as *abertura*, or "opening") gathered speed after starting in 1974. But in the thinking and the rhetoric of the new working-class leaders, changing political conditions did not at first allay their distrust of the parliamentary opposition party and their rejection of party politics.

The second stage of the movement's trajectory was shorter, running its course from 1977 to 1978. With the gradual consolidation of abertura the unions managed to obtain more room to maneuver. Brought on by the public admission of manipulation in calculating cost of living adjustments by the federal administration, the 1977 campaign for wage increases projected the São Bernardo Metalworkers Union to the forefront of national politics. And one year later, the auto industry was the setting for an explosion of strikes which then spread throughout the industrial zone of Greater São Paulo. Novo sindicalismo became a leading faction in the union movement as a whole and a national force, aided by the multiplying effect of the mass media which, freed of censorship controls, covered the new leaders and their programs. With the São Bernardo Metalworkers Union taking the lead, hitherto isolated leaders in other modern industries set up an informal alliance and began to coordinate their activities nationwide. This in turn jolted and resuscitated the spokesmen of a mediocre and virtually impotent union bureaucracy, which had accepted authoritarian controls passively and peacefully.

At this moment, the precise dimensions of novo sindicalismo are difficult to estimate. Its core was a small group of less than thirty urban unions and state federations of São Paulo, Rio Grande do Sul, Minas Gerais and Rio de Janeiro. In some critical events the core group was able to mobilize for specific purposes a far greater number, almost one hundred unions. We know that in 1978 there were nearly nine million unionized urban and agricultural workers, organized in 3,795 officially recognized unions and federations, of which 526 unions and 23 federations were in the state of São Paulo. Nevertheless, the influence of novo sindicalismo among active labor unions was far greater than its numerical expression, since it represented a particularly mobilized part of the urban working classes, the "new working classes" of the modern industrial sector.

This second stage saw a proliferation of congresses, public statements of principles, and plans to reform the labor laws. Union leaders shifted their emphasis from specific demands upon the modern industrial sector to unifying themes which would appeal to urban working masses as a whole. These included proposals for a single legal minimum wage for the whole country; abolition of certain authoritarian laws governing wages and job tenure; the right to shopfloor organization; the right to strike; and union autonomy. Autonomy from the state was confirmed as a fundamental aspiration, the hallmark of novo sindicalismo.

The apolitical stance was now abandoned both in practice and as an ideal. The new union leadership now specifically acknowledged the need to act within the framework of the national political arena. At the same time, the placement of workers' demands on the national political agenda was felt to be a natural continuation of trade union action. When the Geisel administration announced it would reform the political system, by eliminating some of the most blatent authoritarian institutions, the new unionists responded in the following terms:

> "... Once again we are informed that the government intends to decree a package of reforms, without consulting the people or asking them what they want, with the supposed aim of solving the serious institutional and social problems which are faced by the Brazilian people.... In the face of these proposed reforms which are designed merely to serve the interests of the dominant groups, we say that the very top demand of the workers union organizations is the right

> to full union freedom. Restoring the autonomy of labor unions in effect means restoring the right to strike, so that in peaceful, egalitarian and fraternal struggle, we can return to free bargaining between employers and workers. It also means the right to a stable job, and the elimination of controls imposed by the Ministry of Labor."[8]

Labor leaders injected the issue of the rights of citizenship for subordinate classes into the debate on democratization. And they did so by forcing their participation in the closed political arena within which entrenched political elites believed they could liberalize the regime without substantively democratizing it. What should be stressed here is not so much the effect these speeches and actions of the militant unionists had on the progress of liberalization, but rather the perception of politics that informed their words and deeds.

At this moment their aspiration to achieve autonomy took the form of independent political action with regard to existing forces and parties. In the last resort, autonomy meant acting as a pressure group in order to be heard by politicians and parties, and to obtain their support for workers' demands. As the most important metalworker leader, Luis Inácio da Silva ("Lula") put it:

> "... Not only workers but the whole Brazilian people should get into politics, even if it's when they're in the bar drinking *pinga*. I really can't agree that politicians should have any influence inside the unions, but I think the unions are duty-bound to influence the politicians."[9]

Acting on this line of thought, new unionist leaders went to Brasilia in late 1978 to demand that Congress reject a government draft bill that practically banned the right to strike. Though threatened with removal from office by the Minister of Labor, the union leaders went to the capital anyway, only to discover that Congress was indifferent to their demands. This disappointment only fed their traditional distrust of politicians, parties and Congress.

At the same time, a certain notion of class representation began to appear in the thinking of the new leadership. A kind of "descriptive notion" eventually crystallized and became the core value in their striving for autonomous participation.[10] In Lula's words:

> "... Solving the problems facing the working class doesn't depend on the creation of a political party. I believe that the problems of the working class will be solved when the working class participates in politics regardless of whether or not it creates its own political party. Just imagine what things would be like today if we had hundreds of workers representing us, maybe in both political parties.... I believe that if political parties are created in which the working class doesn't take part, the class will stay in the same place it is in today. Irrespective of parties, workers must participate in the nation's decisions. And when they do participate, things will change automatically."[11]

Despite their distrust of parties and the concern with autonomy, union leaders knew they had to face the challenge of elections, and decided to become actively involved in the 1978 Congressional elections. They made a careful choice of candidates from the opposition party through a process of tough negotiations. It was in this way that the main leaders of the new unionism in São Paulo threw their weight behind the campaign of Senate candidate Fernando Henrique Cardoso, the well-known sociologist and opposition figure, and managed to force him to accept a running mate whom they fully supported. Lula recounted his view of this episode:

> "... I think the same about MDB or ARENA. They're both parties of the bosses, of the bourgeoisie, and they won't do much for workers, except in the extremely exceptional cases of a few candidates who really do

> have links with the working class.... When we made contact with Professor Fernando Henrique Cardoso, he was told -- and he himself knew this -- that what we would really like would be to have a union leader as a candidate. Since this would be impossible... we had no choice but to support Fernando Henrique Cardoso, although he himself made a point of saying that he wasn't a workers' candidate."[12]

For many new unionists, taking an active part in the 1978 election campaign reinforced their feeling of social distance between professional politicians and workers. But it also showed them the need for political participation through the party system. The next step would be to create a party of their own, an autonomous workers party. Indeed, the idea of setting up such a party was in the air, but only when the new unionists went through the experience of a mass mobilization and its contradictory consequences did this project take shape. Between 1979 and May of 1980, the union movement discovered the importance of mass action. A wave of large strikes shook the country's Center-South, and definitively placed the question of worker citizenship on the agenda of democratization.[13] At that moment, strikes, mass mobilizations and public demonstrations became the prevailing forms of political action, and were actively organized, promoted or supported (when spontaneous) by the new unionist leadership.

The strategy adopted by the movement was to show that the old labor laws and institutions could not function any more, that they were therefore anachronistic and in urgent need of radical reform. The aim was to make the state system of labor relations collapse under the pressure of the mobilized masses, and to defeat authoritarian politics and laws, while ensuring widespread grassroots participation and democracy. This strategy effectively annulled the relevance and meaning of union action based on bargaining. The 1979 and 1980 auto and metalworkers strikes in São Bernardo raised a set of non-negotiable demands for freedom, autonomy and recognition of the presence of the working class.[14]

Within the labor union itself the strategy of the new unionists did not produce the desired institutional changes owing to a complex set of circumstances. The spread of strikes beyond the frontiers of key modern industries had a paradoxical outcome, in that it simultaneously brought into question and revitalized traditional labor institutions. It gave new importance to rights and forms of mobilization and organization that had been left behind by the modern working class. For the underprivileged sectors of the labor market, simply achieving enforcement of existing labor laws was sufficient grounds for collective action, whereas workers in advanced technology industries wished to reformulate them altogether. For their own reasons, middle-class salaried employees in the public sector, who were intensely involved in the strike movement, made the recognition of minimal social demands and the right to organize in unions the focus of their participation.

The disparity between the situations, experience and expectations of the various participants gave the government far greater room to maneuver. Its policy was to combine the repression of novo sindicalistas with prudent, conservative reformism. One example was the reformulation of the law governing wage adjustments and indexing in order to incorporate some of the labor movement's demands. The diverse composition of the working class also facilitated support for and lent a degree of feasibility to the conservative policies implemented by the "moderate" union leaders, who were always far more numerous than the "authentic" novo sindicalismo group. On the other hand, the experience of a whole year of mass mobilization and the discussion of labor's options with respect to political parties altered the dynamics of the labor movement.

One group, formed by the independent left wing and communist unionists who had joined the new unionists in the 1977-1978 period, began to diverge from them over union and political matters. These leaders moved closer to the moderate, pro-establishment labor officials who controlled the majority of Brazilian unions, or at least found a *modus vivendi* with them over time. The outcome was the creation of the union bloc known as Unidade Sindical.[15] The growing tension between Unidade Sindical and the new unionism bloc, on the other hand, pointed to their increasingly divergent views of union affairs and politics. The result was that for better or for worse, the experience of mass action and the split it produced had the effect of causing a drastic transformation in relations between politics and the new unionism.

At the end of 1978 all the signs indicated that the demand for freedom and autonomy would lead to the creation of a new form of political unionism, that the labor movement, at least its most vocal members, would become political actors alongside the parties, and would be able to bring constant pressure to bear on them while remaining independent from parties. Yet this was not what happened. Novo sindicalismo went into retreat when the flood of strike actions abated in 1980. The retreat was marked by a sharpening of internal conflicts among the movement's constituent factions, and was exacerbated by the early effects of the gathering economic crisis following the second oil shock. Nevertheless, this declining mass mobilization and the shrinking opportunities for trade union action contributed to shifting the new unionist leaders' energies to party politics.

Meanwhile, the complex interplay of forces driving the pace and the shaping the political liberalization process led, in 1979, to the government's reform of the political parties. The MDB and ARENA (the government party) disappeared. This reshuffling eliminated the two-party system imposed in 1966 and opened up new alternatives, within limits, for the alignment and expression of political groups.

These changed circumstances led the new unionism movement to redefine its role in national politics. The goal of autonomy was reassessed and reformulated once again, but now it became the creation of autonomous political representation through a workers party. Lula saw the process as follows:

> "... I was really an apolitical leader until 1977. It was only when the strikes broke out that we realized the need to participate in politics. We realized that the two activities were closely connected, that there

> was no use in getting an extra 10 percent if the men in power had the means to bring in a new wage policy to take away all the working class's victories.
>
> "... To sum up, I'd say that the 1970s -- although I've only had 3 years of experience in the union -- have been very positive for three basic reasons:
>
> 1) The workers have rediscovered themselves as the only part of society which is able to propose the transformation of society.
>
> 2) With this rediscovery, we have done away with the anti-strike law and the wage squeeze once and for all.
>
> 3) All this has led us to even more important discoveries. for example, it's not enough to brush aside the Special Powers acts and go on strike. It's not enough to break the back of the laws cutting wages, because on its own that won't solve the workers' problems. So we discovered the need for workers to organize politically, to provide themselves with support and alternative organization. That's how the idea arose of the Workers Party, or 'PT'."[16]

This was the way the union leadership of the new PT evaluated its mission. In fact, there were several other groups involved in the consolidation of forces making up the new PT.

CLASS IMAGES, POLITICS AND THE PT

The PT was born as a typical mobilizing party in Rochon's definition,[17] in that it tried to build and mobilize a new political identity from several groups. The PT was created in the confluence of political forces that came into being under the authoritarian regime, above all during the decade of abertura. These included leaders and activists in the new unionism movement; militants and organizers in urban popular movements, mostly sheltered under the umbrella of the Church; new social movements (feminist, black power or sexual-minority groups), academics, and militants (or former members) of the radical Marxist left.

What united all these groups was a common critique of authoritarianism, which contained a radical anti-statist ideology and a deeply rooted belief in the resourcefulness of an autonomous civil society. Further, they shared a critique of the behavior of existing political parties, including the MDB, along with the pre-1964 popular parties, such as the PTB and various Communist Parties, all of them thought to be unauthentic and elitist.

The political and ideological positions of the new unionist leaders exerted great influence in shaping the new party's political mood and public image. One can detect a number of key themes that characterized PT ideology from its birth. In the discourse of novo sindicalismo, the idea of autonomy was always accompanied by a strong class affirmation. Thus, the image of the working class as central political actor replaced the more generic images of small people and poor people, which were the hallmarks of populist rhetoric. Leaders proclaimed the working class' rights to full citizenship, including autonomous representation in national politics and also the recognition of its own role in the development process, with its rightful share in the benefits of economic growth.

The PT's platform took shape within the framework of a class critique of the social cleavages in Brazilian society. In Lula's words:

> "... I think the PT -- though I don't like saying this because the press will start to exploit it right away, and say that I'm 'classist,' '*obrerista*,' etc.-- is a party which is much nearer to being a class party than anything else. Now there's another thing: people who think we're a class party shouldn't be horrified by that because all the existing parties belong to the ruling class. So it's right for the PT to be close to being a class party, because it came out of the

workers' organization."[18]

"... We're not creating a party of workers, of metalworkers, but a party of Brazilian working-class people, because we have a very broad concept of what a working-class person is. This includes liberal professionals, teachers, and a number of other groups in society who directly or indirectly live in subordination to a wage- or salary-earning regime. So we're not getting away from this business of being a workers party, which the government is so afraid of."[19]

And as Francisco Weffort, the political scientist and party theoretician who later became Secretary General, elaborated in the same vein:

"... To claim that class-based parties are necessarily incompatible with democracy means to ignore that the major Western democracies (except for the USA) have a firm tradition of class parties. These range from the Social Democrats -- of whom so much is said nowadays, in all kinds of contexts -- to the British Labour Party, and includes the various Communist Parties, such as the Italian and French CPs. It matters little, in this context, how one would critically evaluate today's and yesterday's policies pursued by these parties. The fact is that their existence is a sure sign that it is difficult to conceive of modern democracy without solid workers' political organizations...

"It is certainly true, however, that the idea of a workers party can be expressed in a far broader formulation than the notion of a class party in the narrow sense might lead one to suppose. Although the idea of a workers' party here was born in the labor unions and, it would seem, with a significant level of participation by groups of industrial

> workers, above all the metalworkers, in explicit terms this idea has taken on a broader range of connotations. It is undoubtedly a party without bosses. But what has been suggested ever since discussions began is that it should be an organization of the popular masses, with a broader base than the industrial working class in particular."[20]

In truth, the PT's stance on class was ambiguous, because its notion of what constituted the working class tended to be ambiguous. If some preferred a narrower definition of workers as blue collar workers, others pressed for a version that was broad enough to inclue all wage- and salary-earning employees. Not surprisingly, a compromise version emerged in which "workers" were synonymous with the "popular masses."

But is is not the conceptual ambiguity that matters. Rather, it is what this ambiguity reveals about the way in which a pervasive mass society and its conflicts were perceived. In certain contexts the stress fell on the striking social distinctions of an elitist and authoritarian social and political order. This is where the term "us" overlaid the image of the poor manual laborer. At other times, the fluidity of such social distinctions was emphasized in order to accommodate a society in which the perception of class distinctions was eroded by chances for mobility and participation in a mass-consumption market. The latter view implies a situation in which all wage earners could be seen as equals, however great the differences in their life-styles and levels of income.

In fact, various definitions of the working class coexisted in the discourse, conceptions and practices of the PT. Now one was uppermost, now another, depending on how the party's identity was being built in distinction from that of other parties, as the political struggle was waged.

Based on its previous experience, novo sindicalismo also brought with it into the PT a distinct form of anti-authoritarian ideology, in which advocacy of grassroots democracy and plebiscitary participation went hand-in-hand with a marked opposition to the state's control of society (anti-statism) and an acute distrust of representative institutions which have traditionally made up the political system.

In this way, the political vision of novo sindicalismo intersected and converged with several ideological components of branches of the Catholic Church, specifically its "preferential option for the poor." These Catholic groups were also anti-state and distrustful of traditional forms of politics, while sanctioning the virtues of self-help, community initiative, and popular solidarity. It associated the idea of human dignity with that of equality between citizens.

In studying the Catholic *comunidades eclesiais de base* (Christian base communities), the sociologist Antônio Flávio Pierucci has written:

> "... In order not to limit themselves to a purely religious conduct but to reconstitute and enrich the human values of solidarity, fraternity and mutual aid; and in order to awaken the sense of human dignity, which means demanding rights rather than asking favors, fighting for social justice and equality in the distribution of material and cultural goods, the CEBs have come to the point of placing Catholic militants alongside other individuals and groups of a lay ideological inspiration, in their refusal of authoritarianism and rejection of the centuries-old domination reinforced by the prevailing model of economic growth, which reproduces in a more accentuated manner the existing inequalities and exclusion."[21]

The elective affinities between the political platform of novo sindicalilsmo and the Church's base communities are striking, and they explain how these two kinds of experience could come together in the PT. Yet they became stronger still through action, mainly during the mass strikes of 1979 and 1980 in São Bernardo do Campo. It was then that the resistance movement organized by the unions was backed by the Catholic Church as an institution, as well as getting concrete support in the poor neighborhoods where the Church promoted and organized forms of solidarity in everyday life. The fact that the Church and the CEBs provided leadership in the day-to-day struggle gave them an enormous political and moral advantage over the other political forces, whose backing of the metalworkers on strike was substantial.[22]

Anti-statism and the distrust of traditional machine politics, which were two related themes in the PT world view, were undeniably rooted in the political exclusion under authoritarianism experienced by large segments of Brazilian society. However, they represented a perception of only a part of the experience of living under an authoritarian regime. The same state that denied citizens the right to participate in politics was also present in the day-to-day life of the masses as supplier of goods and services, or as mediators for demands and favors.

Thus, in their actions, the PT militants -- whether members of the unions or of other urban movements -- alternately turned their backs on the state and then dealt with it in order to secure running water, paved streets, day care centers and medical clinics for their constituency. PT deputies spoke strongly against Congress, but made use of their privileges and immunity to reinforce demands from the grassroot sectors.

In short, anti-statism and distrust of the political system, the search for autonomy, class affirmation and participatory democracy were the themes that produced the PT brand of politics. Nonetheless, the party's political actions often conflicted with these very same aims. At such moments, rhetoric and performance seemed to be at odds. The national electoral campaign of 1982 was central to the crystallization of the PT's images of society, politics and the functions of political parties. In the fight for votes the PT had to distinguish itself from its competitors, above all from the PMDB (as the MDB was renamed after the 1979 party reforms). Thus it stressed class appeals in order to differentiate itself from the PMDB's broader appeal to the popular and democratic electorate. This had the effect of accentuating the narrower definition of class allegiance mentioned above.

THE FIRST TEST: ELECTIONS

Since its creation the PT has gone through two election campaigns. These were the 1982 elections for governor and federal and state legislatures, and the 1985 elections for mayor of state capitals. In neither has the PT's performance been yet properly analyzed.

The PT's 1982 electoral campaign was characterized by an extensive mobilization effort and the systematic effort to differentiate the PT from the other opposition parties (PDT, PTB and PMDB), especially the PMDB. This drive was reflected in the choice of candidates, slogans and images for the campaign, which in every case stressed *the class dimension of the party*. The PT's major slogans were "worker votes for workers" and "vote PT, a party without bosses." Red flags, clenched fists and angry workers' faces were shown profusely in the party's television advertisements. The campaign culminated in a stream of attacks on the major opposition party (PMDB) which was accused of being identical to the government's PDS party. The electoral results provide a picture which is highly revealing. In national terms, the PT earned an insignificant number of votes. Table 5.2 provides an overview of this situation.

In six states, the PT received fewer votes than the number of party members enrolled in those states. In eight others, membership figures barely accounted for the total PT share. In reality, it became clear in practice that the PT was, at least in electoral terms, little more than a São Paulo state party: 72 percent of its total of 1,460,000 votes for the Federal Chamber of Deputies came from São Paulo. In this state, the party achieved a significant 10 percent of all votes cast and as much as 14.3 percent for the capital city alone (7.1 percent for the rest of the state). Its candidate for mayor was elected in Diadema, the municipality where most of the grassroots members of the São Bernardo metalworkers union reside. Table 5.3 shows that the votes cast for the PT paralleled the distribution of votes for the PMDB and, as in the latter case, had a strong popular connotation. Indeed, Lamounier's data on the distribution of votes by homogeneous socioeconomic zones in the municipality of São Paulo clearly reveal that the PT grew in strength in the poorest areas.

It is clear that the party's class appeal did have repercussions among certain minority segments of the population in metropolitan São Paulo. Still, the class-based platform of the PT does not seem to have appealed to the broader strata of lower-class wage-earners in the state of São Paulo, nor, above all, those in other parts of Brazil. It also appears to have failed to win over those "other" workers, the white-collar workers, a large group which represents a significant portion of the country's salaried working class and a decisive electoral force. These voted PMDB.

By emphasizing its class character, the PT provided a political identity and voice for a group of metropoliltan workers who experienced injustice, daily lack of respect and social exclusion. This in itself fulfilled a democratizing role in Brazilian society. But given the feeble electoral results in 1982, it could hardly be said that the PT was becoming the democratic mass party as intended by the intellectuals and labor unionists who founded it.

Yet the poor electoral results in 1982 did not have negative consequences for the PT's leading role in the union movement. Confirming an old pattern of Brazilian working class political behavior -- the tendency to separate union political allegiance from party political preference -- the PT's influence upon the union movement grew steadily. The PT's union leaders became almost hegemonic among the mobilized and dynamic sectors of the Brazilian labor movement. In 1983, pro-PT unions formed the Central Unica de Trabalhadores (CUT), a new national labor confederation which gave full expression to the new unionist labor policies and politics.

Moreover, the poor electoral showing in 1982 affected the power relationships within the PT. The emphasis on class politics was held to be responsible for the less-than-satisfactory results at the polls. Consequently, the internal balance shifted towards a more moderate leadership which favored the full integration of the PT into the democratic game and its transformation into a mass democratic party. This facilitated a new strategy for the 1985 mayoral elections in the state capitals.

In the city of São Paulo, one of the PT's largest and most important electoral bases, the party presented itself as an alternative to the right wing candidate Jânio Quadros as much as to the PMDB, which was suffering through the rather traumatic experience of governing the state under an economic crisis and tightened budgets. In contrast to the aggressive class images of the 1982 campaign, the PT now presented itself as a new, democratic and quite de-ideologized alternative to the old party politics. On television, good humored political advertisements replaced the red banners and angry faces of the first campaign. The party's candidate for mayor (Eduardo Suplicy) was a new face -- handsome, rich, gentle and full of good will. His slogan was: "Try Suplicy. He's different from those we've had up to now."

Throughout Brazil the PT presented itself as the only authentic opposition party, and it tried to aggregate the diffuse protest votes which are traditionally important in the large cities of Brazil.[23] As shown in Table 5.4 the results were highly favorable for the PT's prospects. The party became a national force, winning in Fortaleza, an important northeastern capital, and reaping large vote tallies in at least four other cities including São Paulo.

But despite these successes, the internal balance of forces had still not shifted definitvely toward those leaders who wanted the PT to be a mass democratic party fully integrated into the Brazilian political system. The internal struggle between these groups and those favoring a class party, or even a marxist revolutionary party became sharper and more open after the 1985 elections. This struggle is still being waged today. Moreover, the PT labor leaders, who have great authority in the party's inner circles and in setting party policies, seem to move from one position to another without a clear definition.

TABLE 5.2

Performance of the PT in 1982 Elections by State

STATE	PT votes as % of Total (1)	PT Votes per Member (2)	Number of PT Candidates Elected to Office				
			Federal Deputies	State Deputies	Mayors	City Councillors	
						in Capital	in Interior
São Paulo	9.0	14.5	6	9	1	5	73
Minas Gerais	1.8	2.8	1	1	0	0	13
Rio de Janeiro	2.6	2.9	1	2	0	1	1
Acre	5.2	4.4	0	1	0	2	1
Rondônia	3.0	2.8	0	0	0	0	2
Rio Grande do S.	1.1	3.1	0	0	0	1	0
Paraná	0.3	0.8	0	0	0	0	0
Sta. Catarina	0.3	1.1	0	0	0	0	0
Mato Grosso do S.	0.7	0.5	0	0	0	0	0

Mato Grosso	0.2	1.3	0	0	0	0	0
Goias	0.6	0.9	0	0	0	0	0
Bahia	0.7	2.6	0	0	0	0	6
Espirito Santo	1.2	1.9	0	0	0	0	0
Sergipe	0.3	1.3	0	0	0	0	0
Alagoas	---	---	---	---	---	---	---
Pernambuco	0.2	0.7	0	0	0	0	0
Paraiba	0.3	0.7	0	0	0	0	0
R. Grande do N.	0.4	0.6	0	0	0	0	0
Ceará	0.5	1.7	0	0	0	0	0
Maranhão	0.8	1.6	0	0	1	0	9
Piaui	0.6	1.8	0	0	0	0	3
Pará	1.1	1.7	0	0	0	0	5
Amazonas	1.2	2.0	0	0	0	0	4
TOTAL	3.0	5.6	8	13	2	9	117

Source: Raimundo Pereira, "Duas táticas eleitorais," *Folhetim*, January 30, 1983, p. 9.
(1) Statistics on votes for the Federal Chamber published by the Supreme Electoral Tribunal (TSE).
(2) *Em Tempo*, December 12, 1982.

TABLE 5.3

Votes for Candidates for State Governor in the Municipality of São Paulo, 1982, by Homogenous Socioeconomic Zones (as percentage of total votes cast)

Areas	Reynaldo de Barros PDS	Roge Ferreira PDT	Lula PT	Jânio Quadros PTB	Franco Montoro PMDB	Blank	Null	Absolute No. of Voters	% Turnout
I	23.5	1.8	11.2	17.2	41.0	2.9	2.4	318,932	85.3
II	21.7	1.5	11.5	19.2	40.9	2.8	2.4	273,528	83.5
III	20.8	1.5	13.3	21.2	38.1	2.6	2.5	306,745	85.5
IV	20.8	1.5	11.3	23.7	37.7	2.4	2.6	266,558	83.6
V	18.7	1.4	13.4	21.7	40.2	2.1	2.5	626,901	87.7
VI	15.8	0.9	12.2	27.7	39.2	1.8	2.4	691,796	88.3
VII	14.4	0.9	17.2	19.3	44.1	1.7	2.3	721,707	87.8
VIII	14.1	0.6	17.8	15.4	48.2	1.6	2.4	774,497	87.7
TOTAL	17.4	1.1	14.3	20.6	42.1	2.0	2.4	3,980,644	86.8

Source: São Paulo Regional Electoral Tribunal (TRE-SP); Bolivar Lamounier, "São Paulo: a geografia do voto." *Folhetim* 315, January 30, 1983.

Note: Zones are ranked from I (richest) to VIII (poorest). Classification by SEPLAN-SP: Sub divisão do municipio de São Paulo em areas homogêneas, estudos e pesquisas no. 12, 1977.

TABLE 5.4

Votes for Candidates for Mayor of the City of São Paulo in 1985 by Homogenous Socioeconomic Zones (in percent)

Zones	Jânio Quadros PTB	Fernando H. Cardoso PMDB	Eduardo Suplicy PT	Suplicy and Cardoso
I	35.6	43.4	13.6	57.0
II	37.1	40.4	14.9	55.3
III	37.8	37.7	16.3	54.0
IV	41.6	35.1	14.7	49.8
V	37.2	35.1	19.0	54.1
VI	42.8	29.8	18.9	48.7
VII	36.0	31.7	23.1	54.8
VIII	34.3	32.4	24.4	56.8
TOTAL	37.5	34.2	19.7	53.9

Source: São Paulo Regional Electoral Tribunal (TRE-SP).
Note: Zones are ranked from richest (I) to poorest (VIII). See Table 5.3 for similar data on 1982 state gubernatorial elections in São Paulo.

Until now the PT has alternated between instrumental political action within the established rules and an expressly anti-establishment behavior, without being able to choose between these two paths. Sometimes it behaves as a protest party[24] expressing the feelings of political and social exclusion of those popular sectors which are on the outskirts of the Brazilian polity. Sometimes it seems to have decided to take its place within the established party system, to search for political power and to compete for it with the other parties. Can it combine an emphasis on mobilization and grassroots participation, on the self help of the common people, with the role of a real political party, capable of playing the political game while integrating the working classes into the political system?

In the past ten years, from the initial challenge of novo sindicalismo to corporatist labor laws to the establishment of the PT, one can discern a redefinition of forms of public participation by the urban working classes. Whether in the mode of unionist activity or party politics, these forms can be seen as efforts to break from the patterns of control and political exclusion exercised by the authoritarian regime. Similarly, they have also represented a denial of corporatist modes of integration of urban workers into public life through populist politics.

As far as unionism is concerned the institutions and practices of the new labor movement still seem to function inside the old, but now "liberalized" system of corporatist labor relations. Novo sindicalismo is no longer a new issue; it has become the dominant orientation of the Brazilian labor movement. However, until very recently at least, worker demands for autonomy from the state still had to be negotiated within the framework of old corporatist structures, and this meant negotiations between unions and the government.

As for political recognition of the working class, the mere fact that a political phenomenon like the PT could emerge with its profound quest for autonomy means that neither authoritarian exclusionism nor populist inclusionism *cum* manipulation are acceptable to a socially significant section of the urban poor. Having said this, it is by no means certain how the PT constituency will be inserted into national politics. The PT has steadfastly refused to be co-opted into the PMDB. But given the leadership's ambiguous views on its constituency, and its continuing suspicions of party politics in general, it is not certain that the party will be able to move beyond being a force for social democratization to become a viable contender for power in its own right.

NOTES

1. The Sindicato dos Metalúrgicos de São Bernardo e Diadema organizes the manual and non-manual employees of automotive, engineering, foundry, electrical, and metal goods factories of São Bernardo do Campo and Diadema, neighboring idustrial municipalities in metropolitan São Paulo. Almost all the international automobile companies operating in Brazil -- Ford, General Motors, Volkswagen, Toyota, Mercedes Benz, and Scania Vabis -- are located in this region. During the seventies, workers from the major auto companies comprised nearly 60 percent of the unionized workers belonging to this union.

2. Carlos Hasenbalg and Nelson do Valle Silva, "Industrialization, Employment and Stratification in Brazil," Chapter 3 in this volume.

3. Eduardo Matarazzo do Suplicy (1977) cited in Maria da Conceição Tavares and Paulo Renato Souza, "Emprego e salário na indústria: o caso brasileiro," *Revista de Economia Política*, v. 1: 27 (1981).

4. More information on these movements can be found in Frederico Celso, *Consciência operária no Brasil* (São Paulo, 1978); also see John Humphrey's *Capitalist Control and Workers' Struggle in the Brazilian Auto Industry* (Princeton, 1982).

5. "Resoluções do I Congresso dos Trabalhadores das Indústrias Metalúrgicas, Mecânicas e de Material Elétrico de São Bernardo do Campo e Diadema" STIMMMESBCD, mimeo, Sept., (São Bernardo, 1974), pp. 1-2.

6. The apathy and lack of interest in politics of large segments of the population was made manifest by the unusual number of blank and null votes. See Fernando Henrique Cardoso and Bolivar Lamounier, eds. *As eleições de 1974* (Rio de Janeiro, 1975).

7. *Ibid.*

8. Luis Inácio da Silva, *Lula -- entrevistas e discursos*, (São Paulo, 1980), pp. 129-130.

9. *Ibid*, p. 32.

10. Hanna F. Pitkin, *The Concept of Representation* (Berkeley, 1967).

11. Luis Inácio da Silva, *op. cit.*, pp. 48-49.

12. *Ibid*, p. 69.

13. See M.H. Tavares de Almeida, "Tendências recentes da negociação coletiva no Brasil," *DADOS*, 24:2 (1981), pp. 161-170. Also "O sindicalismo brasileiro entre a conservação e a mudança," in B. Sorj and M.H. Tavares de Almeida eds., *Sociedade e política no Brasil pós-64* (São Paulo, 1983).

14. At the final rally of the metalworkers strike in São Bernardo, in 1979, Lula spoke in the following terms:

> "... What really matters is that we keep the flame alight. We are the winners. We must walk into the factories with our heads high tomorrow! This strike must show the bosses that they can never doubt the will of the working class again. Let no one ever again doubt the workers' ability to struggle."

He then asked the Bishop of Santo Andre to lead the group in saying the Lord's Prayer. The Minister of Labor ordered Lula and the other directors of the union to be legally removed from office. See *Entrevistas e discusros* (São Paulo, 1980).

15. It is not easy to assess the real strength of both union blocs. The Unidade Sindical seemed to attract a greater number of unions and union leaders. Nevertheless, novo sindicalismo seemed to have more capacity for mass mobilization.

In the first big congress of the national union after the 1964 coup (CONCLAT), held in 1981, the 5000 union delegates were evenly divided around Unidade Sindical and novo sindicalista positions, and so balanced were they that no controversial proposition could be voted upon.

16. Luis Inácio Silva, *op. cit.*, pp. 232-233.

17. T. Rochon proposes a distinction between two types of new parties: mobilizing and challenging parties. The former "are a response to changing cleavage structures, or perhaps to the softening of existing cleavage structures through electoral dealignment. Such parties attempt to take advantage of changing social and political conditions by emphasizing their association with new cleavages and by mobilizing new identities.... The mobilizing party is based on a program that stresses new issues and looks at old issues from a new ideological vantage point." T. Rochon, "Mobilizers and Challengers: Towards a Theory of New Party Success," *International Political Science Review*, v. 64 (1985), pp. 419-440. Renato Boschi also addresses some of these issues in Chapter 6 of this volume.

18. Luis Inácio Silva, *op. cit.*, p. 299.

19. *Ibid*, pp. 247-248.

20. Francisco Weffort, "Autonomia sim, isolamento não," *Isto E* (August 1, 1980), pp. 8-9.

21. Antônio Flávio Pierucci, "De l'Eglise traditionelle aux communautes ecclesiales de Base," *Problemes d'Amerique Latine*, v. 65:3 (1982), pp. 74-75.

22. For a good analysis of social movements from this perspective, see Ruth Cardoso, "Movimentos sociais urbanos: balanço crítico," in B. Sorj and M.H. Tavares de Almeida, eds., *op. cit.*

23. For an analysis of opposition electoral behavior of mass urban electorates in the Third World see Samuel P. Huntington, *Political Order in Changing Societies* (New Haven, 1968).

24. Protest parties are parties "representing relatively diffuse protest against the present society and they have no real expectation of taking or sharing power." See G.B. Powell, *Contemporary Democracies; Participation, Stability and Violence* (Cambridge, Mass., 1982), p. 94.

6

Social Movements and the New Political Order in Brazil

Renato R. Boschi

The 1970s were a major turning point for Brazilian society. Of the many transformations that took place, the remarkable increase in the rate of urbanization looms as one of the most salient structural changes in Brazil. Rapid urbanization in this decade had broad social and economic implications, including an expansion of the urban middle sectors, the creation of a modern segment in the work force, and high rates of urban employment.[1]

Urbanization was not a new phenomenon. According to the 1970 census, a majority of the Brazilian population had already become urban dwellers. Of these, almost 39 percent of the population lived in cities of more than 20,000 inhabitants. By 1980, however, fully 75 percent of the urban populalation lived in cities with more than 100,000 inhabitants. Moreover, the population tended to concentrate in large metropolitan areas exceeding one million inhabitants, and the number of medium-sized cities increased. These data suggest that Brazil's demographic structure shifted dramatically over the decade.

Concurrently, the structure of the state underwent an impressive transformation as it expanded, diversified, and became better equipped to confront change. The state apparatus grew not only in the sphere of production, but also through the creation of regulatory agencies, leading to an intensification of its activities in the realm of social policy. While it was successful in monitoring the impact of social movements with repression, the growing bureaucracy was unable to deal effectively with problems often induced by its own policies.

Social movements on a large scale, coupled with the spread of the state into a number of social spheres, manifest critical aspects of the interface between deep structural transformations and state expansion. Increasingly, and much more rapidly than one could have imagined just a few years ago, collective social movements have become a key element in the dynamics of Brazilian social change. Whether occurring as sporadic mob actions or as broader social movements, collective action in the form of organized associations has become an important way to protest and make political demands. If there is no good estimate of the size of these movements, their visibility in the mass media, to say nothing of the sociological interest they have aroused as subjects of analysis, suggests that they are widespread.

According to the news magazine *Isto E* there may be upwards of 8,000 neighborhood associations in Brazil.[2] In Rio de Janeiro alone, some 100,000 working and middle class people from 120 neighborhoods belong to about 200 associations. To this total should be added about 350 associations from the *favelas*. For São Paulo the same source lists 900 associations. Similar groups may be found in other major cities, such as Salvador, Curitiba and Belo Horizonte.

If collective movements were restricted only to the phenomenon of neighborhood associations, this portrait of a society organizing at the grass roots would be impressive enough. But the associational drive extends to other groups such as feminists and blacks, to ecological and anti-nuclear groups (Belo Horizonte), to groups calling for better mass transportation (Rio de Janeiro, Salvador and Belo Horizonte), and to those pressing for better health conditions (Rio de Janeiro and São Paulo). No less important are the land invasions which, organized or spontaneous, are ever more prevalent in metropolitan areas. Other less structured collective actions include the sacking of supermarkets and large riots such as the one occurring in downtown São Paulo in April 1983, or the large mass demonstrations calling for direct presidential elections in 1984.

Most of these social movements have been scantily studied, if at all. The literature, while growing, is still more useful for recording cases rather than for interpretation, and it has focused primarily on urban popular sectors. Very little has been written to date about the middle classes, even though their role as mobilizers and participants is evident in many of the events and processes listed above.[3] Favored by economic growth in the 1970s, the middle class expanded only to be pushed back by the recession of the early 1980s. In the realignments of the early 1980s, the middle class emerged as an important political group in opposition to the military regime, and it is bound have a decisive role in the shaping of Brazilian society under the New Republic.

This chapter analyzes one aspect of middle class collective action: association building at the neighborhood level that emerged in the late 1970s. Rio de Janeiro stands out as perhaps the most vivid example among the many cities where the phenomenon is flourishing. Rio's experience with associations is analyzed with research data collected on the early stages of the movement. For comparative purposes, other experiences are discussed, in particular those involving lower class settlements and favelas.

Issues regarding the interpretation of collective movements in general, as well as in the Brazilian context, are addressed in the first section. Several inadequacies in current interpretations are discussed, including the serious theoretical difficulties posed by the relationship of collective action to the political-institutional realm. In the final section, I assess the potential of these movements for aiding the consolidation of a democratic political order in Brazil.

INTERPRETING COLLECTIVE MOVEMENTS

To evaluate collective movements and their impact one must see the coming together of two interrelated processes. On the one hand there is the accelerating penetration of civil society by the state; on the other are the factors that produce collective action.

Since the nation-state was formed, many different types of collective manifestations have been related directly or indirectly to the state's progressive monopolization of civil society.[4] As for collective action itself, the central question is how to account for its institutional impacts and results. This is related to the characteristic dilemma of collective actions: the problem of how to sustain them.[5] The importance of social movements is precisely the extent to which new collectivities can pressure their way into becoming legitimate political actors. In other words, if these movements produce new social alignments, what is their impact at the institutional level?

Any serious analysis of the role of the so-called "new" social movements cannot overlook the complexities involved in both the generation and the outcomes of collective action. It is in the confluence of these processes that the core of a theory of political change can be found. However much analysts may disagree over the causes of collective action, they tend to see this process as a combination of contextual and probabilistic elements.[6] Thinking about the political results of collective action is complex, particularly with regard to the direction of change and its institutional implications, because the realm of political institutions usually corresponds to successful mobilization.[7]

Attempts to incorporate collectivities or excluded interests into the political domain cause tension in the institutions, because of their dual nature: they permit inclusion while legitimizing exclusion. This is true of the mechanism of representation itself. It functions both to mitigate uncertainty in the early stages of identification of interests and the creation of collective identities,[8] but also to contain the possible impact of collective action through participation.[9]

Thus, institutionalization must be thought of as an inherent part of the logic of collective action since it is instrumental in producing the rhythmic ebb and flow seen in the formation of collectivities. Institutions also shape the daily experiences of individuals, giving form to resentments and establishing limits on demands and collective action. They are also an underlying determinant of the forms that protest can assume, in the sense that it is institutional life that aggregates and disperses people, in terms of physical space if nothing else. The neighborhood, as much as the factory, is a case in point.

The existing literature on Brazilian social movements does not seriously address these issues. Despite having posited some dramatic accomplishments for these movements, the analyses use no systematic methodology and tend to be informed by ideological presuppositions that are not made explicit. Ideologically, the assumption is that a society in a state of permanent mobilization is desirable and, moreover, is actually possible. Participation is valued as an end in itself, while the possibility of representation is disparaged. Combined with an ideal of "autonomous collectivism," mobilization and participation are thought to be ways to prevent the cooptation of these movements by the state.[10]

On the empirical level, the actual reach of social movements is exaggerated, particularly with respect to their horizontal links to other social segments, including labor and political parties.[11] The case studies used extensively in this literature do not make use of the proper methodology for making generalizations about this. And finally, on the theoretical level, these studies sidestep the issue of change although it permeates this whole discussion. In sum, the extant literature either takes as a given or simply ignores the analysis of social movements precisely at their most problematic aspect, which is the political-institutional effects of collective action.

Thus an indiscriminate "progressive" content is attributed to the activity of collectivities, whether organized or not. The movements' links to the state apparatus, both with respect to their genesis and to their role in opening space for political representation, are ignored. The idea that political change could take place within such a framework, either theoretically or practically, is discarded. The term "institutionalization" is not used much in the literature, being identified with suspicion as part of the status quo. Instead there prevails a romance with the movements, seen as something to be preserved in a pure state, but stripped thereby of their role in the development process and of their dialectical character.

Finally, these studies rarely address the political-institutional aspects of these movements, how they relate in some way to the achievement of citizenship and other victories in the face of pervasive state control. To the extent that they deal with the matter at all, most of these works manage only to identify differences in the social bases of movements or their degree of organization.[12]

It bears repeating that action taken by the state is a correlative of the emergence of collective action. There may be a variety of collective actions with different impacts -- this by virtue not only of the nature of collective action itself, but also because of differences in the local, discrete performance of the state. This is particularly true of the Brazilian state, which became very complex, diversified, and underwent rapid transition. Moreover, all this collective activity took place originally in confrontation with the state in the attempt to open space for underrepresented interests, or to assure entrance of new groups into the political arena.

Thus the central preoccupation of much thinking on Brazilian urban movements should probably be redirected. Rather than emphasize the radical *potential* of urban social movements for disrupting existing structures, scholars should acknowledge just how limited their short-term impact really is. On the other hand, analyses of the transition of authoritarian regimes tend to hold that change occurs from the "top down," thereby neglecting the role of social movements in the creation of at least the foundations of new democratic political cultures.

Social movements in Brazil are frequently viewed as responsible for a democratization of social relations. From a perspective that combines both the "top down" and the "bottom up" of this transition process, the issue to address is whether this democratization of social relations has as its counterpart the institutionalization of equally democratic processes in such things as political parties and the state. Is there any correspondence between these two processes, each one so pervasive in Brazil in the 1980s?

NEW FORMS OF URBAN ASSOCIATION

Both in the poor sections of metropolitan peripheries and in the middle class districts, neighborhood associations have become so significant that one may truly speak of a national movement.[13] Associations concerned with land use issues and the legalization of land titles have sprung up in virtually all the metropolitan regions, from Amazonas to Rio Grande do Sul. A research project co-directed by the author discovered a large number of neighborhood associations on the urban periphery of Manaus, Belém, São Luis do Maranhão, Fortaleza, Campina Grande, Recife, Brasília, Belo Horizonte, Rio de Janeiro and even Curitiba, which at the time this survey was made in 1980-81 had one of the lowest percentages of favelados in Brazil.[14] Their highly visible campaigns sensitized public opinion while demonstrating an excellent capacity to mobilize resources to carry out collective action.

The role of leaders and of external support agents was critical in sustaining the mobilization. The Church invariably played a key role, either by providing resources or leadership to organize the protest campaigns. Although the Church has recently "retreated" to a less active stance, it has effectively linked grassroots social networks throughout many areas of the country. São Paulo with its active union movement is a notable example: the Church's ecclesial base communities (CEBs) helped to articulate the labor movement in the late 1970s and also the PT, or Workers' Party.[15]

The cases we studied shared another characteristic, a counterpart in fact to the mobilizations whether at their most intense phases or in between campaigns. This was the involvement of various public agencies, amounting to a continuous relationship with the state. This relationship, in turn, helped to determine whether the course of events was more or less conflictual, more or less participatory, marked by growing or declining mobilization. Ranging from rejection of state policies at one extreme to acceptance at the other, the movements nonetheless showed a consistent disposition to negotiate and a clear understanding of the basic interests at stake.

Interaction with public agencies was particularly visible in land invasions or property seizures, which dot the activities of residential associations of poor people. The degree of conflict, and indeed the outcome -- permanent settlement or ejection from the area -- was bound up with the response of public agencies. This response could set a pattern of negotiation, or of repression and social control. Curitiba, with its tradition of successful urban planning and a more liberal mayor, illustrates the first pattern; Brasília, where the authorities attempted to eradicate new dwellings in expensive areas, shows the opposite.[16] In all cases, the political expression of this movement was bound up with a group's identification with its place of residence. Participants attempted to monopolize representation in name of this identity. In turn, this conferred upon them the status of legitimate actors.

Both middle class and popular residential associations tended to join forces to achieve common aims. Federations of residents were set up above the local level, especially in Rio de Janeiro. And there was even an attempt to establish a National Confederation of Residents Associations (CONAM) in 1982. However, it is difficult to place the movements of favelados and other groups on the periphery and the movements of middle and upper sectors on the same plane. Differences in the operating logic of collective action across class lines as well as differing capacities to mobilize resources are important in this regard. The collective expression of each of these sectors was substantially different, both in their sense of priorities and in their sense of efficacy in the persuit of common goals. Even when an identity of interests was stressed, conflicts tended to arise in the course of joint campaigns.

One marked difference was the larger number of favelado organizations. These emerged earlier than their middle class counterparts, and were more structured despite the periods of deactivation that occurred when repression was at its height. Another difference was the political and social sensitivities raised by the popular sector demands. In certain cases the need for action was so great in peripheral areas that the government itself took on a populist facade, adopting policies that would have been unthinkable only a short while before. Changes in the land use statute of 1982 is a good example.

Class differences notwithstanding, it can be said that the neighborhood association movement as a whole displays a a basic repertoire of collective action. This is marked by an entrance into politics by way of alternative channels, channels that are not necessarily competitive with existing institutions but that certainly maintain a tense relationship with them. Whether for middle class or favelado organizations, the possible effect of the electoral process on the degree of mobilization is similar as well.

In Rio de Janeiro, the middle class association movement became highly visible in the late 1970s; even more so since then. Similar middle class neighborhood groups arose in the early 1950s, although their character and content differed from today's. The first recorded association was formed in 1947 on the Ilha do Governador, followed by the Barra da Tijuca in 1950 and by the Lagoa in 1957. Some nineteen associations of this sort existed by 1963.[18]

Unlike the current associations, these precursors were more inclined to monitor policy and less inclined to make demands. Striking was their non-partisan character and their disengagement from larger ideological concerns. This occurred despite the great polarization then affecting national politics. In fact, the demobilization and deactivation of these first associations occurred early in 1962 had nothing to do with the 1964 Revolution, which was solidly supported by the urban middle sectors.

This early neighborhood movement was not confrontational; nor did it represent an institutional alternative to the electoral path of access to the state then still fully functioning. It was quite localized and restricted, and if the organizational format was in some cases similar to current ones -- the existence of general assemblies, working groups, and councils of representatives -- there was little concern for participation or to demonstrate the working out of democratic norms at the local level. While they achieved some visibility, these early associations did not reach very far into the communities that they supposedly represented.

This earlier type of collective organization did not become institutionalized. On the contrary, it kept aloof from the growing opposition being led by different leftist groups which sought to link social forces in the countryside and the city for a radical transformation of the nation. The earlier movement appealed to certain principles but did not organize to produce political actors as is now the case. Today's association movement, from its inception in the late 1970s, opposed the regime, although this was downplayed in its professed objectives. Even more important, it used its identification with the local neighborhood to press for an alternative institutional space both for access to the state and for the realization of democratic principles.

By the late 1970s, the urban middle class was numerically much larger, and it is probable that its standard of living was more threatened by inflation than ever before. The new middle class entered the political arena, but as a previously excluded actor now pressing simultaneously for political change and incorporation in the political system. Downward mobility brought on by the economic crisis of recent years was one factor in this reaction, which did not occur during the expansionist economic "miracle" years.

Politically, the new urban middle class tended to be in opposition, but this did not mean that it shunned the existing institutions or was particularly radical. On the contrary, the vast urban expansion had increased uncertainty and one way to deal with this was to embrace democratic norms, and to call for their consolidation. Thus the massive demonstrations for restoring a fully democratic electoral process which occurred in early 1984, and which had a large middle class contingent, can be so interpreted.

These demonstrations were also a point of convergence for many different social groups and for many of the organized forces in Brazilian society, including the neighborhood and labor movements. They illustrate the somewhat open-ended and unpredictable attempts of broad social movements to build consensus and to create conditions for change. One could not have anticipated that the theme of direct presidential elections would galvanize so much national support, cutting across class lines and other cleavages.

The demonstrations also revealed that what matters is not stability or instability but their potential for institutional change. The direct elections movement had a clear institutional content in that it represented the popular search for lasting political solutions which could, in turn, lead to solving economic problems. But they also revealed the volatile nature of collective action, seen in the difficulties of sustaining a high degree of mobilization and participation. The result was a relative stalemate lasting into the indirect election of Tancredo Neves in early 1985.

The new urban associations themselves thus represent the rise of new political actors and the development of a certain style of political representation. They create a counterpoint to existing institutions but do not, as some would have it, provide an alternative that excludes either parties or elections. These movements practice democracy and produce pressure to democratize social relations. However, their permanent incorporation as legitimate political actors and the consequent institutionalization of these democratic practices through permanent channels of access to the state is doubtful. This is so because they are organized around specific and therefore transitory demands, and because of the internal dynamics inherent in collective action, such as factionalist tendencies. Therefore, in the short run, the institutional impact of these movements will probably be less than what one might expect from just observing the wide extent of this collective action phenomenon on the national scene. They are divided on class lines, marked by regional differences and political contexts from which they emerged, and they differ in the extent to which their demands received attention and were met. Furthermore, their actions were shaped by the most immediate institutional context as well as by their relationship to more global aspects of the political process.

In the long run, however, the movements may operate and diffuse the ethos of a new political culture, especially in view of their emphasis on the values of participation and internal democracy. Beyond narrow community boundaries, the movements inaugurated a political style characterized by collective pressure which defied the rigid structures of the authoritarian regime.

What, then, was the relationship between these associations and the political *abertura*, especially in the period through the 1982 congressional and state elections won by the opposition? Such a relationship did exist even though it is hard trace it empirically because of the interaction between "permissive" tendencies in the system and the pressures originating from the movement. On the one hand, the elections and their outcome tended to demobilize the associations as vehicles for neighborhood interests. But on the other, the associations did stimulate participation in the electoral process, both in 1982 and later on in 1984 when they joined the broader movement for direct presidential elections.

In addition, various forms of social mobilization were activated during the abertura, although it would be exaggerating to say the state alone induced it. There were also internal dynamics of associations that had less to do with the global political process than with their leadership, and the role of the Church, as well as of political militants. Individual involvement also varied widely, creating practical difficulties with respect to mobilization and maintaining participation. The intensity of participation varied over time, revealing the cyclical nature of the movement as a whole. An examination of the processes that govern the formation, structure and functioning of these new social movements is thus necessary in order to clear up these issues.

THE MIDDLE CLASS NEIGHBORHOOD MOVEMENT IN RIO DE JANEIRO

As mentioned above, the surge of associations (including favela organizations) is quite recent. Note that in Table 6.1 the favela movement was larger than the middle class movement. Note also the ebb in associational activity after 1964 and particularly around 1974 at the height of repression. This was much more visible in the case of the middle class associations, although one recalls that demobilization started to occur before the 1964 coup.

The differential effects of repression on the capacity of distinct groups to organize themselves is illustrated in the more durable character of the favela movement over time. This even increased in 1964-68, and was reasonably stable during the 1969-73 repression. In this same period the middle class associations were practically dismantled, suggesting that -- for whatever reason -- for the lower classes the neighborhood movement continued to one of the principal vehicles for the defense of fundamental interests. It had also developed deeper roots than its middle class counterpart.

Clearly, associational activity was enhanced in periods when social segments were allowed to organize freely. However, the removal of censorship and the repressive Institutional Act Number Five had a somewhat differential effect on associational life. On the one hand, it favored the free flow of information. On the other hand, it barely affected the functioning of a governmental system whose basic characteristic was and continued to be centralized decision-making.

Increasingly, successive military government policies affecting the daily life of citizens were handled at the federal level. This tendency to "federalize" continued during abertura had a direct effect upon the party structure and the electoral process. Elections became an outlet for generalized opposition to the regime. Precisely because of this, neighborhood associations were perceived as effective avenues for pursuing more immediate demands.

TABLE 6.1

Residents' Associations Based in the Municipality of Rio de Janeiro, 1947-1981

	Period(a)				
Areas	1946-63	1964-68	1969-73	1974-78	1979-81
Middle and Upper Class Neighborhoods(b)	19 (1.1)	1 (0.3)	5 (1.3)	5 (1.3)	30 (15.0)
Rest of the municipality(c)	105 (6.2)	70 (17.5)	42 (10.5)	28 (7.0)	136 (68.0)
TOTAL	124 (7.3)	71 (17.8)	47 (11.8)	33 (8.3)	166 (83.0)

Source: Registro Civil de Pessoas Jurídicas.
Notes: (a) Survey for 1981 is only through June. Numbers in parentheses are annual growth rates, expressed as percentages. (b) Neighborhoods in North and South Zones; Center and the Ilha do Governador are counted as middle and upper class neighborhoods. (c) The rest of the municipality category includes favelas and residential complexes existing in upper and middle class districts. All the neighborhoods traversed by Central do Brasil and Leopoldina tracks are included, also Cajú given the large numbers of poor people residing there.

The middle class association movement was reactivated with a rhetoric frankly hostile to electoral politics, yet this paralleled the rearticulation of the party structure. Not surprisingly, this process was marked by uncertainties, circumlocutions, and forward and backward steps. Thus, disbelief in the possibility that party politics would be run on democratic principles in addition to skepticism as to its efficacy were major factors motivating a search for alternative channels. Associating at the neighborhood level was seen as the best way to take care of the most immediate problems of everyday life.

Important as this rejection of parties and the electoral system may have been in the movements' early stages, it did not last. For instance, the issue of the "imprisonment" of the association movement by the parties soon came to a head in the favelas with the clientelistic machine of former governor Chagas Freitas, who headed the Popular Party. The favela movement was split into two competing federations, the one pledged to Chagas Freitas, the other independent and both insisting that their representation was legitimate.[19] Although the relationship of middle class associations to the party structure was posed in a less drastic form, it too resulted in a politicization of the movement in its later stages.

Competitive party politics tended to work against uniting people around common, local objectives. With a multiparty system created in 1979, and with the opposition beginning to fragment as a consequence (and as the government had intended), this tendency became even more pronounced. Relations between the associations, which had typically emerged to maximize individual benefits, and the political parties were tense.

An association usually began when an "organizational entrepreneur" mobilized individuals from a locality around some specific issue such as the cutting of a landmark tree, the construction of a highway across their bairro, any and all projects that affected the quality of urban life. The initial mobilization generally produced an assembly, not necessarily representative, and the formation of an effective organization could take years. This happened in the Southern Zone of Rio de Janeiro with the formation of the Neighborhood Association of the Lauro Muller District (ALMA). ALMA was the first such group, and it set the pattern for subsequent developments.

Based on this assembly, the emerging collectivity would try to establish itself as a legitimate spokesman and to monopolize repre-sentation however low the initial membership. The rhetoric would typically involve the discrediting of traditional politicians, a stress on collective problem solving, and a claim that this form of political activity was the "true exercise of democracy." With an identity forming apart from the state and political parties, the association evolved with its own internal dynamics.

After a certain point, however, the association's relationship to the existing institutions would be redefined, without such a counterdistinction to the party structure. New umbrella associations were formed out of the very necessity of the movement as a whole to consolidate. Thus the Federation of Neighborhood Associations of Rio de Janeiro (FAMERJ) was set up to represent both favela and middle class neighborhood associations.

The leadership played a fundamental role by taking initiatives, maintaining levels of mobilization and participation, and building bridges to government agencies. When this research was conducted in 1981, the elected presidents were mostly from the liberal professions -- architects, lawyers, teachers and sociologists. Most were male, with a mean age of 38; and some had previously been politically active in leftist groups. Women headed almost one quarter of the existing associations, and with few exceptions the leaders were educated up to college level.

Regarding the membership, a survey with a sample of 50 participants in a typical Southern Zone association showed that between September and November 1980, some 56 percent earned between 6 and 20 minimum salaries; 62 percent had a college degree including 20 percent who had gone on to graduate school; 40 percent were in the liberal and technical professions; 58 percent were married and 42 percent had one or two children; and 44 percent owned their own apartment in this neighborhood. All affirmed that the participation of women was a key factor in sustaining their association's activities.

Leaders and followers alike reflect the structural changes Brazilian society has recently gone through. The presence of so many women, along with salaried professionals (including lawyers, architects and physicians) points clearly to the emergence of a new middle class. Expanding educational opportunities in the post-"miracle" years had much to do with this emergence. This new social segment seems to be entering the political arena with a new style of politics, of which the neighborhood associations are but one example. The union movement involving typically middle class occupations such as medical doctors, teachers, bank employees and others emerged by 1977, about the same time as the neighborhood movement with which it was complementary.

It is with reference to the electoral process and the party system on the one hand, and to the emerging union movement on the other that the neighborhood movement can be best understood and evaluated. Like unionism, the neighborhood associations attempted to evade state regulation and control while innovating in forms of political participation.

Associations such as ALMA and Gavea were the most active in the early phases of the movement between 1974 and 1977. Then FAMERJ was created in 1978. It motivated the creation of new associations while also producing a sphere of internal competition and a platform for airing political questions of a more general character. This new federative structure had a tendency to develop areas of inequality, and hence for the movement to bureaucratize itself. With FAMERJ consolidated by 1979, the neighborhood movement was marked by a more direct confrontation with the public authorities and by the attempt to be heard and represented at the municipal level. This incursion into the public arena was greatly facilitated by the appointment as mayor of Israel Klabin, a liberal-minded entrepreneur who believed in making urban policy through participatory planning. The associations participated in meetings with the Municipal Secretary of

Planning and thus became actively involved in discussions about zoning. Focussed on discrete issues such as this, the movement under FAMERJ now acquired significance as a collective actor.

At this time a Technical Council was proposed to discuss zoning and the issuing of building permits as a means to control land use and inhibit real estate speculation. This Council with representatives of the local communities was reasonably successful. Laranjeiras managed to change its zoning through this process. But Klabin was replaced in 1980 by Julio Coutinho, who eliminated the Technical Council, thus closing the political space that the association movement had opened.

Meanwhile, the middle class neighborhood movement was expanding rapidly while acquiring immense visibility. Many of the new associations were no longer started to address a particular problem, but to defend the general interest of their communities such as environmental protection, parks, recreation, transportation and police protection. Their campaigns were well publicized, whether successful as in cleaning up Lajé Park and completing the metro station for Largo do Machado, or not as in the handling of the new Barra-Lagoa expressway or parking in Ipanema.

A look at the main campaigns between 1976 and 1982 shows that the associations were relatively successful in their aims, judging from the proportion of their demands that were fully satisfied (see Table 6.2). While the absolute number of demands was greater in the area of state production of goods and services, note that a proportionately greater number of successful demands (72.7 percent) is concentrated in the sphere of state regulation. These demands entail having the public authority control the operations of private real estate firms and even those of state agencies carrying out projects in various neighborhoods.

This pattern confirms what has been said above about the relationship of this movement to the state. If on the one hand the movement attempts to circumvent state regulation over forms of political participation, on the other hand it calls for the state to regulate interests that are potentially in conflict. The movement's successes are intimately linked to the establishment of norms and procedures for urban land use, an area in which particularistic interests come into play under the guise of general public concerns.

TABLE 6.2

Neighborhood Association Campaigns by Nature of Demand and the Outcome Obtained, 1976-1982

Outcome	Nature of Demand: State regulation	State production of goods & services	Non-intervention of state	Total
Totally satisfied	16 (72.7%)	30 (53.6%)	5 (33.3%)	51 (54.8%)
Partially satisfied	1 (4.6%)	14 (25.0%)	3 (20.0%)	18 (19.4%)
Not satisfied	5 (22.7%)	12 (21.4%)	7 (46.7%)	24 (25.8%)
TOTAL	22 (100.0%)	56 (100.0%)	15 (100.0%)	93 (100.0%)

Sources: Jornal do Brasil, O Globo, VID, Rio Zona Sul; disclosure reports of the residents' associations; and information provided by the presidents of these organizations.

In the process of its development, the movement achieved the status of an interlocutor in negotiations with the public authorities. However, one constant permeates the life of these associations: the problem of how to achieve definitive legitimacy as a political actor. This is so because of the nature of the demands, which in some cases conflict with interests that are generalizable beyond the limits of the neighborhood. This is also because the movements represent limited numbers of people. As seen in Table 6.3, the permanent membership is barely large enough in some bairros to sustain the association without great difficulties.

TABLE 6.3

Relationships Between Neighborhood Populations and the Number of Affiliated Members in Selected Associations, 1980-1981

Associations	Estimated population of the neighborhood	Declared regular members	Percent
Botafogo	150,000	400	0.3
Catete, Flamengo, & Gloria	200,000	400	0.2
Bairro Peixoto	30,000	150	0.5
Ilha do Governador	300,000	100	0.03
Meier	200,000	100	0.05

Source: See footnote 18.

If legitimation as a political actor does not necessarily depend on the number of members, these figures at least suggest that the movement suffers a certain vulnerability in overcoming obstacles to its operation as a collectivity. Taking the 19 associations for which membership data was obtained, there is only an average of 251 regular members per association. Other dilemmas aside, just overcoming the barrier of the heterogeneity of a densely populated neighborhood is in itself an essential aspect of the association movement. The most active and visible associations are found precisely among those with the most homogeneous base and with the most clearly bounded or confined geographic areas. The Lauro Muller association has these characteristics.

When the survey was made it had almost 700 declared members, the highest recorded in this research. It was also more active, scoring several victories at the outset.

To these difficulties facing the association movement should be added the superimposition of the party structure beginning with the 1982 electoral campaign. In terms of their central functions, the demobilization of the neighborhoods reached its maximum as the elections approached. According to information collected two weeks before the vote, in only 5 of the 16 associations surveyed in the Southern and Northern Zones were their regular activities not disrupted. In four associations there were debates about the elections, but most wanted to avoid having their solidarity undermined by various parties and their orientations.

Notwithstanding worries about the deleterious effect of ideological cleavages, electoral politics enveloped the association movement. Capturing decision making posts at the state and local levels was now perceived as a way to satisfy collective demands as well as a way for some local leaders to advance their political careers. Candidates for the opposition parties, notably the Democratic Labor Party (PDT) emerged from some of the associations, and two of them were former presidents. Five of the associations surveyed before the elections endorsed candidates from the PDT and the Brazilian Democratic Movement (PMDB).

When the opposition won power at the state level, this seems to have strengthened the political role of associations while weakening their overall effectiveness. The associations gained access to policy issue areas, notably through regular contacts with some levels of state government. But at the same time the movement seems to have reached a stage of routinization in the organizational life of associations. Thus the neighborhood associations assumed a lower profile in national life, while other more topical forms of collective action such as land invasions became more prominent. A number of demonstrations drew upon a middle class contingent, including the one by employees of state enterprises in June, 1983. The demonstrations demanding direct presidential elections galvanized the nation's attention in early 1984.

As mentioned above, the neighborhood movement is but one facet of the new middle class' role as a political actor. In this sense, it should be evaluated in conjunction with other forms of collective expression such as the union movement of salaried professions. This movement involved middle class occupations that were formerly carried out independently but which were now done on a salary basis. Medical doctors are a good example. Starting with a demonstration by 500 resident doctors in São Paulo in April 1977, there were four major national strikes between June 1978 and May 1981 which shut down hospitals in Rio, São Paulo, Porto Alegre and other cities. A National Protest Day on May 7, 1982 involved 60,000 medical doctors throughout the country.

Other professionals were extremely active in the upsurge of strikes during this period. Elementary and high school teachers, joined by university professors, are a case in point. When the Association of Professors of the University of São Paulo (ADUSP) was reactivated in April 1978 the movement soon gained momentum with strikes in Paraná, São Paulo, and the Federal District. In 1979, the entire public school network was totally paralized at least seven times in different states, including a major work stoppage involving 100,000 elementary school teachers in Minas Gerais and Pernambuco. In September 1980, a nationwide strike by university professors shut down 32 institutions of higher learning, including 20 federal universities. In November 1981, 19 out of 21 federal universities were struck, and again in 1982 when 14 of them were forced into total recess. In all, there were 16 strikes and demonstrations in this area between April 1978 and December 1982.[20]

CONCLUSIONS

Two central points emerge from this analysis of Brazilian social movements. The first involves their relationship to the state with respect to getting excluded interests incorporated and represented in the political arena. The second is the extent to which they encourage the dissemination of democratic practices and the consolidation of these in political institutions.

The movements traced above emerged in an attempt to escape the rigid state monopoly over political participation through control of the electoral process and in the official trade unions. And while social movements were suspicious of a system of interests that excluded them, their dilemma was that they also called for state regulatory action to encompass thus far excluded interests. Over and above the obvious risks of cooptation, this double-edged appraisal of institutionalization seems inherent to the dynamics of collective action. Although they initially sought to avoid control, dependence on the state and on an electoral process under tight government control pulls them into these strategic areas. Added to this basic difficulty are problems inherent to the very process of sustaining high levels of mobilization and participation on a routine basis, and the tendencies toward bureaucratization and factionalism within the movements themselves.

The Brazilian literature on social movements tends to sidestep these crucial issues, not only overestimating the impact of so-called urban social movements, but also posing (because of certain ideological assumptions) a fundamental state/society split. Either it is assumed that a highly mobilized society exists from the bottom up, or that the society is manipulated by the state from the top down.

While some of the difficulties and problems would apply equally to social movements elsewhere, the pervasiveness of the state stands out in the Brazilian case. Moreover, associational activities occurred while institution building took place in the political system as a whole. Overcoming the authoritarian regime and consolidating democratic institutions constituted the broader agenda of which the social movements were but one part.

This is perhaps the main difference between Brazilian movements and those occurring in the core advanced democracies of the capitalist system. In the latter, well-established party systems organized on a territorial basis are unable to translate the demands of the very diffuse constituencies that make up social movements. The movements then acquire a dynamic of their own, at once less amenable to control by the state and perhaps more likely to affect the political process directly. In Brazil, while that inability is also present, the degree of uncertainty around a party system still being formed gives the party system a strategic quality which may equal that of social movements.

There is also the question of scale which sets Brazil apart from the other experiences with authoritarianism in peripheral countries. The recent urbanization of this society brings Brazil closer to the profile of some advanced industrial countries than to that of rural underdeveloped countries. The existence of nine very large metropolitan areas and the increasing number of medium sized cities suggests that large "available" populations exist which can search for new forms of social organization. Given the complexity and intractability of many urban problems, neighborhood-centered organizations may well become even more prevalent.

In the advanced countries, some patterns of locally based political and social organization developed gradually, accompanying or antedating the great surge of industrialization. This Tocqueville observed very well in the early industrial United States. Elements of a Tocquevillian society can be found in the new Brazilian urban setting. One finds them in the developing concerns which, despite individualistic overtones, go beyond purely localized interests and provide support for the formation of a civic culture.

The emergence of neighborhood associations in middle and upper middle class districts in Rio de Janeiro is not a phenomenon exclusively linked to the authoritarian period inaugurated in 1964. In fact, associations emerged in Rio as early as the beginning of this century, and more significantly in the 1950s. As a particular format of collective organization then, neighborhood associations are neither a new phenomenon nor a clear cut product of political openings or closures.

However, present day associations differ from earlier ones in several basic respects. In the first place, they differ from one another in the scope and content of political purpose. The earlier associations did not have an oppositional character, nor were they as politicized as the contemporary ones have come to be. The novel aspect of the associations of the 1970s and 1980s is that they are ideologically oriented from their inception as organizations aimed at providing a democratic space within the framework of face-to-face interaction at the local level. In addition, as contrasted to the associations of the 1950s, today's associations formed an organized movement at the supralocal level, having become involved in and affected by major political events.

Another aspect concerns the type of social alignments that the neighborhood movement has come to express. Brazil went through profound structural changes -- economic, social and political -- in the 1970s and one change with far-reaching consequences was the rate and pattern of urbanization which caused the overall quality of city life to deteriorate. Such deterioration, although certainly more dramatic for the lower echelons of society, also affected the emerging middle class of the post- "economic miracle" era.

As noted, between 1979 and 1981 there was an upsurge in the growth of neighborhood movements. Although no clear-cut relationship can be established between this expansion and broad economic and political processes, it is possible to observe an inverse pattern connecting these processes in the moments preceding and coinciding with the associational spurt. The movement's expansion was preceded by economic growth and political repression, and coincided with economic recession and political relaxation. Later, the early 1980s were characterized by increased economic uncertainty, due to high rates of inflation and unemployment, and political uncertainty because of swings in the institutional process of abertura itself. For a short period a thriving and prosperous segment, the middle classes are experienced shrinking opportunities after 1979 and well into 1984.

Some aspects must be highlighted with respect to the relationship of these movements and abertura. The electoral process and party competition are central factors in the dynamics of social momements because the control and timing of abertura were carried out through institutional mechanisms in those areas. The centrality of the electoral process is visible both in the movement's initial rejection of elections and party politics as detrimental to its cohesion, and in its later demobilization during the peaks of the 1982 campaign and the demonstrations for direct elections.

In other areas, however, abertura had a lesser impact. As the curtain of abertura was being drawn, the scenario it revealed was one of a society which had mobilized and organized itself, but in which the possibility of substituting pluralist practices for authoritarian, clientalistic arrangements was still low. For instance, tendencies towards centralization of decision making processes still prevailed in policy areas affecting the daily life of citizens, even while the state's administrative machinery had become more complex and diversified as a result of its expansion in the regulatory and productive domains.

The resulting atomization changed the character of contacts between citizens and the state in a number of ways. One implication was that some form of organized collective action became more central for the achievement of certain goals. In this sense, it is the "deepening" of the bureaucratic authoritarian state rather than its demise which underlies the flourescence of organized collective movements in the earlier stages. Abertura only stimulated that tendency by eliminating institutional barriers to free association.

By and large, the development of the movement over time reveals its transformation from sectoral, demand-specific goals to a more politicized orientation, revealing throughout some of the dilemmas of the art of associating. Even though the goals are still alive and still nurture some of the campaigns, the thrust toward political action became dominant, if for nothing else by reason of factors external to the movement itself. Starting with the 1982 elections and beyond, the neighborhood movements were swept into the large, diffuse, liberal social pact against the authoritarian regime.

The electoral process acquired an even more central and strategic position in the political transformation of the regime. Both the 1982 campaign and the early 1984 mass movement for direct election of the president galvanized society and the movement shifted from its specific, particular goals to a broad political role. If the campaign for direct elections did succeed, it certainly had an impact on the timing of the transition to democracy, making a military candidacy unviable. The role played by social forces from below in this process is usually overlooked by those who emphasize instead the peaceful, gradual transition from the top down. And in the process of consolidating the newly achieved democracy, such a role by the grass roots movements is bound to be even more deemphasized because of the focus on formal institutions. This was particularly the case soon after the New Republic was inaugurated and the mobilization for a new constitution began.

It is however precisely in the runup to the Constituent Assembly that organized interests tend to emerge, thereby enhancing the role of social movements and other collectivities that champion pent-up demands. Two of the most prominent organizations speaking for a number of interests have been the Church through the National Conference of Bishops (CNBB) and the Bar Association (OAB). In the New Republic these two organizations if anything have been even more assertive advocates for democratization.

But in addition to the support provided by CNBB and OAB, social movements have acted quite vigorously on their own within the framework provided by the campaign for the Constituent Assembly and the daily policing of the Cruzado Plan starting in February 1986. The campaign for the Constituent Assembly has prompted a broad spectrum of social movements to voice their demands -- the ecological and feminist movements, the blacks -- all of which have pressed for a vast agenda of specific interests to be included in the Constitution. As for the economic plan, the daily control of the price freeze has stimulated not only a citizen-oriented public consciousness, but also the action of neighborhood associations and other residents' movements.

These last-mentioned groups have been highly visible, particularly through the two supralocal associations representing favelas (FAFERJ) and middle class neighborhoods

(FAMERJ). Residents' associations have gained a more definitive status under the New Republic, frequently being consulted by public authorities on issues affecting local interests such as changes in urban traffic, the preservation of parks, issues of public health and sanitation, and the overall quality of urban life. Finally, FAMERJ has been particularly active on the question of property tax increases early in 1985 and again in 1986.

The grassroot neighborhood movement expanded enormously along with the random and chaotic pattern of urban growth and modernization in Brazil. The upshot is that today "available" and mobilized populations are searching for new forms of social organization to ease and solve some of the problems brought about by unprecedented growth. These neighborhood organizations could well challenge and test the limits of existing structures of participation and interest representation for years to come. But in order for this to happen, the remains of an authoritarian tradition must be eliminated and replaced by new democratic institutions. Some of the elements for creating a Tocquevillean society already exist in Brazil and they will gradually emerge even more through the achievements of these organized collectivities.

NOTES

1. The conference version of this paper was translated by Jeffrey Seward and rewritten by the author while he was a Tinker Fellow at Stanford University.

2. *Isto E*, March 21, 1982.

3. Of recent vintage, the bibliography on urban social movements in Brazil is vast. Much of it has appeared in working papers of the ANPOCS Study Group on Urban Social

Movements, and many of the foregoing comments are based on this literature. These works focus heavily on urban lower class movements. Other recently published works include José Alvaro Moises *et. al.*, *Contradições urbanas e movimentos sociais* (Rio de Janeiro, 1977) and his *Cidade, povo e poder* (Rio de Janeiro, 1981); Paul Singer and Vinícius Caldeira Brant, *São Paulo: O povo em movimento* (Petrópolis, 1980); Carlos Nelson Ferreira dos Santos, *Movimentos urbanos no Rio de Janeiro* (Rio de Janeiro, 1981); and Renato R. Boschi, ed., *Movimentos coletivos no Brasil urbano* (Rio de Janeiro, 1983).

For a critical review of this literature see Pedro Roberto Jacobi, "Movimentos sociais urbanos no Brasil," in *Boletim informativo e bibliográfico das ciências sociais*, no. 9 (1980). One study including some analysis of groups beyond the working class is J.A. Moises, "Experiência de mobilização popular em São Paulo," paper presented at the XXV annual meeting of SBEC, São Paulo, 1975 and also his USP doctoral dissertation: *Classes populares e protesto urbano* (São Paulo, 1978).

4. Charles Tilly discusses this relationship in "Major Forms of Collective Action in Modern Europe," in *Theory and Society*, 3:3 (1976) and later in his *From Mobilization to Revolution* (Reading, Mass., 1978). For a discussion of the social movement as one particular form for the structuring of collective protest see Charles Tilly, "Britain Creates the Social Movement," in James E. Cronin and Jonathan Schneer, eds., *Social Conflict and the Political Order in Modern Britain* (London, 1982).

5. See Gerald Marwell, "Altruism and the Problem of Collective Action," in V. Derlega and J Grzelak, eds., *Cooperation and Helping Behavior* (New York, 1981); Rolf Sartorious, "Benevolence, Collective Action, and the Provision of Public Goods," in Harlan B. Miller and William H. Williams, eds., *The Limits of Utilitarianism* (Minneapolis, 1982), and Lawrence C. Becker, "The Free-Rider Problem" in the same volume. Alessandro Pizzorno, "Interests and

Parties in Pluralism," in Suzanne Berger, Albert Hirschman and Charles Maier, eds., *Organizing Interests in Western Europe: Pluralism, Corporatism, and the Transformation of Politics* (Cambridge, 1981). Claus Offe and Helmut Wiesenthal, "Two Logics of Collective Action: Theoretical Notes on Social Class and Organizational Formats," in *Political Power and Social Theory*, I (1979).

6. This does not mean that regularities are impossible to establish with respect to the outcomes of collective movements, only that there is an imponderable element for each specific combination of events. The more unstructured the pattern of action, the less predictable the outcomes. For views on the probabalistic element in the generation and the outcomes of collective action see Gary T. Marx, "Thoughts on a Neglected Category of Social Movement Participant: The Agent Provocateur and the Informant," in *American Journal of Sociology*, 80:2, (1975); Mark Granovetter, "Threshold Models of Collective Behavior," in *American Journal of Sociology*, 83:6 (1978); and Paul D. Shumaker, "The Scope of Political Conflict and the Effectiveness of Constraints in Contemporary Urban Protest," in *The Sociological Quarterly*, 19 (Spring 1979). For a discussion of other conditioning factors see Hardin Russell, "Collective Action as an Agreeable Action -- Prisoner's Dilemma," in *Behavioral Science*, 16:5 (1971); Norman Frohlich *et. al.*, "Individual Contributions to Collective Goods: Alternative Models," *Journal of Conflict Resolution*, 19:2 (June, 1975); and Jack M. Weller and E.L. Quarantelli, "Neglected Characteristics of Collective Behavior," in *American Journal of Sociology*, 79:3 (November, 1974).

7. In theorizing about political change, the problematic relationship between the realm of social action and the realm of institutions is discussed by Fabio M. Reis in his *Racionalidade e política*, Tese de Livre Docência, UFMG, mimeo, 1981. See also his "Authoritarianism and Political Development: Proposal of Some Leads for the Study of Group Representation and Repression," paper presented at the IPSA meeing in Lisbon, October 1980 and his "Representation and

Autonomy of the Political," paper for the IPSA world congress in Rio de Janeiro, August 1982. The problem concerns the fact that the forms encountered at the level of political institutions are determined by the social base of the conflicts while at the same time the political institutions render opaque the social relations at the base. Conflicting and strategic actions become significant when they acquire resonance on the level of political institutions, translating themselves into organizations or institutions of an operational character.

8. On the relationship between context, the creation of coalitions of solidarity, participation and the emergence of collective identities see Alessandro Pizzorno, "Introduccion al estudio de la participacion politica," in Pizzorno and Manuel Castells, eds., *Participación y cambio social el la probemática contemporánea* (Buenos Aires, 1979), and also Pizzorno's "Identity and Interest," mimeo, Princeton, 1978. In subsequent elaborations this same author explores the connections between exclusion from a system of interests and the creation of collective identities through the mechanism of representation. It is against the rigidity of existing structures, especially the political party, that nuclei of emerging interests express themselves at a certain moment as social movements. See his "Interests and Parties in Pluralism," in Berger, Hirschman and Maier, *Organizing Interests in Western Europe*.

9. For social movements of the economically underprivileged, the argument about institutional relations and their political efficacy is developed by Frances Fox Piven and Richard D. Cloward, *Poor People's Movements: Why they Succeed, How They Fail* (New York, 1979), especially chapter 1. Electoral politics is examined as one institutional alternative which narrows available modes of participation among the poor, though constituting a counterpoint for the emergence of movements themselves.

10. For a critical discussion of the ideal of autonomy see Renato R. Boschi, "Associativismo urbano e democrátização: algumas reflexões teóricas," in *Revista de Ciências Sociais*, vols. 12-13, nos. 1 & 2 (1981/2). In the same vein see Boschi and Licia do Prado Valladares, "Problemas teóricos na análise de movimentos sociais: Comunidade, ação coletiva e o papel do estado," in *Espaço e Debate*, 8 (Jan.-April, 1983). Some of the aspects raised here are treated in other critiques of the literature. See Luiz Antônio Machado Silva and Alícia Ziccardi, "Notas para uma discussão sobre movimentos sociais urbanos," in *Cadernos do Centro de Estudos Rurais e Urbanos*, 13 (1980).

11. For a realistic assessment of the political impact of social movements, and especially the difficulty of predicting a democratizing impact on the structure of the state as an outcome appears, see Ruth C.L. Cardoso, "Movimentos sociais urbanos: balanço crítico," in Maria Herminia Tavares de Almeida and B. Sorj, *Sociedade e política no Brasil pós-64* (São Paulo, 1983).

12. The question of the confrontation with the state and the need to give up an exclusively "basista" perspective is appropriately discussed in Fernando Henrique Cardoso, "Political Regime and Social Change: Some Reflections Concerning the Brazilian Case," *Occasional Papers in Latin American Studies*, Stanford-Berkeley Joint Center for Latin American Studies, Berkeley, 1981.

13. As it is used throughout this text, social movement is defined as: "a sustained series of interactions between power holders and persons successfully claiming to speak on behalf of a constituency lacking formal representation, in the course of which those persons make publicly visible demands for changes in the distribution or the exercise of power, and back those demands with public demonstrations of support." Cited from Tilly, "Britain Creates," in Cronin and Schneer, p. 26.

14. For a synthetic analysis of these cases see Boschi and Valladares, "Movimentos associativos de cámadas populares urbanas: Analise comparativa de seis casos," in Boschi, ed., *op. cit.*, pp. 103-143. For a detailed inventory of these experiences see Boschi and Valladares, "Experiências comunitárias em assentamentos urbanos de baixa renda," IUPERJ/BNH, Relatório de Pesquisa, mimeo, 1981. The favela population of Curitiba was a little under 4 percent in 1979 as compared with 15 percent and up for other large Brazilian cities. A systematic count of these associational experiences is not yet available. For the case of Rio this survey was conducted and analysed by Eli Diniz, "Favela: associativismo e participação social," in Boschi, ed., *op. cit.* She records the existence of 175 favela associations in Rio de Janeiro in December, 1980.

15. The precise role of the CEBs remains to be analyzed, especially their complex connections with the labor movement. For a critical evaluation see Antonio Octavio Cintra and Antônio Luis Paixão, "Movimentos religiosos e mobilização política: Notas sobre as Comunidades Eclesias de Base," mimeo, 1982. A condensed version appeared in "CEBs: Um movimento religioso ou político," in *O Estado de São Paulo* (July 31, 1982). See also Scott Mainwaring, "Grass Roots Catholic Groups and Democracy, 1974-1985," Kellog Institute mimeo, 1985.

16. As mentioned, invasions are a recent phenomenon which have become prevalent in urban areas. For an account of land invasions in Rio see Lícia do Prado Valladares and Regina Kayat, "Invasões de terra no Rio de Janeiro de 1983: uma cronologia," *Serie Estudos*, Rio de Janeiro, IUPERJ, no. 20 (November, 1983). The authors kept track of 14 invasions of public and private land in the first semester of 1983. Invasions differ from favelas as a form of land seizure in that they involve a sudden and fast process of organized occupation.

17. See Offe and Wiesenthal, *op. cit.* for a discussion of the class-contingent nature of collective action. On resource mobilization from the organizational perspective, see Anthony Oberschall, *Social Conflicts and Social Movements* (Englewood Cliffs, N.J., 1973); James Q. Wilson, *Political Organizations* (New York, 1973); John D. McCarthy and Mayer N. Zald, "Resource Mobilization and Social Movements: A Partial Theory," in *American Journal of Sociology* 82:6 (May 1977); and Richard C. Rich, "A Political-Economy Approach to the Study of Neighborhood Organizations," in *American Journal of Political Science* 24:4 (November, 1980).

18. All the information on the middle class associations in this chapter was collected during a research project directed by the author between 1980 and 1982: ("Associativismo de classes médias urbanas," Convênio IUPERJ/FINEP), with Sergio Pechman as assistant researcher. For a more detailed analysis see Pechman, "A construção da solidariedade -- Associações de moradores de classe média alta do Rio de Janeiro (1976-1982)," Masters Thesis, IUPERJ, July 1982.

19. See Eli Diniz, *op. cit.*, and also her *Voto e máquina política* (Rio de Janeiro, 1982).

20. All strike information was systematically compiled in a survey of *Isto E* between 1977 and 1982. Strikes by union organized professionals include stage and screen actors, professional photographers, and journalists. The ecological movement also became prominent in national life. Between February 1978 and August 1982, eight large actions took place including a massive anti-nuclear demonstration in Angra dos Reis and anti-pollution protests in different cities.

PART THREE

Policy and Perceptions of Basic Structures

7

Framing the State: Economic Policy and Political Representation in Post-Authoritarian Brazil

Ben Ross Schneider

INTRODUCTION: BRAZILIAN POLITICS IN FLUX[1]

Much recent theory and evidence suggests that we should expect a significant recasting of the Brazilian state in the wake of the transition to civilian rule.[2] For example, Krasner argues that states evolve in a pattern of "punctuated equilibrium."[3] States change little most of the time, but suffer radical and rapid transformation in periods of crisis, which are often associated with regime change. Recent experience in Latin America confirms this pattern. The generals who took power in Chile, Peru and Argentina (1976) drastically transformed the role of the state. Redemocratization in the last two countries brought significant, though less dramatic, state reform. Moreover, as discussed in this introduction, it is also easy to find in Brazil pressures for remaking the Brazilian state.

Although there are good reasons to expect change, the essence of Brazil's state-centered political economy has suffered little alteration in the first 18 months of civilian rule, and is unlikely to do so in the near future. In Krasner's terms the current transition is more one of equilibrium than punctuation. In the following sections on state intervention in the economy, private participation in economic policy, and political representation, I examine the forces inside and outside the state which are politicking for and against altering elements of the state's role. On the fundamental issues of state intervention, the stasis coalition is likely to prevail, and maintain state investment, enterprise, policy discretion, and the state's strength vis-a-vis parties and Congress.

While the core of the state may retain its essential features, the boundaries will be the locus of numerous, uncoordinated struggles to shape the role of the state in the economy and the polity. These struggles will frame, but not transform, the state in the emerging political order. The frame metaphor captures two aspects of current Brazilian politics. On the one hand, it situates these struggles on the periphery of the state. On the other hand, democratization opens up possibilities for renegotiating aspects of state-society interaction, and the frame metaphor conveys the notion that this renegotiation will give more concrete form to the currently amorphous and fluid boundaries of the state.

In a state-centered political economy, the state is the dominant actor in both the economy and the polity. Little of significance in postwar Brazilian history has occurred without some participation by the state. Through mechanisms Vargas created over 40 years ago, the state has structured society and determined much of how it would organize politically, both in corporatist structures and political parties. The parties that dominated the democratic interlude (1945-64) grew out of the state and never outgrew their dependence on it (see Nunes and Geddes' chapter in this volume). Through the manipulation of credit, investment, state enterprise, tariffs, prices and other instruments, the state played the leading role in transforming Brazil from an agricultural to an industrial economy in the brief span of the second half of the twentieth century. And, as I will elaborate below, the state was not only a central political actor (or set of actors), but also an arena for elite accommodation and aggregation of interests.

Although common knowledge, the foregoing bears repeating when considering how and if the *Nova República* will shape a *Novo Estado* out of the overgrown and over-enthusiastic state it inherited from the generals. In the months leading up to

Tancredo Neves' January 1985 victory in the electoral college and the transition to civilian rule in March 1985, opposition politicians often referred to the upcoming "encounter between the State and the Nation." The implication was that military rule had estranged State and Nation, and that their relationship after re-uniting would be very different. The questions I want to ask in this essay concern what sort of state is going to this meeting. What sort of nation -- society, economy, and polity -- will it encounter? And, who is likely to come away changed by the encounter, and how?

A new political elite, a transformed and more vociferous society, new economic challenges and an ongoing set of legal and institutional reforms all constitute major pressures for change. While many of the faces in the Sarney government are familiar, a new generation of opposition politicians and policy-makers have taken over parts of the state, and they are eager to translate into policy the values they defended throughout their long exile from power. Many feel that democratic consolidation requires a fully revamped regime and a completely made-over bureaucracy. Many (both politicians and citizens) blame the state for many of the excesses of the military regime -- arbitrary rulings, arrogance, corruption and repression. Hence, during the first months of the Sarney government, debate and proposals focussed on flushing the legal system of the "authoritarian blockage" (*entulho autoritário*). Moreover, politicians will get an opportunity to rewrite the state after November 1986 when the new Congress drafts a new Constitution. This Constituent Assembly could enact potentially far-reaching formal change.

As Santos, Boschi (in this volume) and others have shown, Brazilian society is transformed and seeking new modes of organization.[4] Authoritarian regimes have had dubious success in remaking politics in their image, but they are perhaps most effective in stunting new political organization.[5] While the Brazilian military tolerated much more political space than its Latin American contemporaries, the society which became predominantly urban and industrial under its rule has nonetheless had to await the demise of the authoritarian order to redefine its organization and relationship to the state. Industrial unions, neighborhood associations, agricultural workers and business organizations no longer fit the antiquated corporatist legislation. The future evolution and mobilization of these groups will have a deep impact on state-society relations.

The state faces a new economy, and a new set of domestic and international challenges. Mostly by coincidence, Brazil completed a series of programs in heavy import-substituting industrialization (ISI) and infrastructure -- projects of massive capital mobilization and blunt policy tools -- just as it moved to a more open regime. To further industrialization, economic policy-makers in the state now need new instruments and face different economic agents. Both within and without the state, economic actors will hence be looking for ways to define the future economic role of the state.

Lastly, by my definition, the state is already greatly changed. The state is the permanent federal executive, and during the authoritarian regime this state swallowed up much of the judiciary, parts of Congress, and state and municipal government. Although the military maintained constitutional checks and balances, and the federative, legal autonomy of the state and municipal governments, the federal executive came to control these other organs of government either by restricting membership in them, or by directly appointing judges, congressmen, governors and mayors, thereby incorporating these branches and levels of government into the state.[6]

With the 1982 direct elections for governor, the military and Federal executive relinquished its informal appointive powers in the state governments. The 1985 mayoral elections in state capitals and over two hundred other 'national security' municipalities further reduced the appointive power of the state. Finally, the elections of November 1986 produced a Congress which -- while still gerrymandered to over-represent poor, rural and conservative areas -- will have a membership unadulterated by the military for the first time since 1964. Though the practice of stripping congressmen of their political rights ceased in the 1970s, only in 1986 did elected senators replace the last of the "bionic" senators appointed by the military.[7] In 1986 the bloated state returned in formal terms to the normal shape of a still enormous federal executive.

This introduction has emphasized the forces for change, but as I hope to show in the rest of the paper other political forces, such as vested interests, economic incentives, vulnerable capitalists, and actors already well represented in the state, will actively shore up the state bequeathed by authoritarianism. In the next sections I examine selected contacts between state and society, and assess how struggles over these contacts are developing.

PERSPECTIVES ON THE STATE

The Brazilian state has been many things to many observers: *cartorial* (sinecure), developmental, clientelistic, capitalist, dependent, inefficient, techno-bureaucratic, bureaucratic authoritarian, corporatist, patrimonial, fragmented, centralized, insulated, interventionist, penetrated, entrepreneurial, immobilist, even statizing. To others the state overwhelms other aspects of Brazilian social reality: state capitalism, state corporatism, state clientelism, state bourgeoisie, state-led development, state entrepreneurship and state-centered political economy. The Brazilian state is -- at least at times or in part -- all of these things. Depending on the issue, some aspects merit more attention than others. Single, overweening characterizations at best neglect crucial facets of the state and at worst mislead.

Hence, the better analyses also disaggregate the state: direct and indirect administration, productive and non-productive, insulated and clientelistic, militarized and civilian, and so forth. Disaggregation is essential because it forces one to dispense with discussions of the state as a unitary actor or of the state's interest. The state houses many different actors with many different preferences which cannot be reduced to a single interest, be it a state bourgeoisie devoted to state accumulation, a patrimonialist state dedicated solely to its own perpetuation and domination, or an interventionist state bent on destroying the private sector.[8] State officials are quite willing to enter the political fray to defend their preferences. However, these preferences depend on particular contexts and incumbents (who change frequently), and hence they cannot be construed as *state* interests. It is in this sense that the frame analogy is useful. It is not a question of determining one relationship between state and society, but rather of establishing many boundaries between myriad state agencies and diverse social actors.

For the present discussion I consider the Brazilian polity and economy state-centered by which I mean that the most important economic and political actors are in the state, and that many of the most important political and economic activities occur within the state.[9] The position of this state is the result of intra-elite political battles that in general institutions did not channel and that ideologies did not guide.

The Brazilian state lacks institutionalization. Formal organizations and the legal ties between them are not the primary actors or channels for politics. Turnover at the top echelons of the state is high and institutional experimentation constant. Chalmers' "politicized state" is relevant here:

> "... The repeated transformations imply that political institutions are considered tentative and are viewed instrumentally, not as permanent fixtures. Many problems which might be resolved by reference to a fixed set of procedures or laws are likely to be dealt with purely politically, subject to resolution only through a clash of forces. Policy-making institutions are themselves subject to active political questioning and conflict, and their reconstruction is viewed not so much as a violation of basic principles (as it would in the United States) but as the outcome of a particularly important confrontation.[10]

In the politicized state desired outcomes shape politics, and institutions are the result of political battles over these outcomes. Institutions are means -- not ends -- and therefore can change as desired outcomes and/or the constellations of forces supporting them evolve.[11]

In Brazil elite actors -- politicians, bureaucrats, capitalists and the military -- have historically avoided rigid ideologies and strident doctrinal confrontation.[12] While ideological sparring over the state has recently jammed the media, it is highly unlikely that the future state will conform to some triumphant ideology.

In the past ideology has had little direct impact on the evolution of the state. Ever since Vargas, a fervent pragmatist, began extending the scope of state intervention in the 1930s, free-enterprise ideologues -- from Francisco Monteiro Lobato to Roberto Campos -- have opposed it, with little success. By the same token the ideas of modern European socialism (*e.g.*, the British Labour and French Socialist Parties) on nationalizing industry have also had little impact on state expansion.

The irony in Brazil is that those who expand the state protest -- not cynically but too much -- that they support private capitalism. The military rulers insisted on spouting free enterprise rhetoric while they were in fact busy fomenting massive state expansion. Martins' survey of 106 top managers drawn from both state enterprises and ministries reveals a similar inconsistency. Martins administered his questionnaire in 1976 when many of these officials must have been executing Geisel's expansion of the state. Yet when asked to choose which type of firm should be favored for their vision of Brazilian development, 11 percent responded state enterprise against 46 percent in favor of private national enterprise.[13] These anomalies can be explained by the stronger mentalities of nationalism and developmentalism. These mentalities are goal oriented -- *e.g.*, a national steel, petroleum or computer industry -- and largely neutral on the overall issue of state intervention. Imbued with these mentalities, economic policy-makers pursue goals; if the private sector can achieve them, so much the better, if not, they have few ideological qualms over using the state. As in the case of institutions, goals take precedence over procedures.

The pragmatic process through which elite actors have defined the state's role is not likely to change. The consensus among social scientists is that the massive expansion of the state since 1964 (or even since 1945) has been ad hoc, piecemeal and in response to specific problems, without any overriding goal or plan.[14] There is little reason to expect a global approach to supplant this traditional way of changing.

Yet this non-institutional, non-ideological perspective requires some qualification when applied to individual agencies of the state. Surveying the vast sprawl, one finds a range from strong ideologically-backed institutions to fluid, amorphous, practical arrangements, with the mode tending to the latter end of the spectrum. In some cases past political battles and widespread subsequent legitimation create strong institutions, such as Petrobras, the state oil monopoly. But, even previously institutionalized and ideologically-grounded agencies are not immune to subsequent tinkering. For decades the BNDES (National Bank for Economic and Social Development) operated as a strong, ideologically-driven institution, but military governments (particularly the Figueiredo administration) shifted it from Ministry to Ministry, packed its management with outsiders, and fragmented its core mandate by tacking on new, unrelated functions.[15] The general point for framing the state's economic role is that institutions and ideologies do not predominate, but may at times figure in political battles.

The Brazilian state -- the federal executive bureaucracy -- is full of different interests which are not usually ideologically motivated nor institutionally embedded. The position of this state in the economy has been, and is likely to continue to be, determined by elite actors -- inside and outside the state -- politicking to pursue specific substantive outcomes. My argument for the present and near future is that some of the substantive outcomes and some of the actors are changing, and this will produce pressure to frame and redefine the role of the state. Certain economic and political activities such as allocating resources or aggregating interests can be done inside or outside the state. New actors -- and old actors with new goals -- may push to "privatize" or extract activities that up to now unfolded within the state. However, they face powerful countervailing forces.

STATE INTERVENTION I: SETTING THE STATE'S SHARE OF THE ECONOMY

Some of the critical arenas for framing are the economic contacts between the state and the private sector. To simplify the presentation I separate these contacts, or the conflicts between the two sectors, into those concerned with shares of resources and those involving relative power over decision-making. The first category, the topic of this section, includes issues of state investment, ownership, spending and the controversy over the massive state productive sector. The second, addressed below, deals with participation in state decision-making that affects the bulk of both state and private resource allocation. There is of course enormous overlap between these two areas, but in order to pinpoint pressures for and against reshaping the state's role, fine analytical distinctions are necessary.

Given the needs of Brazil's newly industrialized economy, international financial pressures, and the political mobilization of industrialists against statization, one would expect to see a reduced and qualitatively different share for the New Republic's state in the economy. The current political transition coincides with an economic watershed: the sectoral bottlenecks to further industrialization are fundamentally different from twenty or even ten years ago. New policy and economic elites are pushing to use the state differently to meet these new economic challenges. Brazil's international financial situation discourages state expansion. The cheap and abundant international loans that financed the last wave of state expansion in the 1970s are no longer available, and all of the participants in renegotiating Brazil's debt -- the International Monetary Fund, the World Bank, the Reagan administration, and private banks -- favor reducing government spending.[16] On the political side, São Paulo businessmen have waged a decade-long campaign against *estatização* ('statization'). One would expect these businessmen to take advantage of the openness of the Sarney government to promote the privatization they have preached for so long.

The state's massive mobilization of capital -- usually directed and administered by state enterprises -- peaked in the Geisel and Figueiredo governments.[17] Begun in the early 1970s, Tucurui and Itaipu (the fourth and first largest dams in the world) began generating in 1983 and 1985 respectively. Other energy investment in areas such as alcohol and offshore oil exploration will fall off (especially if international oil prices remain depressed). Carajás, the outsized mining project in the Amazon, began exporting iron ore in 1985. The intermediate-goods sector (which absorbed most of the increase in state enterprise activity in the past decade) will not require massive new projects in the near future. For example, over the last four years two huge steel mills, Açominas and Tubarão, came on line and two state-owned aluminum plants began production. As a result, adequate capacity exists in these and other intermediate sectors to meet domestic demand for the medium run, though in the nearer future current exports may have to be redirected to the domestic market. But, more importantly, less costly, incremental expansion which takes advantage of past investment can easily increase capacity.

In short, Brazil has completed at least one phase of "deepening" or difficult import-substituting industrialization. The economy now has a complex productive plant in capital and intermediate goods, and has overcome the most serious obstacles in traditionally state-intensive areas such as energy and infrastructure. As some of the new technocrats have publicly stated, more pressing future challenges lie in areas such as technological modernization, agriculture, developing the Amazon region, industrializing the Northeast, and export promotion.[18] Effective policy responses to these challenges will require very different sorts of state intervention. Unlike dams or steel plants, agricultural, technological and regional development all involve the mobilization of many, dispersed, *private* economic actors. These changing economic conditions by no means obviate a need for state intervention nor do they affect the political will to do so. They do, however, require qualitatively different policies, policy instruments and modes of state/private interaction.

Nonetheless other economic pressures may keep government investment high for the near future. First, while the major projects mentioned above have begun operation, completion will absorb billions more. For example, the dams need more generators and costly transmission lines, Carajás has new mines and processing projects to complete, and Açominas alone requires major investment to reach capacity production. The costly nuclear energy program will be scaled down but not abandoned. State enterprise investment rose in the first year of the New Republic and is slated to rise 19 percent in 1986.[19] Moreover, the Sarney government is committed to increasing social spending. Hence, while activities such as dam-building will probably account for a decreasing share of investment, social investment could rise, thereby maintaining the overall level of government investment.

Lastly, macro-economic policy-makers may feel obliged to increase state investment. Investment in the 1980s has been below the levels attained in the 1970s. However, the 1981-83 recession created immense idle capacity that in turn allowed the recovery of the past three years to proceed despite the lack of new investment.[20] Now that industry is running close to full capacity, somebody has to start investing to sustain growth through the end of the decade. Policy makers will prefer increased government investment to stagnation. Furthermore, private investors have a history of following state investment, and may be waiting for a clear government signal. If this is indeed the case, policy-makers are in the paradoxical position of having to expand the state to privatize the economy.

From a more political perspective one would expect a greater reduction in the state's share of the economy. The *anti-estatização* campaign stirred up a great deal of controversy in the first years of the Geisel government (1974-79), and it helped speed *abertura* by revealing the cracks in the military-industrial alliance. The campaign meant many things to many people, but usually zeroed in on state enterprises. Despite the fulmination, Geisel forged ahead with massive government investment, and created scores of new state enterprises to undertake it.[21] The campaign dissipated, but 'anti-estatização' persisted as refrain of future criticism. 'Statization' became one of the hallmarks of military and authoritarian excess, and a rallying point against which the (capitalist) opposition held apparent consensus.[22]

Though it is a very effective mobilizing symbol, reducing the size of the state is politically much more difficult to bring about. Most of the capitalists who collectively oppose state intervention in general depend individually on specific state programs. For example, industrialists may well oppose state enterprise expansion, but when state firms stop investing, the flow of contracts to private equipment producers, and to private construction and engineering firms dries up. Thus, cutting any one program or firm pits a broad, diffuse coalition based on principles against a small group of intense and material interests. Without ideological cohesion the amorphous state-withering coalition stands little chance. Because of the interaction of these different interests, a case-by-case renegotiation of the bounds, the frame, of the state share of the economy is more likely than sweeping reform.

Selling off state enterprises faces additional political obstacles beyond the self-interest of their dependents. The four largest state enterprise conglomerates -- Siderbrás, Petrobrás, Eletrobrás, and Companhia Vale do Rio Doce (CVRD) -- account for over two-thirds of state enterprise investment and expenditure,[23] and are for all intents and purposes impossible to privatize beyond spinning off a few marginal subsidiaries.

Petrobras was born amid great public mobilization, and in political legend counts as a popular victory over foreign "trusts." Any program to sell it would encounter massive popular resistance. A state petroleum monopoly is also a central component of the military's concept of national security, and the military has always been closely tied to Petrobrás.[24] Furthermore, there is no easy way to sell off an integrated monopoly and the largest firm in Latin America. Such a massive economic presence, if private, would require such intense government regulation that it makes little administrative sense to privatize. Selling Petrobrás might in fact only marginally reduce state presence in petroleum. Electricity firms -- the Eletrobrás system -- present similar difficulties. They are monopolies, and previous experience with foreign power companies has left very little public sympathy for private utilities.

The obstacles in the cases of Siderbrás (steel) and CVRD (mining) are somewhat different. Neither constitutes a natural monopoly, both could theoretically be subdivided into competing units, and the private sector is already heavily involved in both sectors. In the case of Siderbrás' ten operating firms, some are productive and in sound financial shape, and might attract buyers. However, even these sales would encounter opposition. Steel is a risky capital-intensive investment, and the sale price might have to be so low as to provoke charges of public give-aways.[25] In some states Siderbrás steel is an important part of the local economy, and regional elites would not be eager to surrender their power in nominating management and in formulating policy for these firms.

In the case of CVRD, the company has claims covering incalculable mineral wealth, mostly through the control of the vast Carajás deposits in the Amazon. True privatization would constitute another massive and unknown donation to the buyers, and would counter a long-standing distrust of private and especially foreign ownership of sub-soil rights.

"Pulling the state back out" may hence be more difficult politically than imagined. Figueiredo assumed office professing a deep commitment to privatization and publicized a major campaign to sell off state enterprises, but he achieved precious little. The same has so far been the lot of Sarney's privatizing intentions. Over a year after taking office the new government finally sold its first state enterprise; the Grande Hotel Blumenau.[26]

Active withering of the state confronts structural, logistical and political obstacles. However, the secular *passive* trend of increasing privatization is driven by forces that need not abate in the near future. Passive privatization occurs when the private sector grows faster (and hence its relative share of GNP expands) than the public sector, which may nonetheless be growing. By some measures this privatization has been the trend over the past two decades.[27] The state sector led the economic recoveries of the last two decades,[28] but private exporters led the 1984-85 recovery and together with other private producers may well drive future growth. If the trend continues, then cutting the state back is less urgent for advocates of privatization than promoting private sector growth. It is in this sense that the *anti-estatização* campaign -- to the extent that it preaches selling government assets -- is misplaced. Antonio Ermirio de Moraes, the president of the largest private Brazilian conglomerate, put it more succinctly: "Privatization (*desestatização*) is a joke. What's needed is to stop statization."[29]

In sum, the state as investor and direct producer is not susceptible to radical pruning. Despite auspicious economic conditions for increasing the private share, international pressures to curb state expenditures, and a new government attentive to the wishes of industrialists, privatization faces formidable obstacles. More immediate political, administrative, material, macro-economic and social concerns -- both inside and outside the state -- are likely to keep the state share of the economy high.

STATE INTERVENTION II: SETTING THE PRIVATE SHARE OF ECONOMIC DECISION-MAKING

Most of the anti-state controversy in Brazil (and the discussion above) focusses on issues of property, ownership and shares of GNP, in part because these issues are easier to grasp, publicize and rally around. But they have eclipsed the more important issue of the distribution of power between public and private actors in economic decision-making.[30] The vast majority of large private firms depend on government subsidies, price supports, discretionary credit, tariff protection, restraint of competing MNCs or other support. Most would have difficulty surviving without it. Moreover, the resources affected by these policies are far greater than those controlled directly by the state. Few industrialists favor across-the-board modification of their dependence on this political capitalism. However, depending on the firm and sector, industrialists will pressure to change the state's responsibility, and especially to secure greater private sector participation in setting policy.

The first part of this section analyzes 'mature' sectors where the private sector is pressuring for greater control, and other new sectors where the state is increasing its control. This is a fairly constant process in Brazil; the state deregulates established sectors while plunging into new ones that barely exist. However, there is more redefinition, sector by sector, during these years of political change than during the last years of the military regime. The second part of this section analyzes the question not of the state's role in the private sector, but of the private sector's position in the policy centers of the state.

In theory, when a sector reaches a threshold of maturity and complexity, minute, outcome-specific state intervention becomes increasingly ineffective and costly: ineffective because policy-makers lack sophistication, contact and information; costly because industrialists depend on effective decisions. At such a threshold a coalition forms between those producers who bear most costs and those policy-makers keenest on improving sectoral performance. This privatizing coalition forms to liberalize the market, to change state intervention from rulings to rules.[31]

One of the best examples of a state-fostered, but now maturing industry is petrochemicals. The state orchestrated a *tripé* arrangement (a 'tripod' joint venture between state, national private and MNC capital), and shouldered the critical risks.[32] Over the past 15 years this industry has flourished and the national private partners have greatly strengthened their leg of the 'tripe'. The president of Petroquisa (Petrobrás' petrochemical subsidiary) and the vice-president of the industry association declared that the national private sector was ready "to think about walking alone."[33] The Petroquisa president -- perhaps remembering the tripe metaphor -- added that the sector would need a state crutch in the area of technological development. According to another recent assessment, the petrochemical industry is "mature, technologically capable, with significant participation by national private capital, and financially solid."[34]

Today the policy debate revolves around market consolidation and forward integration into more sophisticated products for which producers want a different sort of government intervention. Whereas Petroquisa stepped in initially to produce the basic feedstock chemicals, private producers now want the state to foment private national investment and diversification. Haguenauer claims that the sector does not require further credits, subsidies and finance, but rather "the guarantee of space for national firms."[35] Confirming Barzelay's argument that political signals are critical to private investors, Haguenauer argues that what is most needed is not specific policies but a policy; "the political indefinition to date has certainly constituted one of the obstacles to the development of more sophisticated chemicals."[36]

Private producers are not pressing for complete state withdrawal. They still want the state to define the overall policy for the sector and they want to participate more actively in formulating that policy through representation in the Industrial Development Council.[37] They also want tariff protection, export promotion, technical assistance, and preferential treatment from other government organs, for example from health agencies that buy pharmaceutical products. Furthermore, regional elites in Bahia and Rio Grande do Sul will want the Federal government to insure that market forces do not jeopardize the future expansion of the petrochemical complexes in their states.

My argument that diversification and consolidation create pressures for market liberalization is not functional. These pressures come from private and public actors in pursuit of specific goals that they feel are better served by markets than by administration, by general rules rather than specific rulings.[38] That is, diversification creates new industrialists who may -- once consolidated -- find administrative means costly and prefer to take their chances in freer, albeit highly protected and regulated, markets. Or, to use Barzelay's formulation, some investors prefer market uncertainty to the strategic uncertainty for political products (whose profitability depends on policy).[39] Barzelay uses this formulation to assess what investment strategy an investor is likely to pursue. However, it can be usefully extended to consider what sort of political goals investors will pursue. That is, rather than shift investments to alter the mix of uncertainties in their investment portfolios, investors may decide to lobby the state to change the mix of uncertainties affecting *past* investments.

But while industrial diversification promotes coalitions favoring market-oriented solutions in sectors of extensive past intervention, the momentum (or inertia) of past successes and the dependence of new infant industries will abet the continuation of company-level intervention in new areas. For example, one of the most controversial policies of the Figueiredo and Sarney governments is the Informatics Law designed to protect and promote the domestic computer industry. The law gives SEI (Special Secretariat for Informatics) the right to approve all micro- and mini-computer production, and importation of electronic components used in any industry, from automobiles to machine tools to toys. On paper the law gives the state powers of minute intervention into all aspects of private production.[40]

At a broader level the Stabilization Plan of February 1986 (Plano Cruzado) constitutes deep new intervention. The plan may not be indicative of long-term trends, but through it the government vastly increased its price control powers in an effort to freeze *all* retail prices.[41] Though the price freeze is temporary, never has the state been so directly involved in so many sectors; weighing products, checking specifications, closing uncooperative supermarkets, and importing goods to replace supplies withheld by producers.

While most attributed the spark for the *anti-estatização* campaign to quantitative state expansion, an underlying *political* critique is more significant.[42] At the time the state was expanding, economic policy-making was also becoming more centralized, arbitrary and less subject to private sector (let alone public) input. The process of centralization and exclusion of private sector representatives in deliberative councils began under Finance Minister Delfim Neto and peaked under Geisel before easing somewhat during the second *delfinato* when Delfim Neto returned in 1979.[43]

Industrialists adapted to their changing opportunities for access. Lucia Klein provides a detailed account of how capital goods producers and their association ABDIB lobbied to increase Açominas' purchase of capital goods in Brazil.[44] They were completely excluded from the initial decision, but regrouped and successfully pressured the government to increase the percentage of orders going to Brazilian firms. On one flank they resorted to the recently unfettered press to condemn Geisel's policy. At the same time they courted sympathetic technocrats. In the beginning the bureaucrat/ industrialist alliance revolved around the BNDE and its President, Marcos Vianna. But, Vianna later abandoned his erstwhile allies, and the capital goods producers cast about for another insider ally whom they found in Paulo Bellotti, then the General Secretary (Vice Minister) of the Ministry of Industry and Commerce (MIC).

This ad hoc, personalized influence conforms well to Cardoso's conception of bureaucratic rings.[45] Bureaucratic rings are policy specific, as in the above case of supplying equipment for Açominas, and hence hundreds or thousands of them are in rather constant formation and dissolution. The members of a ring come from both private and public sectors.[46] Cardoso further notes that the bureaucratic ring for a particular policy revolves around one person in a pivotal bureaucratic position. Lastly these rings are informal and personal.

The Açominas case clearly demonstrates how a temporary, informal, bureaucratic ring forms around a top official; the ring formed first around Vianna in BNDE, collapsed when he withdrew, and reformed around Bellotti in MIC.

Bureaucratic rings became the predominant form of interest articulation precisely in response to formal exclusion from policy. At any given moment they may or may not represent industrialists to their satisfaction and provide policy makers with adequate feedback, but they are volatile and are likely to break down at some point. Because bureaucratic rings are informal and dependent on particular bureaucrats they are highly unstable and can be very arbitrary. Private firms and business associations can invest years in perfecting a policy web, a bureaucratic ring, only to see the keystone bureaucrat fired. The replacement may have a very different policy orientation, or may have closer ties to other private interests.[47] They are also arbitrary because there are no mechanisms for formalizing the influence or voice to be accorded to each participant. Major actors can be caught powerless by simple changes in the positions of other members of the ring.

Given a choice, how would industrialists restructure their access and influence? They have three options for 'privatizing' power in economic policy: markets, formal access to and participation in the economic bureaucracy, or an expanded Congressional role in economic policy. I will address the first two means here and leave the discussion of Congress to the next section. The simplest and most absolute way to privatize economic policy-making is to extricate the state altogether. In certain instances (as discussed above) industrialists and/or bureaucrats may push to substitute markets for bureaucratic rings.

Another means of privatization would involve reducing the number of points of contact and access between private actors and the state. This would privatize much of the interest aggregation by forcing private interests to organize and adopt a position prior to meeting the state. This channelling of access -- or transformation of bureaucratic rings into funnels -- would require permanent formal channels, which would mitigate the problems of instability and arbitrariness noted above.[48] The patois for such industrialist-sponsored, formal channels is societal corporatism.[49]

Depending on their market strength, organizational force and experience to date, private sector actors may seek either informal bureaucratic rings, liberal privatization through markets, or corporatist privatization through organized access. To date these strategies and the varying responses of state actors to sectoral demands have had an ambiguous impact, producing neither an aggregate privatizing or statizing trend. So far I have considered only the direct contact between the bureaucracy and the private sector, and the numerous motivations on both sides to revise the terms of their interaction. Of course, businessmen and capitalists have other modes of articulating their interests which is part of a broader political discussion to which the chapter now turns.

THE STATE AND THE POLITY: REPRESENTING THE POWERFUL

The Brazilian state is as dominant in the polity as it is in the economy. In Brazil's state-centered polity the bureaucracy internalizes political roles that in most democracies other political actors and institutions perform. Eisenstadt was one of the first to note the political consequences of an overweening bureaucracy in developing countries:

> "... [A] major aspect of the bureaucracy's involvement in the political process ... is its tendency to develop as one of the main instruments of political regulation. It is one of the main channels of political struggle in which and through which different interests are regulated and aggregated. Its role in this aspect of the political process may be not only important but predominant....
>
> "Thus ... the bureaucracy may tend to fulfill different types of political functions and, like parties,

> legislatures, and executives, become the center of different types of political activity. Through these activities it may establish some of the basic frameworks of modern politics, but it may also minimize the extent of differentiation of various types of political roles and activities. It thus impedes the development of autonomous and differentiated political activities, organizations and orientations."[50]

In Brazil, the state -- the bureaucracy, not the legislature -- leads in policy formulation. The state, not Congress or the political parties, is the central arena for interest articulation, elite negotiation and compromise. The state, not political parties, holds the key to electoral support.[51]

The elements of Brazil's state-centered polity include: a constitutionally weak legislature (especially as regards budgets and economic policy); tens of thousands of political appointments which absorb much of the political elite; a politically active military which can only affect policy within the state; extensive government intervention in the economy and society (which therefore draws politicians and the military to the state); a coalition tradition based on individual cooptation instead of programmatic alliances; and historically (and currently) weak parties which depend on state resources. This section assesses some of the interplay between these elements by examining the relationships between the state on the one hand, and Congress, political parties and the military on the other. The goal again is to identify the potential backers of continuity and change.

Prior to 1964, Congress played a minor role in formulating major policy.[52] After 1964 the military completely cut Congress out of any significant participation in policy. Now, through the new Constitution, political and economic elites have an opportunity to revamp relations between Congress and the Executive. However, both elites also have motives for keeping the legislature subordinate.

As discussed above, economic elites may prefer to leave allocation decisions within the state or to privatize decision-making through markets or societal corporatism. For the pursuit of specific interests, Congress offers few advantages in terms of regular, strong influence.[53] Moreover, in general terms it is not clear that parliamentary mechanisms are best suited to represent the economic elites generated by late industrialization. Peter Evans argues that bourgeois democracy functioned well during early European industrialization because it adequately represented the major factions of capital and gave them a suitable forum for working out their differences. However,

> "...in the context of dependent development, ... the need for democracy is small. One of the functions of parliamentary regimes is to provide a forum for the resolution of differences among the bourgeoisie.... But when accumulation depends on the triple alliance of multinationals, state enterprises, and their local private allies, parliamentary means of achieving consensus are inappropriate. Neither the multinationals, nor the state bourgeoisie are likely to be politically represented in proportion to their economic importance. For the local private bourgeoisie the disproportionate (relative to their economic position) representation of small capital could be a real problem. The lack of representative political bodies may make it harder for the local private bourgeoisie to forge an internal political consensus, but, since its role in accumulation is ancillary rather than dominant, an overall consensus is not crucial."[54]

Designing a political system to represent adequately the powerful is a question that prompts speculation on the nature of the current transition. Extrapolating from Evans' argument, we might in fact be witnessing an historic climacteric. The diversification and strengthening of local capital may have made it less ancillary, rendering bourgeois democracy or "parliamentary means of achieving consensus," therefore less inappropriate. The São Paulo bourgeoisie has become quite active in electoral and party politics. Its social democrat wing was a decisive force behind Tancredo Neves' candidacy, and Antônio Ermírio de Moraes -- whom Evans once described as "Brazil's best candidate for membership in a classic conquering bourgeoisie"[55] -- recently ran for governor of São Paulo. I do not mean to enter into the larger debate on the relationship between capitalist development, the bourgeoisie and democracy.[56] It is still far too early to know whether or not we are observing a lasting political reorganization and reorientation of the bourgeoisie. Nonetheless it is worth remembering Barrington Moore's famous dictum, "no bourgeois; no democracy," as democratization unfolds in Brazil.

My goal here is to examine a second-order issue within a more competitive regime: who -- Congress or the bureaucracy -- is to lead in economic policy-making? In other late industrializing democracies such as France and Japan the pattern has been to limit the economic powers of the legislature. To the extent that state, MNC and large national capital -- the 'tripé' -- are currently well-represented in the state, they may favor following this executive-centered pattern. Elements of the same politically active São Paulo bourgeoisie are also very well represented in the economic policy bureaucracy and in Sarney's inner circle of close advisors. For example, Dilson Funaro, the Minister of Finance, is an archetypical representative of medium, São Paulo capital, and Sarney regularly consults with Matias Machline who is a prime example of the modern, internationalized capitalist created by the 'miracle.'[57] The 'tripé' members may well favor less open, state-centered arrangements for economic policy-making. However, we might expect small capitalists and the growing number of industrialists who are denied stable representation within the state to promote alternative mechanisms of representation in Congress.

The new Constitution will determine major issues of Congress and economic policy, in particular Congress' role in the budget process. Since the *Congress* -- not an independent Constitutional Assembly -- elected in November 1986 will draft the new Constitution, some expansion of its role is to be expected. However, so far the transition to civilian rule has not reinvigorated Congress. Congress has had little impact on the major policies of Sarney's first year (*e.g.*, the Plano Cruzado), and has mostly managed to tarnish its public image, through a series of well-publicized scandals.[58] Hence, public opinion, the 'classe polit́ca', 'tripé' participants, the military and others who are already well represented may pressure Congress not to "abrogate" too many economic powers unto itself.[59]

When it comes to the relations between the state and political parties, the question is whether or not forces exist that will push to take state resources out of parties by reducing patronage, and to take party functions out of the state by making parties the major independent arena for interest aggregation and political recruitment. On both counts current pressures reinforce the past melding of state and parties. Brazilian parties have historically been very clientelistic, and if Shefter's comparative analysis holds for Brazil, the Sarney government will be tempted to use government spending for patronage.[60]

Shefter distinguishes between internally and externally mobilized parties. The former comes to power without a mass electoral base, must build such a base while in power, and is likely to use state resources to do so. The externally mobilized party is out of power, must use non-material appeals to build a mass base, and is unlikely to revert to patronage politics once in power because it already has a loyal programmatic or ideological following.[61]

Of the parties in the 'governing' Democratic Alliance (AD), the smaller Liberal Front Party (PFL) lacks a mass base, while the majority PMDB enjoys respectable, though somewhat unstable, voter preference.[62] The PFL is clearly an internally mobilized party. The PMDB is a hybrid. At first glance the PMDB appears to be externally mobilized. It established a mass base while out of power during 20 years of military rule. However, the generals' exit in 1985 ended the PMDB's major appeal to voters -- opposition to military rule. To escape its reputation as a referendum party, the PMDB must redefine its appeal to its mass base.

Thus, the temptation to use state resources exists, and the heterogeneity of the PMDB further reinforces it. To forge a coherent ideological/programmatic appeal in a party that groups together very diverse factions would probably require splitting off of at least some factions of the PMDB. Given the still tenuous nature of the Democratic Alliance, the PMDB may think it unwise to risk internal division.[63]

Beyond the difficulties of redefining its ideological appeal, the PMDB's mass base is shifting and unsteady. The PMDB is losing politicians and voters in the south and gaining in the northeast in what the press has called the "northeasternization" of the party. The November 1985 municipal elections made this trend very evident. Recent PMDB converts won in northeastern cities where the PMDB was traditionally weak, and the PMDB lost in São Paulo, its core for over a decade. The PMDB's electoral base is shifting at the same time its appeals and resources are, which make it start to resemble closely an internally mobilized party.[64]

Patronage politics may well be the norm for party influence on the state in this 're-encounter,' but the state, or the salience of politics within the state, may also have a decisive impact on parties. Parties have historically been weak, and continued state-centered politics may keep them weak and render the state the preferred arena for politics.

The ruling AD is an intra-state coalition, not a programmatic alliance. The PMDB and PFL cemented their pact in mid-1984 through the distribution of top appointments, and have managed further accommodations through the state.[65] During the first months of the New Republic the members of the AD shocked even cynical observers as they divied up the spoils of victory -- tens of thousands of appointments and jobs.[66] AD leaders and supporters now permeate the bureaucracy, while outside the state the AD is tenuous. The alliance is unreliable in Congress,[67] and in only one of the major municipal contests in 1985 did the PFL and PMDB join forces.

Political leaders the world over distribute cabinet positions to their supporters, but in Brazil the practice goes much further.[68] Political appointments penetrate the bureaucracy more deeply, and because of the state's power in society and economy, more political leaders are attracted to "administrative" posts. Moreover, appointees do not merely express the voice of their faction in the policy process, but rather use their positions to continue their own politics. This often takes the form of patronage, but also includes furthering ing one's own career in the 'classe política' by aggregating interests and forming policy coalitions, often in areas outside the appointee's formal policy responsibilities. To the extent that political appointees continue politics as usual and because top political leaders are drawn into the state, parties and Congress are deprived of the roles and talent that give them greater importance in other democracies.

Lamounier and Meneguello argue that, among other factors, the tendency throughout this century for the ruling elite to coopt opposition leaders and bring them into the ruling coalition weakens parties because it preempts the development of a strong opposition party capable in the longer run of capturing the state as a party.[69] This analysis of cooptation neatly describes Tancredo's succession; 12 of his 21 civilian ministers had served in some top-level, 'confidence' capacity in one of military governments. Sidestepping the question of who coopted whom, it is nonetheless clear that an amalgam of old and new elites leads the New Republic and that this elite accommodation could have deleterious consequences, as before, for strong party politics.

Another indicator of just how critical intra-state politics are to the New Republic is the position of the military and their emerging accommodation with civilian elites. The most important military participation comes through the six military ministers[70] who involve themselves in top policymaking, something Sarney considers perfectly legitimate. As his spokesman said, "the military ministers can talk about politics because they occupy *political* posts."[71] To date the head of the National Information Service (SNI) has been active in formulating the government response to strikes and in drafting the new labor code, and the head of the Casa Militar helped revise and attenuate the proposed land-reform program. In November 1985 the military informally vetoed a bill which would have restored the rights of 2,600 officers discharged during the dictatorship. Sarney's strong lobbying on the military's behalf helped defeat the measure. Furthermore, and as before 1964, military participation continues at lower levels since Sarney has not moved to purge the top civilian bureaucracy of retired officers.

From Evans' perspective, the problem is once again the poor fit between parliamentary representation and de facto power. Parties are not suitable vehicles for military representation, and -- barring Constitutional alchemy -- the military is very unlikely to find a comfortable institutional niche in the New Republic that adequately represents its wide-ranging policy concerns. Thus, the state becomes the only arena for its continued informal participation, which the current government in any event considers essential to its survival.

Brazil's state-centered polity also contains mutually reinforcing components which form a vicious circle (certainly to those who oppose state dominance). For instance, because the legislature is weak, political (and military) leaders are drawn to the executive and, once there, are loath to relinquish their prerogatives.[72] Since parties rely so much on patronage, political leaders are drawn to large executive budgets and accept administrative appointments, but their absence in turn further weakens parties and Congress.

To summarize, in a state-centered polity, politics of all sorts transpire within the state. Many elite political actors stand to lose through the political equivalent of privatization: taking the state out of politics and taking politics out of the state. Big capital, MNCs, much of the 'classe política', and the military are adequately, albeit informally and imperfectly, represented within the state. They face isolated opponents and are unlikely to trade their current privileges for an uncertain place in a new order dominated by parties and legislatures.

CONCLUSIONS: STATE LEARNING AND STATE-SLOWED DEMOCRATIZATION?

In this essay I have tried to disaggregate the state, and, in specific cases of state-society interaction, to analyze which forces are likely to push for an expanded or a reduced role of the state in the economy and the polity. Reaggregated, these cases support the present tendency to leave the state where it was before 1985, and in some important respects where it was before 1964. The much heralded 're-encounter' between State and Nation has so far left the former little changed.

The transition to civilian rule offers Brazilians an opportunity to reorder state intervention in the economy. Other countries have attempted this, but often only after the state's role has become the dominant theme in acrimonious political contention. Fortunately, Brazil has avoided the ideological polarization that has distorted the debate elsewhere. This pragmatism should spare Brazil experiences similar to the havoc the Chilean "Chicago boys" visited on their economy, Thatcher's costly war of attrition, or the French horsetrading in state assets.

Without this sort of radical experimentation, Brazil will retain its form of political capitalism and state-led industrialization. The current juncture still provides an opportunity to learn, adjust and fine tune. In this there are few theories or examples to follow. Social scientists still know much more about how and why states initially intervene than about how they learn and refine that intervention.[73] Chalmers Johnson documents the Japanese experience, which resembles the Brazilian in that it is pragmatic and goal-oriented.[74] Over the past half century the Japanese have refined state intervention into what is now a model of successful state-led industrialization. Brazil may be able to learn from Japan's errors, but there is little to copy directly. The general lesson the Japanese experience underscores is the importance of rethinking policies in the light of their past record and present opportunities.

What would be the consequences of continued state-centered politics, should the proponents of its perpetuation triumph? State-centered politics are necessarily informal, and therefore elitist and opaque. A limited democracy at best. The state is structured as the executive arm of government, and the politics of policy and the aggregation of interests must be superimposed, informally, on this administrative structure. The state is designed institutionally to execute the business of government and therefore lacks the institutional means to conduct inter-elite negotiations, appease the military, or incorporate new elite or non-elite groups. Furthermore, because politics are informal, the powerful are not accountable; policy making and elite negotiation within the state are opaque. Informal politics provide no basis for holding individual actors publicly accountable.

This is not to argue that small government is beautiful or more democratic; the size of government is immaterial. It is the state as privileged locus or arena that has negative consequences for democracy. Cardoso has also argued that democratic control, not size, is the issue.[75] However, to control what currently goes on inside the state requires first extracting it.

I would not want these pessimistic consequences to be construed as predictions, nor am I practicing what Simon Schwartzman has called the "sociology of lamentation."[76] Perhaps two factors not discussed could reverse the tendencies analyzed here. First, I tried to show in each disaggregated instance which forces would politick for which outcomes. However, the task of interrelating these individual battles is beyond this paper. The synergy of overlapping struggles or the impact of galvanizing crises could well generate unexpected coalitions. For instance, contrary to their immediate interest, industrialists might prefer a greater Congressional role in order to neutralize military meddling within the state. Second, by focussing exclusively on economic and political elites, I have neglected non-elite actors who may be able to counter the tendencies noted here. A central assumption of this paper is that for the immediate future elite actors will continue to set the political agenda. Over the medium run, however, the still disenfranchised majority may challenge elite actors and dramatically alter the elitist state-centered politics analyzed here.

In this essay I have followed Albert Hirschman's counsel for would-be political economists to avoid the quest for grand macro-links and instead to focus on the myriad micro-intersections between economics and politics.[77] In much of political economy, political scientists analyze the economic bases of political behavior, and economists (and a growing number of political scientists) assess the economic consequences of political intervention. While largely following the political science tradition, I have also tried to analyze some influences that flow in other directions: the political consequences of extensive state intervention in the economy, and the economic consequences (translated through policy) of the changing political strategies of economic elites. I examined only a few of these micro-intersections and agree with Hirschman that this is still fertile ground for future research.

Furthermore, by focussing on specific issues and actors I wanted to avoid the distortions of macro-political explanations for state continuity. For example, Claudio Veliz' centralist tradition sweeps across the centuries (five of them) to confront us today with a state constructed of barely weathered and seemingly immutable granite.[78] While enduring currents in Brazilian political culture do support the idea of a broader state role, they play a decidedly secondary role in the types of struggles I have discussed. If industrialists and policy-makers see gain in shrinking the state out of certain markets, cultural heritage and historical tradition should present few obstacles.

Other perspectives exaggerate the power and greed of bureaucrats themselves. Some lay exclusive blame for state expansion on these administrators who are characterized as a state bourgeoisie or as power-hungry technocrats bent on the self-aggrandizing and lucrative expansion of their own bureaucratic fiefdoms. In interviews with them they seem to be foggy and/or divided on their own interests and preferences, usually weak against outsider superiors, and incapable of collective action.[79] What I hope to have shown here is that most bureaucrats supporting state intervention can find ready allies in the military, in the 'classe politica' or in the pri-vate sector. Without these allies state withering would be a much simpler proposition.

To close, though the political mood is effervescent and the expectation of change great, we should not expect a metamorphized Novo Estado. Though politicking for change will be great on the margins of state intervention, the core role -- the fundamentals of a state-centered political economy -- remains. Retouched and reframed, this portrait of the state will likely be recognizable for some time to come.

NOTES

1. I am grateful to Albert Fishlow, John Wirth, Kathleen Thelen, Helen Shapiro and Ron Archer for comments on an earlier version, and absolve them of responsibility for its final form. I also thank the Berkeley-Stanford Joint Center for Latin American Studies for its financial support.

2. I use a seemingly prosaic definition; the state is the Federal executive bureaucracy. For some, not including Congress and the judiciary in the definition may cause consternation. However, as I hope to show, much more goes on within the Brazilian executive than administration, including some of the functions that parties and legislatures perform in other countries. Hence, the Brazilian executive deserves a more encompassing label than bureaucracy.

3. Stephen D. Krasner, "Punctuated Equilibrium: An Approach to the Evolution of State-Society Relations" (Department of Political Science, Stanford University, 1982).

4. Wanderley Guilherme dos Santos, "A pós-Revolução' brasileira," in Hélio Jaguaribe, *et. al.*, *Brasil, sociedade democrática* (Rio de Janeiro, 1985).

5. On the political impact of authoritarian regimes, see Karen L. Remmer, "Redemocratization and the Impact of Authoritarian Rule in Latin America," *Comparative Politics* 17, no. 3 (April 1985) pp. 253-275.

6. One of the secular trends in the military regime was the tendency to give the central government, the state, greater control over these positions. Castelo Branco began stripping politicians of their political rights, thereby altering the composition of Congress. Costa e Silva and Medici relied heavily on this mechanism to conjure up Congressional majorities, and Geisel appointed senators directly. After the election of opposition governors in 1965, Castelo Branco made subsequent elections (through 1982) indirect, *i.e.* appointive positions. Lastly, more and more cities became 'national security concerns,' which meant that the (appointed) governors appointed mayors. In sum, the military government appointed the incumbents of local government, Congress, and the judiciary making these office holders beholden to and dependent upon the state.

7. In 1977 when Geisel decreed the indirect election of some senators, the TV show, "The Six Million Dollar Man," was enjoying some success. The "bionic" label stuck apparently because it distinguished these senators from mere mortals (their elected colleagues), and because "bionic" conveyed the sense that these senators derived their power from contrived engineering.

8. Fernando Henrique Cardoso is of course correct when he says state actors act as a bloc when the defense of capitalism is at issue, *Autoritarismo e democratização* (Rio de Janeiro, 1975), pp. 183-4. Bureaucrats might also act as one to save the state. However, since neither the destruction of capitalism nor of the state is high on the political agenda today, this defensive unity is unlikely to coalesce.

9. See the penultimate section for an expanded description of the state-centered polity. Eric Nordlinger also uses a

state-centered model, *On the Autonomy of the Democratic State*, (Cambridge, 1981). However, his is a theoretical construct valid for all industrial democracies, whereas I use it as an empirical referent to distinguish Brazil from other countries.

10. Douglas A. Chalmers, "The Politicized State in Latin America," in James M. Malloy, ed., *Authoritarianism and Corporatism in Latin America* (Pittsburgh, 1977) p. 24.

11. This institutional malleability would also contribute to inflated expectations of change in the New Republic. Space does not permit a full discussion of the lack of institutionalization in the Brazilian state. For a lengthier treatment, see my "Politics within the State: Mining, Steel and State Enterprise in Authoritarian Brazil, 1967-85," (Ph.D. Dissertation, Department of Political Science, University of California, in progress).

12. For a complete discussion of elite ideology in Brazil, see Peter McDonough, *Power and Ideology in Brazil*, (Princeton, 1981).

13. Luciano Martins, *Estado capitalista e burocrácia no Brasil pós-64*, (Rio de Janeiro, 1985) p. 228.

14. See for example Nunes and Geddes in this volume; Martins, *Estado capitalista e burocrácia no Brasil pos-64*; Werner Baer, Richard Newfarmer and Thomas Trebat, "On State Capitalism in Brazil: Some New Issues and Questions" *Inter-American Economic Affairs* 30, no. 3 (Winter 1976) pp. 69-91; and Nathaniel H. Leff, *Economic Policy-Making and Development in Brazil*, (New York, 1968).

15. For an excellent history of the BNDES see Eliza Jane Willis, "The State as Banker: The Expansion of the Public Sector in Brazil," (Ph.D. Dissertation, University of Texas at Austin, 1986).

16. International pressures deserve more attention, even though policy makers proclaim that these pressures will not determine domestic policy. However, international factors are beyond the scope of this paper, and I confine my discussion to domestic forces.

17. See Henri Reichstul and Luciano Coutinho, "Investimento estatal 1974-1980: ciclo e crise," in Luiz Gonzaga Belluzo and Renata Coutinho, eds., *Desenvolvimento capitalista no Brasil: ensaios sobre a crise*, (São Paulo, 1983); and Anibal Villanova Villela, *Empresas do governo como instrumento de política econômica: os sistemas Siderbrás, Eletrobrás, Petrobrás e Telebrás* (Rio de Janeiro, 1984).

18. See *Isto E*, 25 September 1985.

19. *Conjuntura Econômica*, February 1986, p. 27.

20. Antonio Barros de Castro and Francisco Eduardo Pires de Souza, *A economia brasileira em marcha forçada* (Rio de Janeiro, 1985).

21. Castro and Souza, *A economia brasileira em marcha forçada*, p. 40.

22. See especially the enduring campaigns waged by the business magazine *Visão* and the newspaper *Folha da Tarde*.

23. Brazil, Presidência da República, Secretaria de Planejamento, Secretaria de Controle de Empresas Estatais (SEST), *Cadastro das empresas estatais* (Brasília, 1984).

24. On Petrobrás' history and outside support see John Wirth, *The Politics of Brazilian Development, 1930-54*, (Stanford, 1970), and "Setting the Brazilian Agenda, 1936-53," in John D. Wirth, ed., *Latin American Oil Companies and the Politics of Energy*, (Lincoln, 1985); Sérgio H. Abranches, "State Enterprise and Modes of Privatization:

A Critical View Based on Brazilian Examples," Serie Estudos no. 27 (IUPERJ, junho 1984) pp. 24-28; and Getúlio Carvalho, *Petrobrás: do monopólio aos contratos de risco*, (Rio de Janeiro, 1977).

25. The Figueiredo government negotiated for years to sell a minor steel firm, Cofavi, to a private group, but the government could never bring itself to accept the private bids.

26. Besides being a money-losing proposition, with no economic justification for belonging to the state, the Hotel is also a political embarrassment because the military had confiscated it from an opposition deputy 17 years ago (*Veja* 2 July 1986).

27. Santos, "A pós-Revolução' brasileira," p. 249, Table 6.

28. See Reichstul and Coutinho, "Investimento estatal 1974-1980."

29. *Veja*, 26 March 1986.

30. Abranches, "State Enterprise and Modes of Privatization."

31. One critical "market" where many industrialists have long demanded government withdrawal is in collective bargaining (see Renato Raul Boschi, *Elites industriais e democrácia: hegemonia burguesa e mudança política no Brasil*, (Rio de Janeiro, 1979)). Because the labor market involves much more than questions of market vs. administration, the issue is beyond the present scope. See Tavares de Almeida, Chapter 5 in this volume.

32. On the petrochemical industry and the *tripé* see Luciano Martins, "The State-Transnational Corporation-Local Entrepreneurs Joint Venture in Brazil: How to Relax and Enjoy a Forced Marriage," in Harry M. Makler, Alberto

Martinelli and Neil J. Smelser, eds., *The New International Economy*, (Beverly Hills, 1982); and Peter Evans, *Dependent Development: The Alliance of Multinational, State and Local Capital in Brazil*, (Princeton, 1979); and "Collectivized Capitalism: Integrated Petrochemical Complexes and Capital Accumulation in Brazil," in Thomas C. Bruneau and Philippe Faucher, eds., *Authoritarian Capitalism: Brazil's Contemporary Economic and Political Development*, (Boulder, 1981).

33. *Gazeta Mercantil*, 15 October 1984.

34. Lia Haguenauer, "O complexo químico brasileiro: organização e dinâmica interna," (Instituto de Economia Industrial, Universidade Federal Rio de Janeiro, January 1986) p. 103.

35. *Ibid*., p. 106.

36. *Ibid*., p. 107. Michael Barzelay, *The Politicized Market Economy: Alcohol in Brazil's Energy Strategy*, (Berkeley, 1986).

37. *Jornal do Brasil*, 9 September 1985.

38. I follow Karl Polanyi's reasoning that major markets are political creations, not natural phenomena, see *The Great Transformation: The Political and Economic Origins of Our Time*, (Boston, 1971).

39. Barzelay, *The Politicized Market Economy*, 45-77 and *passim*.

40. See *Veja* (16 August 1986) for a summary of the Informatics Law and the controversies over it.

41. The Plano Cruzado also stands firmly in the tradition of technocratic wizardry, which arose in the 1950s, infused the military's new technocratic age in the 1960s, and did

yeoman's work propping up the flagging legitimacy of the authoritarian regime. When the military regime's policies failed, it appeared that this myth would follow the military's economic miracle into oblivion. However, the popularity of the group of young advisors who drafted the Plano Cruzado in secrecy demonstrates that the technocratic, state solution still figures favorably in popular mythology.

42. Alfred Stepan notes this less publicized critique of government intervention: "My interviews in Brazil indicate that Paulista entrepreneurial arguments against statism were arguments not against the state as producer, but rather against the state as regulator." "State Power and the Strength of Civil Society in the Southern Cone of Latin America," in Peter Evans, Dietrich Rueschmeyer and Theda Skocpol, eds., *Bringing the State Back In*, (Cambridge. 1985) p. 335.

43. See Boschi, *Elites industriais e democrácia*, p. 151-55. The evolution of Consider (National Council for Steel and Non-Ferrous Metals), the National Monetary Council (CMN) and the Council for Economic Development (CDE) clearly demonstrates this process. In the case of Consider and CMN the government gradually packed the membership with government appointees and excluded private sector representatives. The CDE was Geisel's economic council from which he excluded private participation. On CMN and CDE, see Cesar Guimarães and Maria Lúcia Teixeira Werneck Vianna, "Autoritarismo, planejamento e formas de centralização decisoria: os casos do Conselho Monetário Nacional e do Conselho de Desenvolvimento Econômico," (paper presented at VII Annual ANPOCS, 1983); Maria Lúcia Teixeira Werneck Vianna, "A administração do 'milagre': o Conselho Monetário Nacional, 1964/1974," (Tese de Mestrado, IUPERJ, 1982). See also Sergio Henrique Abranches, "The Divided Leviathan: The State and Economic Policy Formation in Authoritarian Brazil," (Ph.D. Dissertation, Cornell University, 1978) and Schneider, "Politics within the State: Mining, Steel and State Enterprise in Authoritarian Brazil, 1967-85."

44. Lúcia Klein, "A implantação dos grandes projetos governamentais nos setores siderúrgicos e hidroelétricos, 1974-79," (FINEP, June-December 1980). Açominas is a state enterprise created by Geisel in 1975 and slated to become Brazil's largest integrated steel mill. In 1977 ABDIB (Brazilian Association for the Development of Base Industries) grouped together over 110 companies in the capital goods sector. For an excellent case study of ABDIB, see Boschi, *Elites Industriais e Democrácia*, p. 181-223.

45. Cardoso, *Autoritarismo e democratização*, pp. 206-209.

46. The ring metaphor quickly breaks down when identifying the actual participants. Cardoso designed his original formulation to capture the idea of horizontal links which crisscross middle levels of private and public hierarchies. However, ring participants occupy various levels of the same hierarchy, and any one policy may involve myriad contacts between two or more public and private hierarchies. For clarity, the bureaucratic ring is an appropriate shorthand for a dense mesh, a bureaucratic web, extending vertically and horizontally through various agencies of the state, private firms and including other private actors (*e.g.*, business associations and regional elites).

47. As Cardoso writes, "Through these rings classes ... do not organize as a social form, though specific economic and political interests can be present in the decision-making system. The state guarantees itself...the capacity, by removing a key functionary of a given ring...to provoke a radical disarticulation of the pressures that were becoming institutionalized. This assures the limited cooptation (and not representation) of civil society, and its extreme weakness as an autonomous political force." F.H. Cardoso, *Autoritarismo e democratização*, p. 209.

48. One of the last major state councils that the Figueiredo government legislated and Sarney implemented was CONIN (National Informatics Council). Eight of its 23

members are from the private sector, many of them heads of business associations in the sector. But, CONIN has yet to exercise any real power (*Veja* 16 July 1986).

49. Philippe C. Schmitter, "Still the Century of Corporatism?" *Review of Politics* 36, no. 1 (January 1974) pps. 85-121.

50. S. N. Eisenstadt, "Bureaucracy and Political Development," in Joseph LaPalombara, ed., *Bureaucracy and Political Development*, (Princeton, 1963) p. 112.

51. It is for these reasons that defining the state as the executive bureaucracy, and excluding other components of government such as Congress, is justified.

52. See Nunes and Geddes, Chapter 4 in this volume and Leff, *Economic Policy-Making and Development in Brazil.*

53. Leff (*Economic Policy-Making and Development in Brazil*, p. 113-18) notes that before 1964 capitalists were not well organized for parliamentary politics. Interest groups and lobbies lacked legitimacy, and clientelist electoral machines preempted a strong role for economic lobbies. Philippe Schmitter confirms the weakness of economic interest groups, *Interest Conflict and Political Change in Brazil*, (Stanford, 1971). Boschi takes issue with this weak-lobby school because of the emergence in the 1970s of strong groups such as the ABDIB discussed in the previous section, *Elites industriais e democracia.*

54. *Dependent Development*, pp. 48-9.

55. Peter Evans, "Reinventing the Bourgeoisie: State Entrepreneurship and Class Formation in Dependent Capitalist Development," *American Journal of Sociology* 88, Special Supplement (1982), p. 232.

56. See Barrington Moore's classic, *Social Origins of Dictatorship and Democracy: Lord and Peasant in the Making of*

the Modern World, (Boston, 1966). On what has been a lively debate in Brazil see Cesar Guimarães, "Empresariado, tipos de capitalismo e ordem política," *Dados*, 14 (1977) pp. 34-47; and Eli Diniz and Renato Raul Boschi, *Empresariado nacional e estado no Brasil*, (Rio de Janeiro, 1978).

57. Funaro was the owner of Trol which manufactures plastics and toys. Machline is the president of Sharp (17 percent foreign capital) which grew rapidly in consumer electronics before moving into computers as well. See *Veja* (30 April 1986) on the history of Machline and Sharp.

58. In one, photographers recorded eight congressional "pianists" voting twice on a bill by pushing their vote button and the one of an absent neighbor. Another erupted over press charges of fraudulent payments because Congressmen were receiving attendance bonuses for sessions they did not attend. On the public's generally low esteem for politicians see Da Matta's article in this volume, Chapter 9.

59. Even the political elite is split between its internal elite -- governors, party leaders and Congressional whips -- and the rank and file of the *classe política*. Party leaders and governors enjoy enormous powers in appointing ministers and top bureaucrats, and could stand to lose power were policy initiative to pass to Congress. The political elite is also split in immediate terms between those who currently hold top appointed positions and the colleagues they left behind in Congress.

60. Martin Shefter, "Patronage and its Opponents: A Theory and some European Cases," (paper presented at Conference of Western European Area Studies, University of Wisconsin, Madison, 1976). By patronage politics I mean the distribution of public resources for personal (political not private), clique or party benefit normally through clientelistic networks.

61. Shefter's overall analysis includes other factors such as the orientation and preferences of voters and politicians. For this discussion the resource base is most relevant. For a similar though historically broader argument, see Simon Schwartzman, *As bases do autoritarismo brasileiro*, (Rio de Janeiro, 1982).

62. The PMDB, the Brazilian Democratic Movement Party, is the renamed MDB, the single opposition party (by law) through 1979. The PFL split off in mid-1984 from the pro-regime PDS (Democratic Social Party), and joined the PMDB to form the Democratic Alliance which 'elected' Tancredo Neves and Sarney in January 1985.

63. Chalmers notes that heads of politicized states with tenuous institutional bases tend to pull in all significant political factions in "maximum coalitions." "The Politicized State in Latin America," p. 31.

64. Tancredo Neves and Sarney implicitly recognized these patronage temptations by appointing state managers without partisan ties to head the four largest state enterprises: Siderbrás, Eletrobrás, Petrobrás and CVRD.

65. The PFL demanded the Vice Presidency, Mines and Energy, Interior, Justice, the Banco do Brasil and the important economic organs and state enterprises subordinate to the first two ministries (*Jornal do Brasil*, 27 July 1984). In the end, the PFL got the Vice Presidency, Mines and Energy and three other ministries, as well as several of the largest state enterprises and banks.

66. See *Veja*, 17 July 1985.

67. Despite an AD majority, Congress blocked several PMDB/Sarney bills, including a proposal for two-step, runoff municipal elections, and several proposals on elections for the Constituent Assembly.

68. *Veja* (17 July 1985) calculates there are 15,000 Federal positions, *Visão* (7 January 1985) estimates a total of 50,000, and the *Jornal do Brasil* puts the total at about 100,000. By comparison the U.S. president appoints about 1,000 top bureaucrats and the Japanese Prime Minister about 20, Chalmers Johnson, *MITI and the Japanese Miracle: The Growth of Industrial Policy, 1925- 1975*, (Stanford, 1982) p. 52.

69. Bolivar Lamounier and Rachel Meneguello, "Political Parties and Democratic Consolidation: The Brazilian Case," (Working Paper No. 165, Latin American Program, Woodrow Wilson Center, Washington, D.C., May 1985) pp. 4-7.

70. Each active service -- the Army, Navy and Air Force -- has a minister. In 1974 Geisel made the head of the National Information Service (SNI), the head of the joint chiefs of staff (Estado Maior) and the head of the Casa Militar (a liason position between the Presidency and the active military) ministers.

71. My emphasis, *New York Times*, 23 January 1986.

72. This also contributes to the poor records of the past two governments in their attempts to sell state enterprises.

73. See Dietrich Rueschemeyer and Peter B. Evans, "The State and Economic Transformation: Toward an Analysis of the Conditions Underlying Effective Intervention," in Peter Evans, Dietrich Rueschemeyer and Theda Skocpol, *Bringing the State Back In*, (New York, 1985).

74. *MITI and the Japanese Miracle.*

75. Fernando Henrique Cardoso, "Expansion etátique et democratie," *Revue de l'Institut de Sociologie* (1981) pp. 231-238.

76. *As Bases do Autoritarismo Brasileiro*, p. 144.

77. *A Bias for Hope: Essays on Development and Latin America*, (New Haven, 1971) pp. 1-38.

78. *The Centralist Tradition of Latin America*, (Princeton, 1980).

79. B. Schneider, "Politics within the State: Mining, Steel and State Enterprise in Authoritarian Brazil, 1967-85."

8

Brazil's Role in New World Regions

John D. Wirth

The purpose of this paper is to specify a phenomenon that is rapidly transforming the relationships among large states in the Western Hemisphere, and is now mature enough to have a contemporary history but whose outlines and implications are still unclear.[1] I refer to the clustering of nations into two geographically contiguous regional systems in part through policy design, in part through the process of what has been called "silent integration," in effect when contacts, transactions and exchanges of all sorts take on a life and momentum of their own, creating a new context of interdependency. It is within this context that major trade negotiations between the United States and Canada, on the one hand, and Brazil and Argentina, on the other, are currently underway.

North America is one regional system, comprising Canada, Mexico and the United States as the leading partner. No less geographically specific, the Plata Basin is the other large regional system, including Uruguay, Bolivia and Paraguay with Brazil the leading nation in partnership with Argentina. (The deepening of ties to other national units on the continent may create a Southern system sometime in the future, centering on the Brazilian-Argentine dyad, but this is still a Bolivarian dream.) Neither regional system is compart-mentalized: the logic is for a greater flow of factors, to use a term from economics, for a greater density of relations, to use the language of diplomacy, especially among the larger nations such as Mexico, Venezuela, Argentina and Brazil. There is also movement toward the formation of subsystems, such as the Caribbean Basin in which both Venezuela and Mexico are slated to play a major role with the United States, and, perhaps, toward an Andean subsystem as well.

Neither regional system is a formal entity, with a political, juridical, and institutional identity in the sense of a super-national state -- something nobody wants. Lower levels of formal integration, such as economic unions or, more likely, a customs union are still far off in the North except in the campaign rhetoric of North American politicians. As for the Plata system, the stated long range outcome of July 1986 trade agreements between Argentina and Brazil is a common common market, but simply intensifying what is still a low level of exchange would be a major achievement. Whatever, integration among these old and well-established nations would not lead inevitably to political union. On the contrary, high levels of economic integration will probably foster demands for greater national self-awareness, Canada in recent years being a good example.

Informal ties that bind have received much more attention in the literature, especially the imperial role which the United States, a superpower, was said to play until the first oil shock in 1973 closed the post-war era. The obverse image, that of a Panamerican commonwealth centering on the United States has also been discussed. Neither concept is adequate for the interdependencies of our times. Brazil and the United States, the leading partners, are more powerful relative to the other states. But because they are loath to appear hegemonic they must make concessions to weaker units, all of which are eager to preserve both sovereignty and national identity. Since 1973, the historical trend has been away from U.S. hegemony to a newer set of interactions and special relationships. These will deepen if, as seems probable, the flagging world trading system becomes more compartmentalized into regional markets due to rising protectionism and the unresolved debt crisis.

The nation state is being pushed very hard to accommodate this new interdependence. And not all nations are happy with the results, which are already taking the strong and weak alike along unexpected paths. The formal impulse toward integration is political and strategic, but it is also economic, sector by sector. Thus the growing reality of economic interdependence is building incrementally, and in fact much of it is not consciously designed. If the cumulative effect of this integration is silent, today everyone is (or should be) listening.[2]

Conceptually, the first vague outlines of a Plata regional system were raised after World War II by Argentina under Juan Peron, whose plan for an ABC bloc was well received by Getulio Vargas but not the Brazilian military, or his domestic opposition, or the United States. In fact, the two nations did not resolve their decades-long military rivalry and mutual hostility -- a state of pre-conflict verging at times on cold war -- until the late 1970s with the landmark hydroelectric dam treaties (see below). Economic cooperation was conceptualized after the war by the Economic Commission for Latin America (ECLA). It took shape in the early 1960s as an Argentine-Brazilian project to create a free trade zone, then a common market along EEC lines for South America. (There was the sense that this could lead eventually to political union.) In time this global approach which inspired the original Latin American Free Trade Association (LAFTA) project was scaled back, but the Plata regional system had become something more than a geographical trading zone with cultural affinities. By the late 1970s, in short, interdependency in this region was recognized by both nations. Faced with a persistent debt crisis after 1982, both nations discussed expanding bilateral trade on special terms, and in July 1986, as mentioned, these once hostile neighbors signed a comprehensive trade pact.

The North American system was born out of military and economic necessity on the eve of World War II, but since the late 19th century there was a long history of intensifying economic relations. Until very recently, however, it could not be called a system embracing all three North American nations. For Mexico and Canada both, the dynamic was one of intensifying bilateral relations centering on the United States rather than transactions with each other. But this is changing as all three nations target a larger share of their foreign trade on the continent-sized North American market, while recognizing that problems such as acid rain have a truly continental scope.

Conventional wisdom maintains that regional solutions are outgrown after a certain point, when a nation such as Brazil enters the international market and differentiates the sources of trade and finance. This holds for the expansionary post-war era, especially for the 1960s and most of the 1970s, when Brazil's reliance on the U.S. market waned as trade with Europe and Third World nations (including Latin America) grew. It may no longer describe how large industrial nations or, better yet, groups of nations, behave in a time of slower growth in the 1980s. Furthermore, in an increasingly unforgiving world economy, at once highly competitive and more protectionist, regional solutions may well become more attractive.

When calamity strikes, as in the current debt crisis, nations such as Canada and Mexico do not differentiate; they move closer to their major partner. Slower growth in world trade should propel Argentiana and Brazil together, even though as discussed below in their initial response to the debt crisis each nation has cut back trading with the other, and for that matter Mexican imports from the United States are down substantially. However, it is likely that among nations in the two regional systems I have specified the movement toward integration goes on regardless. Clark Reynolds and Carlos Tello say as much for Mexico and the United States: both are, "regardless of their respective preferences, certain to become increasingly interdependent economically and socially over the coming decades."[3]

Exchange among unequal units will not lead inevitably to integration. In fact, unless the partners perceive that each is benefitting, the result will more likely be conflict, and *disintegration* of important parts of the relationship.[4] For integration to proceed, there must be understanding of (if not full agreement on) the political and economic terms of what are, fundamentally, geopolitical relationships among contiguous states. Quite likely, therefore, the nations under review will continue to seek out, elaborate and expand upon a wide range of special relationships with one another -- because agreement decreases risk in a highly competitive and uncertain world economy, and out of necessity because as neighbors they must live together. Recent examples of special relationships at work are U.S. purchases of Mexican oil for the Strategic Reserve to facilitate Mexican cooperation on the debt crisis, and Brazil's willingness to ease some restrictions on U.S. commercial bank operations in Brazil in exchange for help on the debt. Canada is pushing hard for a comprehensive free trade agreement with the United States, and in return has brought computer pirates to court while easing restrictions on cross-border data flows -- items high on the U.S. trade policy agenda.

Trade in the Western Hemisphere has actually decreased because of the debt crisis, and to meet IMF-mandated adjustments and make interest payments on their foreign debt the Latin American nations as of current writing are exporting more and importing much less. If indulged in for long, this would produce a "fallacy of composition" when everyone sells but nobody buys, something that cannot last, and is particularly harmful to the United States with its persistent trade deficit. When liquidity returns, however, trade may pick up; but in the interim, barter agreements as for example between Brazil, Mexico and Venezuela are intensifying the search for complementarities between nations that to date have had weak trade relations.

Exchange creates interdependence; interdependence, however, may promote further integration -- or forms of conflict causing disintegration. The history of the Argentine-Brazilian case shows that states can easily disrupt integration either deliberately or indirectly by abrupt policy shifts, furthered by domestic political instability and/or periodic crises in the balance of payments. The two rivals were politically out of phase with each other for much of the post-war period. More recently, Argentina returned to civilian rule almost two years before Brazil did on March 15, 1985. This prevented a common stand in negotiations with the banks, something that the Alfonsin government proposed but the Brazilians turned down. In 1986, however, Brazil's Cruzado Plan followed Argentina's Austral currency and price control program and the two democratic nations were again politically in phase. Constraining this new relationship is the fact that Argentina, unlike Brazil, has not yet returned to growth. This also makes it dependent on the IMF, again unlike Brazil which is cushioned by a large trade surplus with virtually all its trading partners.

Brazil and Argentina may have crossed a threshold beyond the conjunctural and ephemeral that marked their brief periods of cooperation until now. In the words of Felix Peña, the Argentine political scientist, "se ha operado ya un aumento y una diversificación [demasiado] significativo de las interacciones económicas reciprocas como para considerar que en adelante lo que ocurra en un pais pueda ser indiferente al otro. A ello debe sumarse el mayor dinamismo e interdependéncia que se observa en el sistema regional latinoamericano en el cual están insertos ambos paises."[5] Given this interdependence among contiguous nations in the Plata Basin, writes Celso Lafer, Brazil and Argentina should take the long view of their interests based on points of convergence, rather than divergence as in the past.[6] The timing is ripe to move beyond eposodic cooperation, in short, to manage the relationship of two interdependent states.

Does integration provide a hierarchy of benefits mostly favoring the leaders, or is it is mutually beneficial and benign? Smaller states naturally sense dependency, while Brazil and the United States, the continental leaders, have a different interpretation of the integration process. Measures to assure a more equal distribution of the benefits can be devised, as well as equal treatment. The strong must continually reassure the weak that they, too, can reap benefits and concessions. This is the logic of the special relationships that are cropping up today.

It may well be that sustained integration can only take place between units of relatively equal size and power. But in the world of contiguous neighbors necessity is the mother of invention. Geopolitics, as well as silent integration, are driving it. One thing is certain: the post-war ECLA dream of "national, autonomous development" is over -- finished, as much for Latin America as for Canada and the United States. Not since the 1930s has the hemisphere faced such times of sweeping, and disruptive change. In this context, everyone is a "developing" nation. Among the alternative futures imaginable, interdependence seems the most attractive to prepare and plan for, especially if movement in this direction is already well under way.

Interdependence is no code word to mask unequal power; properly interpreted, it can be used to address inequalities among states while at the same time reducing risk and uncertainty for everyone, and while also allowing an aspiring economic power like to Brazil to find room at the top. To give an example: it would be naive to assume that Mexico's decision to follow OPEC's pricing structure but not to join it in the mid 1970s was made in isolation. On the other hand, the U.S. Federal Reserve Board's decision to increase the money supply in August 1982 had much more to do with enabling Mexico to avoid default than it did with stimulating Wall Street, a most visible domestic byproduct.

Formal procedures to manage interdependence would mark a step beyond ad hoc measures (such as special relationships) and silent integration. If rules can be agreed upon, this would be desirable. The quickening pace of sectoral integration in North America, at least, makes possible the next steps, while Brazil and Argentina may well begin by integrating their capital goods industries. Speculation on the nature of these new institutions is not my purpose, which is to offer a sort of past-is-prologue rather than a vision of how interdependence might work. Suffice it to say here that the outlines are probably apparent to the next Jean Manet.

Four main premises underlie this presentation on New World regional systems:

1. These systems have a contemporary history, which can be perceived in the light of geopolitical realities, and after realizing that sweeping, disruptive changes have overtaken the post-war dream of autonomous, independent development.

2. Each system will take on more weight if (as now appears likely) the great cycle of post-war growth in the world trading system is over. If we are on the threshold of slower economic growth, with an increasingly anarchic and uncertain world economic system, this would focus attention on regional systems which are both less risky and more predictable.

3. Even without slower growth, the Northern and Plata Basin regional systems may be a more manageable, even the appropriate locus for working out great changes in technology, in the changing industrial base, and the world redivision of labor. North America is undergoing such sweeping changes that it should now be redefined as a developing area, albeit with much greater wealth, power and technological capacity than the relatively impoverished Plata system.

4. The two systems interconnect for economic and geopolitical reasons, including security considerations (although South America is marginal to the East-West conflict). Old relationships are ripe for rethinking and upgrading after atrophy and decline in the 1970s, which was the heyday of the independent foreign policies adopted by Brazil, Mexico and Canada.

Today the great debt crisis of the 1980s has relinked North and South. Is the Plata Basin once again a subsystem of of the North dominated by the United States? A benign reading of the logic of interdependence would say no, but we will know more when we see the terms and conditions for resolving the debt crisis. Rapid movement and uncertainty has created opportunities as well as constraints on everyone: interdependence works both ways.

LINKS BETWEEN NORTH AND SOUTH

Let us begin with the Brazil-U.S. relationship, not only because it is an ongoing preoccupation of Brazilians -- and, I hasten to add, of the Reagan Administration which does not regard with equanimity the straying of an old and once intimate ally from the security fold -- but also because the relationship in its economic aspects has been thrust into dramatic, unexpected, and painful prominence by the current debt crisis. The developmental nationalism of Brazil in such areas as computers and transborder data flows has also been colliding with the free trade nationalism of the United States to produce an escalating series of trade disputes. Bearing in mind that this is a contemporary history of two regional systems, I will briefly review how the two continental powers connect, after a word of definition.

Continentalism to the two leading powers denotes a range of options. Hemispheric interests are important to them but they also enjoy a complex web of global commitments extending well beyond the region. (Cuba with its Third World projection through the Soviet connection has a global foreign policy but it is obviously not a continental nation). To Canadians, Mexicans and Argentines, however, the larger partner *is their major relationship*, and continentalism denotes a redefining of their space by that partner. In the words of John W. Holmes, the well-known Canadian diplomat and writer, "Perhaps the greatest difference between American and Canadian policies is that the Unites States, unlike Canada, does not have an American problem."[7]

Brazilian-American relations are again at the crossroads. The old alliance, with Brazil playing the role of junior partner in shared security concerns toward the Western Hemisphere, and with the United States supplying the lion's share of foreign capital, markets and technology, declined in the 1970s although the Reagan Administration made some attempts to revive it. Security concerns writ large, encompassing the political-economic relationship as well, *were* the main thrust of American policy in towards Brazil from war-time alliance in 1942, through the post-war settlement and into the late 1960's. America's post-war hegemony enabled it to support, to accomodate and to condone Brazil's rise as an industrial power under the umbrella of U.S. power. In return, Brazil was expected to support the Western bloc of nations in the East-West struggle.

To Brazil, developing the country took priority to supporting U.S. security goals during the Cold War. Since the late 1950s, therefore, the nation sought to develop an essentially economic foreign policy in order to support rapid economic growth. As an economic partner, the United States filled a progressively less important role in the working out of this policy so that by the late 1970s it was but one of several relationships in a global strategy to diversify trade, investment and finance. Brazil's trade dependence on the United States declined rapidly as a percentage of total trade, starting in 1969 (see Table 8.3).

That the national interests of the two nations were diverging seemed evident, propelled by differing views of the world system and by the evident decline of America's will, prestige and power, above all of its economic power after the first oil shock. To knowledgeable foreign policy analysts, the old special relationship was dead; the United States by 1980 could not offer enough through even a reintensified bilateral relationship to offset the manifest advantages that Brazil was achieving through an independent foreign policy.[8] Such was the logic of differentiation. Brazil was said to have outgrown the American connection, stretching nearly 70 years from the Barão do Rio Branco era -- when the United States, with its large coffee market, was also used politically to counterbalance Argentina -- to the vastly different world of detente between the superpowers. This attractive vision, at once consonant with Brazilian aspirations, national self-confidence, and rising economic power was soon overtaken by events.

Following the second oil shock in 1979 and world recession came the extraordinary debt crisis (post August, 1982), based as it was on a payments crisis aggravated by falling export prices and high dollar interest rates. The debt crisis revealed the extent of Brazil's vulnerability to externally imposed prices while showing that the links to Washington still mattered very much. Both nations were driven, reluctantly, into an association that was unforeseen. Today, overextended American banks are hostage to Brazil just as Brazil finds itself again heavily dependent on exports to the United States (more than 25 percent in 1985). In the world financial system, Washington has in fact become the guarantor of Latin America. This role will grow if the U.S. government assumes political responsibility for restructuring the debt.

Moreover, the decline of Latin American markets in the early 1980s has hurt the United States badly through loss of export sales and jobs. But it was greatly increased sales to the United States in 1984 that enabled Brazil to grow out of its worst recession in fifty years (see Chapter 2 in this volume). Thus there has been a relinking, but on terms unexpected by either nation, and quite different from the old Cold War alliance.

Whether the debt crisis marks the beginning of a new era as the Great Depression did, cannot yet be known. The United States remains profoundly divided over whether the national interest is defined in the context of the by now traditional East-West struggle, or by the newer North-South relationship. To all but the most convinced cold warriors, America lives in the twilight of the postwar era, in which bipolarity, the former governing principle, has lessened but not disappeared. But the newer issue of global poverty, which drives inequalities and overpopulation, is not yet securely on the agenda of official Washington.

Beginning in the late 1950s, however, and certainly since the late 1960s, Brazil has sought successfully to identify its national interest almost exclusively with economic development within the North-South context, while retaining but also redefining its close links to the industrial nations.

From Brazil's perspective, we have entered a new era beyond the postwar settlement. From this perspective, also, the Soviet military buildup in recent years, and the American response begun by Carter and augmented by Reagan, is vectoring history backward. But this view, too, is under pressure from events, witness the rapid projection of Soviet military power into the Pacific Basin, the most dynamic area of the world trading system, and the Central American crisis with its dimension of East-West conflict. Moreover, the United States no longer has the resources to project itself on East-West and North-South axes simultaneously. A greater selectivity in the application of still formidable resources, coupled with measures to protect American power such as selective protectionism and differential trading access would seem to be a rational response for a newly aroused, more assertive and nationalist United States. This has serious implications for Brazil with its U.S. markets for a wide range of industrial and agricultural exports.

Were the 1970s, then, the beginning of an era of greater independence for Brazil? Or were they an interlude, a fleeting conjuncture that for a few years provided more space for Brazil? Just as historians have tended to exaggerate President Vargas' freedom to maneuver between Hitler's Germany and Roosevelt's United States in the years of movement before World War II, so analysts of the more recent past may well have overplayed the extent to which Brazil could manipulate the world system for national purposes. The long-term consequences of the debt crisis are unclear, but the short-term result is that Brazil, and the other Latin Americans nations, are again reliant on Washington and New York. As for renegotiating the terms and conditions of this debt, it is clear that the 1982 crisis specified a very large area of mutual interest, something scholars writing on the independent foreign policy initiatives of the 1970s did not foresee.

In the early 1980s, the United States tried without much success to link debt negotiations to other strictly bilateral issues on the American agenda such as obtaining Brazilian support for American security objectives in Central America and access to protected sectors of the Brazilian market, especially computers and data processing. In reacting to an assertive Brazil, which has centered its own foreign policy on economic issues, the United States has the power to play short-term linkage politics but unless there are concessions to Brazil this will be counterproductive.[9]

Brazil, in turn, has attempted linkage politics of its own. If the United States doesn't buy a satisfactory amount of Brazilian steel, the Minister of Commerce and Industry warned recently, Brazil's U.S. creditors "won't get paid."[10] While decrying protectionism, Brazil nonetheless accepted lower market shares for this key export. For the first time, Brazilian courts are accepting foreign suits against patent infringement, another U.S. demand in its effort to safeguard so-called intellectual property against software counterfeiting, especially. Whether Brazil will make further concessions in the areas of services, patents, trademarks and counterfeiting to forestall U.S. protectionism remains to be seen.

Consider, by comparison, how the negotiating style differs in the much more interdependent North American region. Mexico's vulnerability on the debt issue and the shift to a buyers market in petroleum have not (so far) been used as leverage on them to change their own, quite different views on Central America.[11] With rare exceptions, U.S.-Canada issues have been free of linkage politics, a point stressed time and time again in the literature.[12] Judging from the North American example, the web of special relationships and arrangements has made them obsolete although Canadians are acutely aware of their vulnerability to policy shifts in Washington.

It is very much in the interest of Brazil and the United States to reestablish a close relationship based this time on economics, for their growing vulnerability to global events puts both nations at risk. Growing trade disputes -- with Americans railing at export subsidies and market reserves, and Brazilians decrying protectionism -- are counterproductive. Aggressive trading practices are bound to create conflict as Brazil seeks to increase market share and the United States to protect its trade, including the world market shares of multinationals.[13] How to manage Brazil's growing industrial power should be given sustained attention by both nations. Geopolitical factors enter in, as well. That Brazil can now lay claim to being the world's third largest democracy is very important, whatever the risk to U.S. economic interests from short-term trade disputes, because this underscores and may even by force of example guarantee the trend to democratic regimes throughout South America. This could be the political rationale for any large program of debt relief, coupled with negotiated access to U.S. markets as well as capital and high technology transfers to the South along with increased U.S. sales to that region.

There are even more important reasons for putting economic relations into a new framework. This would be predicated on the recognition that the United States is undergoing a very rapid and profound transformation away from basic industries. The reindustrialization of America must include a Brazilian component. Brazilian industry under competitive conditions to be negotiated should have a substantial piece of this substitute production stemming from the world redivision of labor. A process already well underway since the 1970s to supply the American market through vertical integration should be accelerated. Steel has become the classic test case. Whether U.S. political factors will outweigh market forces which in steel favor Brazil, Argentina and Mexico among others, remains to be seen. (Voluntary quotas were imposed during the 1984 presidential campaign.) By contrast, Brazilian access to the rapidly growing U.S. market for commuter aircraft has been virtually free of the protectionism effecting steel, and other manufactured exports.

The terms of access for American high technology products to the large Brazilian market for computers and information services should be specified as well, including protection by Brazilian courts against rampant pirating. At issue are the closed policies in communications and high technology which, in part for military reasons, in part to nurture infant industries the Brazilians have imposed.

What has been called the "solução caipira" (home-grown variety) has found several nitches in the dynamic world of high technology, but not without costs. If politics drive economics (as they apparently do in the U.S. steel industry), then market reserve policies that protect Brazil's burgeoning informatics industry are just as entrenched.

Countervailing these national policies to protect specific industries are international market forces, which force costs down, changing technologies, and the redivision of labor. Older, established markets are more important to Brazil with the decline of Third World purchasing power, including Africa and Latin America. Yet Mexico and Argentina can also supply the American market for basic industrial goods, a market which in the immediate future at least, and certainly for the long term if we are entering a phase of slower growth, will be more important to Brazil. The rise of Pacific Basin nations as major, and increasingly important trading partners with the United States is for Brazil another complicating factor. The entire basis for economic complementarity is ripe for review and negotiation. Gone are the the days when Brazil shipped mostly coffee and the United States sent manufactures and capital goods that others, first Western Europe and Japan and then Brazil itself, could supply. The new relationship is a major test case of the world redivision of labor, which also does not have to imply a high technology society for the one, and a low tech future for the other as Brazilian nationalists fear. Risk and conflict both can be lessened if not resolved through sectoral negotiations of the sort set up after President Reagan's 1982 visit. However, steps to work out new forms of the special relationship have scarcely begun.

To be sure, for both countries in the expansionist 1970s developing nations were the fastest growing markets. Brazil's strategy to diversify its markets was spectacularly successful: the share of Brazilian exports going to the United States and Western Europe fell from 69 percent of total value in 1972 to 43 percent in 1981. Latin America as a whole grew not through a regional approach, but by reaching global markets of which the intra-regional flows were only a relatively small part of a larger whole, especially when finance and technology transfer are considered.[14]

But will this diversification continue in the 1980s? The share of trade in regional market systems may become relatively more important, especially if ways are found to restore South American purchasing power, including barter. The Brazil-Mexico agreement in April, 1983 to exchange up to $1bn of goods each way on barter is a good example. Even more important is what will happen to the Brazil-Argentina dyad, the basis of the La Plata stystem and still the point of departure for a South American system. This raises anew the question of hegemony.

Placing Brazil first among the Latin nations is an old, if inconsistently applied, policy of the United States, a policy fought by Argentina when it was the major southern power. What is new is that Brazilian economic primacy on the continent is now a fact. Americans find it easy to proclaim this for the other continental power, while usually downplaying when they do not ignore entirely their own role with respect to Canada and Mexico. Assigning to Brazil the role of "leading nation" (pais chave) in the region probably did contribute to Brazilian isolation from the rest of South America a generation ago, especially with respect to Argentina.[15] But times have changed and Brazil has become much more Latin American in policy and outlook (see below).

Following this brief look at Brazil-U.S. relations, I want to both evaluate and give conceptual life to the two regional systems specified at the outset of this paper. A poor country, Brazil shares with Mexico structural features of the Third World that Argentina, for example, does not. A rich country, Canada has certain affinities with the United States rather than Mexico; on the world scene, it shares with Brazil the status of a middle range power. Both Mexico and Brazil share a longer colonial heritage than the temperate climate nations, an important distinction in its own right. In the New World context, this makes them "old" nations, in contrast to the other three nations of recent settlement. Until the 1930s Argentina and Canada both belonged to the British economic system, preserving, thus, important extra-continental links. But internally, it is Brazil and Canada which have had the strongest regional cleavages in this century.

Blurring a number of these differences, however, is location -- the fact of contiguity. Furthermore, by including Mexico in the North American region, and by associating relatively well-off Argentina with the southern regional group it is possible to blunt the structural dissimilarities between the two regions, while not ignoring the asymmetrical power relationships within systems, and among systems. Recall, also, that I defined both as *developing* regions facing change and uncertainty. This also helps to create a new policy context. Specifying the historical identity of these North and South American regional systems is a first step.

THE PLATA BASIN SYSTEM

The first regional system was conceived by ECLA after the war. The impetus for a global, regional approach began as an Argentine-Brazilian project for Latin American development based on foreign investment and a free trading zone (LAFTA) which was set up in 1961. Inspired by the developmentalism of Arturo Frondizi and Juscelino Kubitschek, the project had a continental focus and was predicated initially on cooperation and close, continuous consultations between the two governments. This was formalized between Presidents Quadros and Frondizi in April 1961 at Uruguaiana, the frontier town. Quadros soon resigned, and Brazil entered a period of political and economic instability. Frondizi was deposed in 1962, to be replacd by military geopoliticians who defined Argentina in terms of its rivalry with Brazil, which from their perspective was a growing threat. Deeply divided politically, and beset with balance of payments problems, Argentina declined relative to Brazil, which replaced it internationally as "the rising power of South America."[16]

Brazil distanced itself from continental projects and resumed its traditional policy of limited, bilateral relations with Latin American neighbors. By 1969 *grandeza* was the order of the day as Brazil reached outward beyond the continent, using a global foreign economic policy as the best means to assure rapid economic growth. While Argentina continued to see itself as a European nation and stagnated, Brazil forged economic links to Africa and the Middle East, followed an independent foreign policy, and well beyond the first oil shock in 1973 reaped benefits from debt-led growth financed by the private banks.

The next conceptual breakthrough came when Brazil took the initiative to end the tense confrontation over hydroelectric dam systems in the Plata Basin, and in 1979 the multilateral Itaipu Treaty was signed between Brazil, Argentina and Paraguay, followed by the 1980 exchange of visits between Presidents Figueiredo and Videla.[17] These actions cleared the way for a series of bilateral agreements between Buenos Aires and Brasilia, with frequent consultations between the two governments. What Itamaraty refers to as a "deepening" of relationships began. This was solid enough to survive the Falklands crisis which nonetheless hurt trade with Argentina while revealing, also, how fragile was the web of relationships that bound South America.

Coincident with the dam treaties Brazil abandoned its traditional distance from multilateral initiatives in the hemisphere. By 1980, it was becoming an enthusiastic sponsor of the Cuenca de la Plata development plan, and the Amazon Pact, while joining the Andean Pact and taking the lead in revitalizing the southern market concept (LAFTA having become defunct) with the more realistic and modestly conceived Latin American Association for Integration. As of current writing, the new Sarney government says it will continue to put Latin America first on the list of foreign policy priorities, and in July, 1986 signed a series of trade agreements with Argentina looking toward the eventual establishment of a common market.

Within the emergent South American system, the Plata Basin growth pole running from São Paulo to Buenos Aires has great potential: energy, transportation, and consumer markets with the strongest purchasing power in South America,

Venezuela excepted. Parts of this region are more favorably en-dowed than the U.S.-Mexico border zone, which is integrating rapidly, or the Rocky Mountain energy states/provinces with their sparse populations. In 1980 Brazil and Argentina agreed to integate their power grids, to end dual taxation, and to cooperate in a number of sectors including nuclear power, aircraft, informatics and computers. Recent agreements with Argentina to supply natural gas are a hopeful sign, coming on the heels of an earlier agreement with Bolivia. The July, 1986 agreements to intensify trade in agricultural and industrial goods were presented as a reaction to the industrial nations keeping shackles on the development of their two economies by protectionism and inflexibility on debt negotiations.

Yet these moves toward integration are still tentative and fragile. Argentina and Brazil have only begun to face the problems of interdependency, let alone to manage them. Railroad gauges are still incompatible, in contrast to North America where the railroads have been integrated since the 1870s. Investments in each other's economies by Argentine and Brazilian nationals do not go much beyond $20 million each way. Trade between the two nations is still far below potential. There is a tradition of exchange based on the natural complimentarity of temperate climate goods such as wheat, fruit and animal products for tropical commodities such as bananas and nuts, a condition which lasted into the 1950s. Twenty years later exchange was occurring on a very different basis. Brazil now exported a wide variety of manufactured goods to Argentina in exchange, primarily, for agricultural products.[18] Smaller and less efficient Argentine industry was hard-pressed to compete and serious questions were raised about the advantages to Argentina of trade on this basis. For this reason the 1986 agreement specifies that trade will be balanced, a concession to Argentina by Brazil, which has a big trade advantage with its up to date, export oriented industries. For this reason it may not go much beyond a machinery for grain barter deal.

Plans to move beyond commercial exchange to sectoral integration among certain private and state companies --

chemicals, iron ore and nuclear technology are often mentioned -- have not yet gone forward. "Mucho se ha hablado y, en verdad, poco se ha hecho, para que la complementación económica, financiera y productiva argentinas y brasileñas sean una realidad," an Argentine industrialist commented in 1981. "Pelo menos no que se refere ao lado brasileiro, a visão que se tem das condições concretas da indústria argentina e do mercado do pais para produtos industriais e extrémamente precária e impressionista. Acredito que o mesmo ocorre do lado argentino," the president of the São Paulo Federation of Industries (FIESP) said at the same seminar in Buenos Aires.[19] Sectoral integration to date has been spearheaded by the multiationals, who were the first to take advantage of LAFTA-inspired trade liberalization measures twenty years ago.

Trade in capital goods and engineering services between Brazil and Argentina was still modest by the early 1980s, but strongly in Brazil's favor -- $120.8 million to $13.4 million in 1983, whereas it had been balanced at just over $40 million in 1975. Nearly one quarter of Brazil's capital goods exports to Latin America were sent to Argentina. *The Economist* reports that "Brazilian exports to Argentina were worth $831m in 1984 (the latest year for which figures are available) and included $644m in manufactured goods, the greater part of it in capital goods. Argentina's shipments to Brazil, worth $478m, included only $85m of industrial goods." (Mexico, which had been a growing export market for Brazilian capital goods in the 1970s, had reoriented its trade toward the United States and the debt crisis severely constricted other Latin American markets). In 1984, a Latin American multinational firm LATINEQUIP was founded by banks in Argentina, Brazil and Mexico to foster this regional trade in capital goods and engineering services, and, with recovery, to capture a larger share of the market for Latin American firms. And if the new trade agreements go forward, greatly intensified trade in industrial machinery and equipment was was expected to spearhead a doubling of bilateral trade, which in 1985 totaled slightly more than $1 billion.[20]

Understandably, Argentina has been reluctant to accept the role of unequal partner in this new growth area, but this is what the new trade patterns could imply unless both nations work to avoid it. Brazil's rise to economic primacy in South America has not been accompanied by Argentina which, though self-sufficient in petroleum and better endowed in argicultural resources, is a classic conflict society whose stop-go economic policies have produced stagnation. Interestingly, Brazil's expanding trade with Uruguay, Bolivia and Paraguay in the 1970's did not displace Argentine exports to these traditional buffer states.[21] But the expanding land frontier of Portuguese-speakers into Paraguay and Uruguay confirms traditional geopolitical fears among the Argentines of Brazilian expansionism -- that most traditional form of hegemony.[22]

One result of the Malvinas disaster was to make the Brazilian military less willing to integrate the electronics industries, while the Argentine military purchased but a small amount of the war materials offered to them during the war and since then have been unwilling to rearm with Brazilian weapons. Nor with rare exceptions has Argentina made its wheat available on competitive terms with the United States and Canada. (One of the new trade agreements calls for much larger purchases of Argentine wheat.) Whether through association with Brazil the nation can find the coherence it has lacked for almost 50 years since being cut adrift from the British economic system in the 1930s is the key question. The military have been, and remain, central players. Peron's main objective in proposing an ABC pact after the war seems to have been strategic and political, to defend the South Atlantic and gain leverage on the United States[23] There were certain affinities between the labor populism pioneered by Vargas and then elaborated by Peron that might have given a right-wing social base to it, including Ibañes' Chile which was to have provided the fleet. Later, in the mid-1970s the two military regimes talked about setting up a South Atlantic alliance with South Africa. Integration along these lines was unattractive to Brazil; the overall political and economic costs far outweighed the benefits of defense collaboration with an unstable military regime, isolated from its own people and at war with civil society. The Plata Basin was, however, given sustained policy attention by the two governments in the late 1970s and attractive opportunities for strategic cooperation may again arise if the Alfonsin administration continues to remove from the strategic agenda or downgrades traditional territorial disputes over the Falklands with Britain and the Beagle Channel with Chile.

Following the historic Quadros-Frondizi meeting in 1961, integration along the Argentine-Brazil axis was in part restrained by Argentina's difficulty in developing a coherent economic foreign policy; in part by nationalist protective measures to prevent imports of Brazilian railroad equipment, trucks and busses and the coordination of sectors such as the automobile industry; and in part by the cumulative effects of political and economic instability. For its part, Brazil until recently has not wholeheartedly pursued the Argentine, and by extension, the South American connection, out of preoccupation with internal growth and success in reaching less problematical export markets. The domestic economy still accounted for 90 percent of GNP in 1980, making Brazil far less trade dependent than Canada, for example.

Thus in comparative perspective, Argentina as a contiguous trading partner is still far from reaching the status of a Canada, or even of a Mexico. Argentina's relative position in Brazil's total trade fell in the 1970's (although it remained the first market in South America for Brazilian exports: see Table 8.2). Mexico's role in terms of the percentage of total U.S. exports rose to the high levels (proportionately) held by Argentina with Brazil in the post-1964 period. For the United States and Canada the level of trade integration by the 1960s approached that of the European Common Market.[24] And by 1986 fully four fifths of Canada's total exports were sent to the United States.

Furthermore, from the perspective of Brazilian trade within the LAFTA/LAAI region, Argentina's share had fallen from 60 percent of total Brazilian merchandise exports to the region in 1966 to just over 30 percent in 1975. In part this was because Brazil purchased more from other Latin American nations. But a glance at Table 8.2 also shows the value of this trade declined rapidly at the height of Argentina's internal troubles, starting in the early 1970s. For most of the 1970s Brazil actually imported more than it exported to Argentina (see Table 8. 1). The free market policies of Finance Minister Martinez de Hoz halted the relative decline of Brazilian exports in 1979-80, years when the large surge of manufactured goods in the export list led Argentine nationalists to fear for the demise of their industrial base, that their country was slipping into a sort of neo-colonial status with Brazil. Led by manufactured exports, Brazil has continued to enjoy a trade surplus with Argentina since then.

Brazil achieved considerable success in the Latin American market which by 1966 was already a significant part of the nation's foreign trade. As mentioned, the lion's share was at first with Argentina, but other Latin nations have become increasingly important, and the most notable recent addition was Mexico. By the mid-70s, one half of Brazil's exports of light manufactured products went to the LAFTA countries. With the debt crisis, however, these export markets contracted and the Mexican trade declined.

Such were the results of the first export drive to Latin America, which was implemented in the early 1960s by the Goulart government in a general climate of alarm that, in Brazil and Argentina especially, economic growth based on import substitution industrialization was slowing. The outlines of this first export drive are known in general, but the period itself is ripe for historical investigation.

Economically, this export drive was seen as the solution to the import substitution crisis, and indeed the decision to seek external markets was charted in 1961, the same year the Treaty of Montevideo creating LAFTA was signed. What came to be seen as the hallmark of the military government in its first ten years --the transition from growth by import substitution to export-led growth based on the new capacity created by import substitution -- was conceptualized before 1964, but with a different distributional policy. In addition to finding new markets, Goulart's advisors wanted to meet social needs through wealth created by export-led growth; later, under the military, building infrastructure while avoiding what the authoritarian regime called "premature restribution" was the order of the day.

Finance Minister Santiago Dantas articulated the new trade policy in 1961. Without larger markets, he said, Brazil faced a payments crisis; it was unable to purchase the inputs to sustain rapid economic growth of 7.5 percent, the rate needed to provide for a rapidly urbanizing and expanding population. Latin America was targeted as the top priority, with the United States in second place as the less dynamic market, and with the EEC downgraded as a trading partner because it was expected (wrongly, it turned out) to freeze out Brazilian products due to preferences toward ex-colonial possessions.[25]

Argentina also wanted LAFTA to expand rapidly, as its ambassador told FIESP in 1962. Both nations faced similar difficulties in having to find ways to accelerate their economic development, he said. "Temos a consciência de que nossos mercados classicos não solucionam o problema da expan são e diversificação de nosso comércio externa. Pensamos no mercado regional latinoamericano a título de sócios comerciais naturais." As for the recent accords between the two governments, "dada a interdependência entre as economias nacionais," he said optimistically, "Uruguaiana e a frente comúm indispensavel para tornar efetivo, no mundo internacional, o direito de desenvolver as duas economias, até as suas últimos consequências."[26]

Although the dynamics of this first export drive remain to be investigated, the early indications are that multinational corporations responded quicker to the export signal than the Brazilian private sector, which was slow to venture beyond the large, protected domestic market. FIESP complained that the Goulart government failed to provide export incentives and was not taking LAFTA seriously.[27] Yet there were tariff and non-tariff advantages for Brazilian exporters through the LAFTA system which, furthermore, accepted government export subsidies for manufacturers, and these were provided increasingly after 1964. For those firms that did export, "There seems to be a natural preference expressed by

Brazilian business to export to other Latin American countries. Many producers think that their products, if exportable at all, are only exportable to Latin America because of their inability to compete in world markets in either quality or price terms with products from the developed countries. This pessimism, either real or imagined, is compounded by the widespread belief in the Brazilian business community that LAFTA has been successful in reducing barriers to intra-regional trade."[28]

This competitiveness argument lost force as the decade wore on and Brazilian exports including manufactures penetrated developed country markets, *especially* the EEC. By the late 1970s, however, Brazilian exports of manufactured goods to Latin America were again on the rise until the debt crisis.

LAFTA itself collapsed as a free trade vehicle, the victim in part of the first oil shock which reduced purchasing power for member states. Brazil preferred bilateral exchange to system-wide negotiations while actively seeking markets elsewhere. But Brazil was also less trade oriented than Argentina: the value of exports during the 1970s was approximately 6 percent of GDP in contrast to Argentina's 10 percent. "Brazil exported a larger proportion of its manufactures to industrialized countries with market economies than Argentina, whereas for the latter country the Latin American market was much more important than for Brazil."[29] Certainly Brazil's own imports from the LAFTA area declined drastically in the 1970s as a percentage of total trade (see Table 8.2), and the level of exports going to LAFTA did not increase until the late seventies. But in 1982 this pattern was reversed. Brazil with its stronger regional economy now imported more than it exported to the rest of Latin America.

Politically, the independent foreign policy emerging in the late 1960s was designed to create policy space in the bipolar world still dominated by the superpowers. This enabled Brazil to maintain close ties to the West while successfully cultivating the Third World. In the thinking of Ambassador Araujo Castro and others, the world was not predestined to be divided into two blocs, especially now that the balance of nuclear terror made world war most unlikely, and made coexistence possible.[30] This was a Latin American conception of the future, which also fit Brazilian national requirements for an economic foreign policy to reach new markets while diversifying its sources of finance capital. As detente between the superpowers dawned in the late 1960s the new policy was in place and Brazil, distancing itself from Washington, reaped benefits. (In the 1970s, Mexico and Canada attempted a similar course, combining economic nationalism with independent foreign policies and a downplaying of *their* special relationships with Washington). Having diversified its trade and sources of finance, Brazil created room to maneuver on the world stage but the new foreign policy also left room for the integration process to begin close to home. Centers for the study of Latin America were set up, and students from nearby nations were invited to attend Brazilian universities. Brazilian academics developed a self-consciously Latin American analysis without being defined as regionalists. Television programming was nationalized, and then "continentalized": Brazilian *telenovelas* became an important foreign policy asset in relations with Hispanic America, as well as a commercial success. Until the late 1970's, however, Brazil preferred bilateral relations to hemispheric initiatives of the sort proposed by Mexico (SELA) and Venezuela.[31] Latin American sales of Brazilian goods were financed by the government. The process of integration began, above all, because Brazil for the first time had the political and economic weight to activate it.

Yet the extent to which this foreign economic policy was now more vulnerable than ever to rapid shifts in the international conjuncture was revealed by the first oil shock. The response was to reemphasize import substitution while securing nearby sources of raw materials and, especially hydroelectric power.[32] The second export drive to Latin America became a scramble with the next oil shock in 1979. As Brazil sought to diversify its petroleum suppliers away from the unstable Middle East, this opened up the possibility of major joint ventures with Venezuela and Mexico. In 1979 the three nations planned PETROLATIN, a joint exploration and development company which is delayed indefinitely or cancelled due to the debt crisis. But the cornerstone of what can be called Brazil's new Americanist policy was close cooperation with Argentina, starting with the 1979 dam agreements, followed by the presidential visits. These contacts were intensified after 1983 under Alfonsin: consultations by the new civilian governments on their anti-inflation plans helped pave the way for the recent trade agreements.

The upshot is that there is now something of a history of continentalism under Brazilian leadership -- in partnership with Argentina which began it. The cumulative effect is something more than "responsible pragmatism," a term often used to describe the style Brazilian foreign policy begun by President Geisel until the debt crisis. As leader of an emergent Plata system, Brazil has not articulated a grand design for Latin America; nor would this be accepted. But there is coherence to the Argentine relationship and this gives stability to the continent.

Yet there are many obstacles to enhanced interdependence, as well as opportunities. On the domestic side, Brazil's regions would not benefit equally from greater integration with the La Plata Basin. Since the early 19th century, Southern Brazil has been pulled into the domestic market through tariffs which promoted inter-regional trade. Since 1930, São Paulo has depended heavily on the domestic market, selling more to the other regions than it buys. (Fiscal redistribution makes up some of the difference.) Deep-running patterns of national coherence could be impinged upon if the developed South were pulled toward the Plata growth pole, away from the impoverished Northeast.

Continental unity in the geo-strategic sense is still very fragile, as the Falklands war revealed. Furthermore, as Brazil completes the transition to democracy, political instability at home could weaken its voice abroad, although this seems more likely for Argentina which faces more serious domestic challenges than Brazil. Today the debt-ridden continent lacks liquidity. In fact, the lack of foreign exchange to finance trade between the two soft currency countries of Argentina and Brazil has put a brake on commerce. (LATINEQUIP was set up in 1984 to address this problem.) Commodity prices are still weak, and protectionism limits exports to the hard currency countries, a serious problem. This could again enhance the importance of the Latin American market, especially if the world trading system becomes more compartmentalized. For Brazil, this would mean a relatively greater emphasis on the Plata Basin, especially, within its overall global foreign economic policy. But the greatest long term weakness in such a Southern regional system may well be the lack of capacity to generate advanced technology.[33] This the other system has in in abundance, coupled with a much richer history of interdependence. To the North we now turn.

THE NORTH AMERICAN SYSTEM

Until very recently, one would have focussed on bilateral relationships -- Mexico-U.S. or Canada-U.S. -- rather than on North America as something more than a geographic unit. But the basis for a larger continental focus first emerged with the military-strategic crisis of the late 1930s, and then took on definition during the energy crisis of the 1970s. In North America, the classic mix of geopolitical relationships and sectoral integration is far more advanced than in the other system. This comparison reveals just how tentative the La Plata system still is.

Interdependence will not please everyone. True to form, it is the Americans who are prone to welcome prospects for a North American community while the Canadians and Mexicans are more likely to denounce it, although opinion is far from monolithic in either country. Thus, elites in Mexico and Canada both reacted negatively to Ronald Reagan's vague plan for a "North American Accord" during the 1980 presidential campaign. (Governor Jerry Brown of California raised it earlier in his abortive 1976 bid for the Presidential nomination.) If the idea resonates well with Americans, it rattles the cages of nationalists on both sides of the border -- Canadians who wish to preserve political and economic independence in the face of what they call continentalism, and

Mexicans who see it as contradicting the goals of national economic autonomy emerging from their revolution. Taken as a sector by sector approach, however, the idea commands attention because the three nations *are* integrating rapidly.

Factor endowments of labor, capital and resources are dynamically interrelated in the Northern continent. "Basically there are two choices" facing Canada, political scientists from McMaster University wrote recently. "The first would be to embrace Mr. Reagan's early proposal for a 'North American accord,' and move deliberately toward closer economic integration with the United States. This path would, however, be fraught with electoral problems for any Canadian political party rash enough to take it. It is thus likelier that the government will choose, as it has in the past, to pursue the other alternative: negotiating piecemeal agreements over specific issues, arguing periodically for special treatment of Canada."[34] Taking power in 1984, the Conservative Mulroney goverment is following something like the first choice. With his large parliamentary majority, and a large favorable trade balance with the United States to safeguard, Mulroney is pressing the Reagan administration to accept freer trade across the board. Whether Canada's free trade initiative will succeed in the face of rising U.S. protectionism and cleavages among Canadian regions remains to be seen.

The weak Canadian dollar, export problems to Europe and the Far East, and the revival of East-West tensions all make exchange with the United States more attractive. Trudeau's Third Option, a multilateral foreign policy based on more attention to North-South issues and with relatively less reliance on Washington, collapsed. His Foreign Investment Review Agency (FIRA), which attempted to both monitor and channel foreign investment was abolished by Mulroney. The national energy policy (NEP) to capture the benefits of ever higher oil prices for a Canadian industrial policy was overtaken by price declines, although Canadianization of the petroleum industry remains popular. Trudeau suffered from poor timing: these measures were adopted in the late 1970s, with the world economic system becoming less stable and when the incoming Reagan administration would soon reveal its hostility to FIRA and the oil policy. Consider that Brazil began *its* independent foreign policy a decade earlier, under much more favorable conditions. Yet within Canada itself there were many who felt all along that the two economies were far too intergrated for even such judicious measures as Trudeau's to succeed. Conflits over a range of issues could escalate to a crisis in relations. And by 1982 the recognition of shared intervulnerability led Washington to devote sustained attention to better managing the relationship.[35]

Whether Ottawa will reap benefits from an intensified bilateral economic relationship with Washington remains to be seen. One of the strongest arguments is that greater access to U.S. markets would stimulate Canadian industry to become more competitive in an increasingly harsh and unforgiving world trading system. As for Washington, it seems clear that holding Canada and Israel up as partners who benefit from greater access to U.S. markets under free trade is useful in GATT negotions and in strengthening its ideological and negotiating stand against, for example, protectionist Brazil, which also enjoys a trade surplus with the United States.

Mexico, for all its nationalist ideology, rhetoric and legislation, has in fact been integrating with the United States since the early 1950s when the financial systems were linked. The recent decision by Ford to invest $400 million in small car production for the North American market is a harbinger of things to come, including more production-sharing as in the *maquiladora* program. (It is worth noting that U.S.-Canadian automobile production was integrated in 1968; the multinational auto companies with all the associated industries in their tow have been the main force for integration to date between Argentina and Brazil.) Mexico is under pressure to do more. "Perhaps Mr. de la Madrid and his Cabinet ought to forget the past [historically one-sided relationship] and join unequivocally in increased and sustained economic cooperation with the American private sector," a business consultant wrote recently in the *New York Times*.[36]

But few Americans are sensitive to the ubiquitous nature of state intervention in the Mexican economy. Given the great demands on the economy in what remains a poor country, it is hard to imagine the state foregoing its central role in planning, ownership and allocation. Canada also has a tradition of state intervention, if less stridently proclaimed. At the Quebec summit in March, 1985 Reagan and Mulroney called for a "bilateral mechanism to chart all possible ways to reduce and eliminate existing [trade] barriers,"[37] although Canada has historically been leery of joint bodies that could signify a loss of sovereignty. The political formula for anything more ambitious than an incremental, sector-by-sector approach is much harder to imagine for Mexico, with its centralized state, hybrid capitalism, and low purchasing power of the masses. Having said this, the two nations are already tightly bound in a set of special relationships of the sort that characterize interdependence. Furthermore, one consequence of IMF austerity measures will be greater reliance on foreign investment and exports, factors which should deepen the already strong attraction of the U.S. market.

Moreover, in geopolitics the North American system rests on two well-established bilateral relationships, both of which started in 1938 when Canada and the United States began mutual defense planning and when the Roosevelt Administration came to terms with the Mexican oil expropriations (and loaned the funds for compensation, in return for defense planning under the hemispheric Rainbow Plan). Canada accepted the production-sharing of defense goods (which continues), and became a wartime, then a NATO ally and partner in North American air defense. "Wars, both hot and cold," two Canadian historians write, "have forced new relationships on both countries, with profoundly important effects on the weaker of the two."[38]

Canada's defense alliance again looms larger as East-West tensions revive; contacts with the small, but increasingly influential Mexican Army have intensified in recent years; but each of the smaller powers is selective in its support of American security objectives, Mexico especially. Because of this defense relationship, (and also trade and finance), Canada abandoned its traditional triangular policy, and in any event post-war Britain could no longer serve as the major market or as a counterweight to the United States. Mexico has won policy distance by retaining ties to Cuba which, it is interesting to recall, both Quadros and Frondizi wanted to do as well. By 1980, Mexico with its oil, markets and migrants for strategic reasons loomed as a highly important and, some would say, the single most important U.S. foreign policy relationship. By 1986, the strains of austerity and political unrest were adding to official Washington's concerns about Mexico.

Antedating defense is a long history of economic exchange in North America. Trade with Canada intensified after Confederation in 1867. U.S. investments in that country accelerated after World War I and particularly since World War II, when branch plants of American corporations came in behind tariff walls, in part to secure supplies of strategic raw materials. In turn, Canandian industry received privileged access to the U.S. defense market and finance.[39] Thirty percent of Canada's gross national product is generated by foreign trade (about 80 percent of Canadian exports now go to the United States) -- a marked contrast with Brazil, with its much lower trade dependency. Exchange with Mexico began its modern dynamic in the Porfiriato when Mexican labor helped to open up the West and American capital built the mines, railroads and early factories of Mexico until the Revolution. The Mexican economic miracle from 1940 into the early 1970s was predicated on very close ties to American capital markets, although Mexico (preoccupied with the internal market) did not become a major exporter. Yet by 1980 Mexico with its new oil reserves had become the United States's third largest trading partner, with Canada first. And, as mentioned, Mexican exports to Latin America, including capital goods, declined accordingly.

While both nations were still large receivers of U.S. direct investment, Canadians were for the first time moving aggressively into American urban real estate markets, retailing, and manufacturing, which improved their bargaining position. "Dependence on the U.S. economy has been offset somewhat by increased Canadian investment in the United States," Bromke and Nossal conclude. "Similarly, Canada's natural resources continue to be vital to the United States. Increased trade works to mutual advantage -- and mutual dependence."[40] It would be logical for Mexico to link forward to gasoline distribution at the pump, in U.S. filling stations, now that Pemex is supplying around 20 percent of U.S petroleum requirements (including the Strategic Reserve). Joint ventures abroad with American oil companies were talked about in Mexico before the debt crisis and could be raised again. (Interestingly, Petrobras may start exploring for Argentine oil and gas under the new trade agreements.)

If the economic links are fundamental, cultural integration does not necessarily follow as a consequence. Canadian efforts to boster national media and reduce the inflow of U.S. job-seekers have been successful. Cultural intergration with Mexico, by contrast, is increasing -- because of the massive migration. For example, the private Mexican television network TELEVISA reaches through the Spanish Information Network a potential audience of 14 million people in the United States.[41] News stories favorable to the Mexican government and Mexican culture are beamed by satellite across North America. As for the Americans, they still seem blithely indifferent to cultural issues except bilingualism. The new tabloid *USA Today* began distributing in Canada without changing its slogan, "The Nation's Newspaper," -- a mistake, which ruffled the Canadians. "It didn't occur to our circulation people that there would be a problem."[42]

Today the timing is right for a close look at the industrial policies of all three nations. Continental markets for certain raw materials are likely to develop. Mexico wants to increase sales of non-oil goods to both nations. Governors and premiers from the Rocky Rocky Mountain region met together in June, 1983 to formalize closer ties. Their counterparts from the Maritime Provinces, Quebec and New England have been conferring since 1973 on hydroelectric power sales among other issues. (The North American power grid is integrated, as is transportation). Constrained by the highly centralized Mexican system, border state governors have nonetheless been consulting regularly for the last five years. The flow of official and private interactions across the frontiers is large, something Argentina and Brazil are just beginning to experience.

I am not suggesting that change will come without difficult tradeoffs or that all will welcome it. California with its very strong economy is perhaps the American state most attuned to interdependence. Mexican migration and significant numbers of Canadian expatriots living in the state are harbingers. Canadians are divided. According to the late Carl Solberg, "the three western Canadian provinces are much more enthusiastic proponents of interdependence than the protected industrial core areas of Ontario and Quebec (Quebec's hydro deals notwithstanding). The resource-rich westerners want the American market opened as much and as fast as possible; the Ontario-Quebec axis (which holds the most seats in Parliament) wants cheap oil and supports the national oil company Petrocan. All this means that closer relations with the United States cause deep regional tensions and cleavages in Canada."[43]

Institutionally, therefore, relationships between a powerful United States, where the states have a certain latitude to cut their own deals and a much more regionalistic Canada where fears of absorption have prompted federal intervention in the economy to deflect continentalism, defy simple solutions. However, the recent deep recession and low oil prices have negatively affected policies to Canadianize investment and restrict the flow of electronic data across its borders. The economic logic for reaching new levels of integration is strong today, and Canada is in fact taking the lead. The highly centralized Mexican system has long held the border region under tight political control. That most of the migration is generated from central Mexico, however, means that the industrial heartland is subjected to strong socioeconomic pulls toward the North. Mexican oil is a valuable resource, which also generates fear of not using the resource well, so that (as Jaime Corredor puts it) "the inertia of Mexico's dependence, far from being broken, will be aggrevated through a process of 'silent integration' that is automatic, out of control, and incompatible with the strategic objectives of the nation."[44] However, now that autonomous national development has been overtaken by events throughout the hemisphere, what will be the outlines of Mexico's new strategic objectives for an increasingly interdependent region?

Having recently joined GATT, Mexico wants to broaden its manufacturing export base, to make the difficult transition from inward-based growth that Brazil accomplished in the 1960s, to become less reliant on petroleum. The political base for such a shift is still unclear. Furthermore, outside pressures (including the IMF) for a relatively more open economy are unlikely to be well received by large segments of the Mexican elite, however much they recognize the logic of such a trend.

Interdependence is so advanced, the web of interests so complex as to render linkage politics almost inconceivable between Canada and the United States.[45] The same can probably be said for Mexico and the United States today, despite a more conflictual relationship historically. But if skills in conflict management are well developed, what Clark Reynolds calls "managed interdependence" has just begun and elites are divided over the costs and benefits.

Americans welcome the *idea* of integration, although they, too, are sharply split on costs and benefits of developing a less *ad hoc* national industrial policy on which the management of "complex interdependence" would depend. Perceptions differ. For example, Mexicans tend to see migration North as an American problem, in large part caused by the demand for cheap labor, whereas to Americans it raises fears of having "lost control of our borders," an essential aspect of sovereignty. On the other hand, Americans regard foreign investment as benign, a benefit for all concerned; Mexicans and Canadians often disagree. Asymmetries in power simply do not concern the Americans, whereas their less powerful neighbors are acutely aware. As one Canadian phrased it, "The problem of integration as a principle for our structural relationship, either economically or politically, is that Canada becomes a minor shareholder in the policy-making instrument which is bound to be controlled largely by the major shareholder. Because of the implications of integration, however, the minor shareholder is bound by the decision." Such is the logic of movement toward what has been often referred to as "dependent continental integration." And a Mexican scholar warned recently that a relationship the United States projects as harmonious "would not be the result of collaboration but of the dependent nature of Mexican capitalism and United States domination of it.[46]

Underlying these negative assessments is a common realization that there are powerful pressures to utilize factor endowments rationally, employing comparative advantage but setting up a policy framework to structure the political economy of this new relationship. The disruptive effects of an unrestrained free flow of factors would be great for both the United States, where wages would fall, and even harder on Mexican industry.[47] Changing sectoral relationships in the North American system are high on the research and policy agenda. That new policies are needed to deal with intrasystem issues is clear enough. The projected binational entity to oversee free trade between Canada and the United States may be a model for the new sorts of institutions we will need.

Living in a developed country, Canadians tend to return again and again to the question of whether or not free trade would present a tradeoff between more rapid growth and the loss of political identity.[48] In a recent poll of opinion leaders,

> "... one group argues that the two are either unrelated or that there is a positive relationship, since economic integration will strengthen the Canadian economy and thereby provide a better basis for autonomy than an ailing economy. The other group sees in greater economic integration a direct threat to Canada's survival as an independent nation."

Living in a poor, developing country, Mexicans have great difficulty dealing with the idea in public, while recognizing that for geopolitical and economic reasons the United States has to forge with them new forms of the special relationship to accelerate Mexican economic growth.

AFTERWORD

What is still a trickle in Brazil and Argentina is now in North America a flood. Regionalism, once the rage in Latin America twenty years ago became old hat with globalization of the world economy, the collapse of LAFTA, and the many opportunities to develop independent foreign policies afforded by expanding trade. At the same time, trends toward integration began, in part by policy design, in part incrementally. If the world economy has indeed slowed down these trends may well become more important as contiguous nations seek to minimize risk and forge special relationships. But these trends also go on, regardless. Linking inderdependency with regionalism, thus, is not farfetched. In this essay I have attempted to fix the outlines of this process, to assess its *historicity*. And if I am right, then the past is indeed prologue to a future few would have imagined just a decade ago.

TABLE 8.1

Brazilian and U.S. Trade with Major Partner, 1958-1984
(percent of total trade in dollars)

	Brazil-Argentina		U.S.-Mexico		U.S.-Canada	
Year	Exports	Imports	Exports	Imports	Exports	Imports
1958	8.6	6.5	5.0	3.5	19.7	20.9
1959	3.8	7.6	4.2	2.8	21.6	20.0
1960	4.4	6.4	4.0	3.0	18.5	19.7
1961	4.8	2.0	3.9	3.6	18.2	22.2
1962	3.9	5.7	3.7	3.5	18.6	22.3
1963	3.2	5.9	3.7	3.4	18.2	22.3
1964	6.3	9.2	4.1	3.4	18.5	22.6
1965	8.8	12.0	4.0	2.9	19.7	22.6
1966	6.5	7.9	3.8	2.9	21.9	23.9
1967	5.9	7.3	3.8	2.7	22.7	26.5
1968	6.4	7.1	3.9	2.7	23.3	27.1
1969	7.4	7.0	4.2	2.8	24.0	28.8
1970	6.9	8.0	3.9	3.0	21.0	27.7
1971	8.9	3.6	3.6	2.7	23.4	27.9
1972	3.8	4.6	3.9	2.9	24.9	26.8
1973	3.1	4.9	4.1	3.3	21.1	25.4
1974	3.8	2.7	4.9	3.3	20.2	22.0
1975	4.4	1.8	4.7	3.1	20.2	22.8
1976	3.3	3.5	4.3	2.9	20.9	21.7
1977	3.1	3.8	3.9	2.9	21.2	20.0
1978	2.8	4.0	4.6	3.5	18.2	19.4
1979	4.7	5.0	5.4	4.2	18.2	18.4
1980	5.4	3.3	6.8	5.1	16.0	16.9
1981	3.8	2.6	7.6	5.2	16.9	17.7
1982	3.3	2.8	5.6	6.4	15.9	19.1
1983	3.0	2.3	4.5	6.5	19.1	20.2
1984	3.2	3.5	5.4	5.5	21.6	20.0

Source: Brazil: Banco Central, *Boletim Mensal* 1966-1985; U.S. Dept. of Commerce, Bureau of the Census; *Historical Statistics of the United States, Colonial Times to 1970*, v. II, Washington, 1975; *Statistical Abstract of the United States*, various years; and *Survey of Current Business* for recent data.
Note: All data is for merchandise trade. Brazilian exports are given in FOB. imports are CIF until 1976, when they are given in FOB. 1984 data is first 10 months for Brazil, first 9 months for the United States.

TABLE 8.2

Brazilian Trade with LAFTA/LAAI Region, 1966-1984
(in dollars)

Year	% of Total World Trade		Argentina as % of Brazilian Regional Trade	
	Exports	Imports	Exports	Imports
1966	10.8	15.9	60.2	49.1
1967	9.7	13.6	60.5	54.4
1968	10.3	13.0	61.5	55.1
1969	11.0	12.9	67.2	53.5
1970	11.1	10.9	61.2	55.1
1971	12.2	8.4	56.6	44.3
1972	10.2	8.2	37.8	55.4
1973	9.0	8.7	35.5	56.6
1974	11.5	7.1	32.8	37.8
1975	13.8	5.6	31.8	32.0
1976	11.8	4.8	27.5	36.5
1977	12.2	3.9	25.9	33.7
1978	12.8	3.8	21.5	38.2
1979	16.2	12.2	29.0	40.5
1980	17.2	14.7	31.5	28.1
1981	18.1	14.1	20.9	18.7
1982	14.2	16.9	23.3	16.7
1983	9.4	14.3	31.8	16.2
1984	10.4	15.5	30.4	22.6

Source: See Table 8.1.

TABLE 8.3

Brazil-United States Trade, 1958-1984
(percent of total trade in dollars)

Year	United States-Brazil Exports	United States-Brazil Imports	Brazil-United States Exports	Brazil-United States Imports
1958	3.1	4.4	42.9	35.6
1959	2.4	4.1	46.1	33.5
1960	2.2	3.8	44.4	30.3
1961	2.5	3.8	40.1	35.5
1962	2.0	3.3	39.9	30.9
1963	1.7	3.2	37.7	30.7
1964	1.5	2.8	33.1	34.4
1965	1.2	2.3	31.2	29.6
1966	2.6	2.3	33.4	39.5
1967	1.7	2.0	32.2	34.2
1968	2.0	2.0	33.2	32.4
1969	1.7	1.7	26.4	30.1
1970	1.9	1.6	24.7	32.4
1971	2.1	1.6	26.2	28.7
1972	2.4	1.6	23.3	28.0
1973	2.6	1.7	18.1	28.6
1974	3.1	1.6	21.8	24.2
1975	2.8	1.5	15.4	24.8
1976	2.4	1.4	17.9	22.9
1977	2.0	1.5	17.7	20.0
1978	2.0	1.6	22.7	21.4
1979	1.8	1.5	19.3	17.9
1980	1.9	1.5	17.4	17.9
1981	1.6	1.7	17.6	15.9
1982	1.6	1.8	20.0	14.8
1983	1.3	1.9	23.1	15.6
1984	1.2	2.3	27.6	16.0

Source: See Table 8.1.

NOTES

1. An earlier version of this paper was given at the Nova Friburgo meeting in July, 1983, at which the comments of Maria da Conceição Tavares were particularly helpful. A later version, prepared for the Berkeley follow-up conference, was commented on by Steven Krasner. In addition to his critique, this chapter also benefited from written comments by historians Carl E. Solberg, Joseph L. Love and David M. Kennedy.

2. For bibliography and discussions of these themes consult Clark W. Reynolds and Carlos Tello, eds., *U.S.-Mexico Relations, Economic and Social Aspects*, (Stanford, 1983); The Dean Rusk Center, *Comparative Facts on Canada, Mexico and the United States: A Foundation for Selective Integration and Trilateral Cooperation*, School of Law, University of Georgia, (Athens, 1979); and the special issue of *Revista Brasileira de Politica Internacional*, "Brasil-Argentina," 14:93-96 (1981). See also Wayne A. Selcher, "Brazilian-Argentine Relations in the 1980s: From Wary Rivalry to Friendly Competition," *Journal of Inter-American Studies and World Affairs* 27:2 (Summer, 1985), pp. 25-53.

3. *U.S.-Mexico Relations*, p. v.

4. Krasner argued this point at the Berkeley conference.

5. Felix Peña, "Perspectivas futuras de las relaciones Brasil-Argentina," in *RBPI* (1981), p. 148.

6. Celso Lafer, "Bacia do Prata: conflito ou cooperação?", in *O Estado do São Paulo* (October 29, 1983).

7. *Canada: A Middle-aged Power* (Toronto, 1976), p. 201.

8. Celso Lafer, "Brasil-EUA: História e perspectivas de um relacionamento diplomático," in *Paradoxos e possibilidades* (Rio de Janeiro, 1982), especially p. 187; Wolf Grabendorff,

"Brazil and West Germany: A Model for First World-Third World Relations?" in Wayne A. Selcher, ed. *Brazil in the International System: The Rise of a Middle Power* (Boulder, 1981); and Riordan Roett, "Brazilian Foreign Policy: Options in the 1980s," in Thomas C. Bruneau and Philippe Faucher, eds. *Authoritarian Capitalism: Brazil's Contemporary Economic and Political Development* (Boulder, 1981).

9. "During the meeting, officials said, [Ambassador] Motley asked the Brazilians in general terms to consider actions to help the U.S. in its Central American activities. implied that it could show its 'appreciation' by looking for more ways to ease Brazil's severe economic crunch. The meetings included discussions of Brazil's difficulty in making its international debt payments, officials said. 'Certainly a linkage was implied, and certainly discussed,' one White House aide said." Gerald F. Seib, "Reagan Seeks Latin American Support for U.S. Initiatives in Central America," *Wall Street Journal*, (June 17, 1983), p. 2. See also "Redefining relations with the USA," *Latin American Regional Reports (Brazil)* (April 29, 1983), p. 4. Evidently, the Brazilians are also cooperating to remove Cuban influence from Suriname, the former Dutch colony. (Washington at one point proposed a joint occupation with Brazil to forestall the Germans from occupying Suriname in 1940.) Lee Lescaze, "Politics of Suriname May Matter to U.S., But What Are They?," *Wall Street Journal*, (December 7, 1983), pp. 1,18.

10. "Brazilian official links foreign debt payments, steel imports by U.S.," *The Wall Street Journal*, (May 14, 1984), p. 29.

11. Robert S. Greenberger, "U.S. Encouraged by Mexican Leader's Tougher Stand Toward Sandinistas," *The Wall Street Journal* (May 15, 1984), p. 34.

12. "One is struck by the general absence of attempts on the part of either country to link negotiations on separate

issues. The conscious avoidance of such linkages is a well-established tradition in U.S.-Canadian relations, and one that has survived despite the period [in the early 1970s] of considerable strain in their relationship." Harald von Riekhoff, John H. Sigler and Brian W. Tomlin, *Canadian-U.S. Relations: Policy Environments, Issues, and Prospects* (Montreal and Washington, 1979).

13. According to *Business Week* (February 28, 1983), p. 62, Petrobras recently said it would demand that oil suppliers purchase Brazilian oil-field equipment. In particular, Mexico and Venezuela should buy from Brazil pipe, valves, and pumps that they now import from the United States. On multi-national market shares by subsidiaries see Baer and Von Doellinger, "Determinants of Brazil's Foreign Economic Policy," in Joseph Grunwald, ed. *Latin America and the World Economy: A Changing International Order* (Beverly Hills, 1978), pp. 155-7.

14. Albert Fishlow, "The Debt Crisis: Solution by Economic Integration?" Unpublished paper (U.C., Berkeley, January, 1983).

15. Oscar H Camilion, who as Argentine Ambassador to Brazil worked so effectively to bring about rappochement in the late 1970's, made this point in "As relações entre o Brasil e a Argentina no mundo atual," *RBPI*, 12:45/46 (March-June, 1969), p. 30-1, 40-2.

16. Argentine reactions to this decline are traced by Joseph S. Tulchin in "Una perspectiva histórica de la política Argentina frente al Brasil," *Estudios Internacionales* 13:2 (October-December, 1980), p. 469.

17. Celso Lafer and Felix Peña helped to conceptualize the new relationship with an influential transnational conference series. See their earlier pioneer formulations in *Argentina e Brasil no sistema das relações internacionais* (São Paulo, 1973), in which Peña argued that his country

should abandon its defensive attitude and seize "the privileged status of a new context, both contiguous and regional," p. 78. Economic and geopolitical aspects of the Itaipu and Yacyrita dams are discussed by J. Eliseo da Rosa, the Paraguayan economist, in "Economics, Politics, and Hydroelectric Power: the Parana River Basin," *Latin American Research Review* 18:3 (1983), pp. 77-107.

18. Alencar D'Avila Magalhães, "A economia Argentina e seu intercâmbio econômico comercial com o Brasil." In period 1977-9, when Argentina's economy was exceptionally open, the share of manufactures by value was only 25 percent of the Argentine export list but almost 56 percent of Brazil's. Yet this is what complimentarity now implies unless it is carefully managed. In FUNCEX, *Trabalhos do I seminário de relações comerciais Brasil-Argentina,* 11-12 June 1980 (São Paulo, 1980), pp. 31-2.

19. See section 6, "A cooperação industrial: suas dificuldades e possibilidades," in *RBPI* (1981). The quotes, by Osiris G. Villegas and Luis Eulalio Vidigal, respectively, are on pages 93 and 98.

20. *The Economist* (August 2, 1986) p. 54, p. 56; and *Wall Street Journal* (July 29, 1986) on the trade agreements. On the unexpectedly rapid pace of implementation, see Alan Riding, "For Brazil and Argentina, New Amity," *New York Times*, (December 14, 1986), p. 3. Daniel Chudnovsky, "El comércio de bienes de capitál en América Latina y las exportaciones de Argentina, Brasil y México, LATINEQUIP, documento no. 1 ([Buenos Aires], 1985), p. 34, p. 25. Latinequip offers trade services, including counter-trade, and export coordination among Latin American capital goods producing and engineering firms. It was founded by the Banco de la Provincia de Buenos Aires, the Banco del Estado de São Paulo, and the Nacional Financiera of Mexico in late 1984. *LATINEQUIP*, (Buenos Aires, 1985).

21. Maria Regina Soares de Lima, "As Relações Econômicas e Políticas do Brasil com a América Latina: Balanço de uma Década," Paper for the Nova Friburgo conference, 18-20 July, 1983.

22. For a Paraguayan view of Brazilian trans-frontier land purchases see Domingo Laino, *Paraguai, fronteiras e penetração brasileira,* (São Paulo, 1979), and scholarly articles in the *Revista Paraguaya de Sociología.*

23. In addition to fortifying the Southern Cone, Peron wanted to resolve the Parana dam dispute, set up a customs union with Brazil as a prototype for South American union, and believed that coming world food shortages would propel the ABC region into world economic leadership -- all according to Baptista Lusardo, long-time Vargas crony and Ambassador to Argentina. In Glauco Carneiro, *Lusardo, o último caudilho* v. 2 (Rio de Janeiro, 1978), pp. 401, 438-41, and 464*ff.*

24. Trade integration for Canada is specified in Robert O. Keohane and Joseph S. Nye, *Power and Interdependence, World Politics in Transition,* (Boston, 1977), pp. 209-10. "Exports to the United States rose from half to over two-thirds of Canada's total exports between 1948 and 1970... Each country was the other's largest trading partner, and their exports to each other rose from 26 percent to 36 percent of their total exports during the 1960s." The analogous figure for LAFTA in 1966 was only 10 percent.

25. San Tiago Dantas, *Política externa independente* (Rio de Janeiro, 1965), especially his lucid presentation to the Chamber of Deputies on 23 November, 1961, pp. 45*ff.*

26. Address by Ambassador Arnoldo Musich to CIESP/FIESP, in which he also said that both nations had to make the transition from agro-pastoral economies to agro-industrial economies. FIESP, *Boletim Informativo* 13:648 (7 March, 1962).

27. Humberto Dantas, "O disinteresse do governo pela ALALC," FIESP, *Boletim Informativo* 13:654 (18 April, 1962).

28. William G. Tyler, *Manufactured Export Expansion Industrialization in Brazil* (Tubingen, 1976), Chapter V on the export sector. For the quote, see p. 146-7.

29. Simon Teitel and Francisco Thoumi, "Las exportaciones de manufacturas de Argentine y Brasil: Crecimiento, estabilidad y diversificación en la década pasada," Unpublished paper, The Inter-American Development Bank (June, 1983), pp. 3 and 27.

30. The collection of his speeches and writings entitled *Araujo Castro* as organized by Rodrigo Armando for the Universidade de Brasília (1982) is important.

31. Maria Regina Soares de Lima, *loc. cit.*, note 20.

32. Werner Baer and Von Doellinger summarize these policy stages concisely in "Determinants of Brazil's Foreign Economic policy," *op. cit.*

33. Edmundo Fuenzalida, the Stanford sociologist, always emphasizes the acute problem of technological dependency, which to him is the grave drawback of any Southern system. Hélio Jaguaribe comments on managing the multinationals as a way to accelerate technological innovation and sharing between Brazil and Argentina, in "Conflito e cooperação," *RBPI* (1981), pp. 131-41. For his efforts on behalf of Argentine-Brazilian integration, especially, an honorary degree was recently conferred on Jaguaribe by the University of Mainz. He also helped to inspire LATINEQUIP, the new export-promoting firm, on whose board he serves. For his efforts on behalf of Argentine-Brazilian integration, especially, an honorary degree was recently conferred on Jaguaribe by the University of Mainz. He also helped to inspire LATINEQUIP, the new export-promoting firm, on whose board he serves.

34. Adam Bromke and Kim Richard Nossal, "Tensions in Canada's Foreign Policy," *Foreign Affairs*, 62:2 (Winter 1983/84), p. 349.

35. Stephen Clarkson, *Canada and the Reagan Challenge; Crisis and Adjustment, 1981-85*, updated edition, (Toronto, 1985), p. 332. In addition to a sympathetic portrait of Trudeau, Clarkson gives an excellent assessment of Canada's struggle to achieve policy coherence in the face of ideological and policy disputes with Washington.

36. Amal Nag, "Big Investment by Ford is Seen in Mexico Plan," *Wall Street Journal*, (January 9, 1983), p. 3. "The aim of the [Mexican] decree is to force the car companies to build cars that can be exported at competitive prices, thus generating much-needed foreign currency for Mexico," which is considered to have the single largest market for autos outside the U.S., Canada and Europe. Benjamin Weiner, "Back from the Brink: Mexico's Miracle of Mirrors," *The New York Times* (January 15, 1984).

37. Summary of the joint communique in *Wall Street Journal*, March 19, 1985, p. 10. See also Bruce Stokes, "The Economic Ties that Bind Canada and the United States May be Broadened," *National Journal* (March 9, 1985), pp. 530-3.

38. R.D. Cuff and J.L. Granatstein, *Ties That Bind, Canadian-American Relations in Wartime From the Great War to the Cold War* (Toronto and Sarasota, 1977) p. xii.

39. *Ibid.*

40. Bromke and Nossal in *Foreign Affairs*, p. 353.

41. Consult Felix F. Gutierrez and Jorge Reina Schement, "Spanish International Network: The Flow of Television from Mexico to the United States," in Everett M. Rogers and Schement, eds., *Media Flows in Latin America*, papers from a 1982 Latin American Studies-Communication Department

conference at Stanford, in *Communication Research* 11:2 (April, 1984).

42. "Whose Newspaper?", *Wall Street Journal* (January 11, 1984), p. 24.

43. Carl E. Solberg, letter to author, February 7, 1984. For the Westerners' perspective consult John Richards and Larry Pratt, *Prairie Capitalism: Power and Influence in the New West* (Toronto, 1979).

44. Jaime Corredor, "The Economic Significance of Mexican Petroleum from the Perspective of Mexico-United States Relations," in Reynolds and Tello, pp. 138-9.

45. Keohane and Nye, p. 294: "The norm of nonlinkage that tends to separate issue areas in Canadian-American relations represents an accommodation of foreign policy to conditions of [what they call] complex interdependence. When multiple issues and actors are involved, linkage is often too costly in terms of domestic politics. No group wishes to see its interests traded away. Threats of retaliation on an extraneous issue involve mobilization of different sets of actors and promote domestic politicization, which bureaucrats fear may get out of control."

46. Holmes, p. 229, elaborating on a long report he presented to the House of Commons Standing Committee on External Affairs and National Defense. Carlos Rios F., "Prospects for Economic Cooperation," p. 194 in Susan Kaufman Purcell, ed., *Mexico-United States Relations*, issue of the *Proceedings of the Academy of Political Science* 34:1 (1981).

47. Clark W. Reynolds, "The Structure of the Economic Relationship," pp. 125-135 in S.K. Purcell, *op. cit.*

48. For Canadian thinking see the study sponsored jointly by the C.D. Howe Research Institute in Canada and the National Planning Association (U.S.A.): *Canadian-U.S.*

Relations, p. 127. (Cited in note 12.)

9

The Quest for Citizenship in a Relational Universe

Roberto da Matta

In this chapter I address the following question: If the concept of citizenship implies, on the one hand, a fundamental idea of the individual (and in the ideology of individualism), and, on the other, a set of universal rules (a system of laws valid for all across all social domains), then then how is this notion perceived and experienced in societies in which *relationships* play a critical role in the conception and dynamics of social order? How is the idea of citizenship, as a specific form of belonging to a given social totality, understood in the case of Brazil?

These are interesting problems to begin with, for if "citizenship" has a history, the role it plays is essentially a social one. But what kind of role is this when it is obscured by discussions of a political character which are frequently moralizing and normative?[1] In this sense it is important to point out that discussions of "citizenship" are always of a moral-political-juridical character, while the concept itself carries a basic sociological dimension. To be a "citizen" (and an "individual") is to assume a role that is learned and demarcated by singular expectations of behavior.

What is truly extraordinary in these discussions is the degree to which the concept of citizenship (and the notion of the individual) has been politically institutionalized. "Citizenship" has come to be taken as a given fact of the human nature -- a sort of spontaneous element -- and not as a social role, or something which is socially institutionalized and morally constructed. In fact, I believe that the perception of the individual as a social role and as an assumed (and critical) component of western society, is a recent and still quite rare concept in the social sciences. In social anthropology, it is related to the perspective opened by the French school of sociology, specifically by the work of Louis Dumont. Dumont has recently done a series of studies on the idea of the individual and its concomitant institutions, comparing a civilization where the whole dominates its parts and hierarchy is a basic principle of social life (the case of India), with Western Civilization, where exactly the opposite takes place. In Western Civilization, Dumont argues, the part is more important than the whole and relations between men and things encompass relations between men themselves. This system has experienced what Dumont calls the "individualist revolution," a movement which institutionalized the individual as the moral center and whose ideology sees society as the instrument of his happiness.[2]

But if the notion of citizenship (and of individualism which it contains) is critically studied and is not considered spontaneously as something natural, spontaneous, and present wherever society and human beings exist, then the discussion can be recast. As citizen I belong to an eminently public domain and I define myself in terms of a complex of rights and duties vis-a-vis another entity -- also universal -- called the "nation." My participation in this entity, moreover, is conceived of as founded upon consent, in such a way that the government of the nation is part of this consent, and derives its fundamental legitimacy from this source.[3] This means that individuals (as citizens) permit the formation of public authority by means of consent and the free representation of their interests. The nation and the society are no longer a source of humanity (and of meaning), according to the traditional theory which conceives society as *universitas*.

In moral-juridical discussions, society is an entity conceived of as a club or a political party; a *societas* or association of citizens with multiple interests.[4] In fact, as a member of a nation I have other citizens as interlocutors, and cannot single myself out (as a citizen) in terms of any other social dimension because citizenship is a role which contaminates all of my behavior. Here, obviously, we are speaking of a social identity informed by the political dimension -- a totalizing identity that is continuously operative in all spheres of life.

Movements for the rights of women, children and the elderly are all around us as proof of this political contamination, which in many contexts has come to be more important than traditional social complementarities based on the dimensions of gender and age. The role of "citizen" (and, I repeat, of the "individual"), performs the sociological function of excluding all the complementarities and gradations that are part and parcel of traditional social roles.[5] As a citizen, therefore, I cannot define myself by age or gender, since if I present myself as a "47 year old man," I can produce an effect contrary to the universalization that the role of the individual (and of the citizen) promises. The proof is that in individualistic systems the expressions "male chauvinist pig" and "don't trust anybody over thirty" which as gender and age referents no longer serve as legitimate social dimensions for raising certain questions in some political and social contexts. In the role of citizen, thus, I learn (and many times learn the hard way) that I should be universal and I have to abandon the complementarities, contrasts and gradations which Linton mentioned as crucial elements in the definition of social status.[6] I stop being a middle-aged man, stop having a family name and a color, I stop being from a given geographic location and having a given profession. I also give up my peculiarities and singularities and turn myself into a generalized, universal and abstract entity, endowed, as Dumont and Lukes tell us, among others, with autonomy, internal space, privacy, liberty, equality and dignity. I suggest that it is necessary to *learn* to be what is called a "citizen" and "individual," just as an American needs to learn to be a "cowboy," a "husband" or a "sociologist," and a Brazilian needs to learn to be a "*malandro*" (rascal), a "politician," or a "*caxias*" (a martinet; a stickler).

I cannot help but observe, at the expense of anticipating my final discussion, that the nature of the social role of "citizen-individual" is molded in universal terms. This is to say that the role should operate in a homogenous social medium which can guarantee its recognition within the boundaries of society. Nothing should come between the "citizen" and the society (or "nation") as a whole. I will return to this point, for I consider it central to the entire discussion.

Here, however, I have to continue calling attention to some of the characteristics of this role with the intention of demonstrating that when we speak of "citizens" we are not speaking of specific traits that define each person in relation to a stage of the human condition, or that in the last instance would permit the construction of relations and complementarities of all as pairs of matching identities, as Goodenough would say. (As man/woman; old/young, rich/poor, etc., for example.) On the contrary. The concept demands that we generalize these traits and that we speak of identities that everyone can and should possess.

The social role of the individual (and citizen) is a social identity that has a levelling and egalitarian character. This would be its ideal and normative characteristic in the sense that as a citizen, I can only claim rights equal to those of all other "men." The group of citizens forming a society therefore, is a complex of units theoretically identical and as absolutely equal and parallel as the stripes of the United States flag.

In another fundamental sense, the semantic idiom of this concept engulfs the singular and the local, as revealed by the social and political history of the phenomenon as it developed in Western Europe and the United States. In fact, in these areas, the idea of citizenship as a universal social role with a political character contaminated all other social identities and made possible the liquidation of the particular laws and *privileges* accorded to nobility and the clergy.[7] Within the specific political dynamic of Western Europe, the concept of citizenship was a powerful instrument for the establishment of universal rules as a way of counterbalancing and offsetting (even terminating) the set of privileges crystallized in social differentiations and local hierarchies. If, as Karl Polanyi argues, market forces made the great transformation in our era, allowing land and human energy to be bought and sold in a social space demarcated by money and price,[8] the idea of citizenship complemented this revolution, establishing the individual as a central and absolutely dominant social role in our society. In both cases the revolution terminated private domains and particularist ethics which operated simultaneously within the same society.

But did this occur in linear fashion across all social sectors? Is the idea of citizenship as a social role related to the essential equality of all mankind (the notion of man as citizen of the world), actually validated by social practice? The facts of daily experience makes this question problematic. Observe, first, what happens in an international airport in the United States. You are a foreigner arriving in New York and line up for the passport check. What do you observe? In this context the concept of citizenship as a universal role no longer serves as a mechanism to abolish privilege. Here, the North Americans have a priviledged space, a special area that is clearly hierarchized, while all others are lumped together in a common line.

In the same sense, when one observes the social sphere of so-called "selections" and "preferences," institutionalized as "invitation," something similar is revealed. In a society with an egalitarian creed, whose basic social unit is the individual (or the citizen), the choice that would make it possible to establish a hierarchy and set of privileges, as well as the primacy of such a relationship, would be theoretically impossible, and would not make social or moral sense. After all, everyone is equal before the law and within society. Yet how can moral or legal equality result in an unequal and effectively hierarchized practice? The question was (and still is) a ghost that astonishes all who theorize about equality and individualism in capitalistic societies where citizenship is demarcated by universal laws.

One need only examine what might be termed a "sociology of invitation" to see that the ideology of merit permits discrimination, recreating privilege and hierarchy. In fact, I would even say that it is precisely because egalitarian consciousness (based on the fundamental concept of citizenship) allows the implementation of the "invitation" to be used that this mechanism of social and political discrimination comes to be so critical and important in the United States, and in other egalitarian societies. Thus, in America there exist many highly prestigious social institutions where one may enter only by means of an "invitation," or a summons which is theoretically personal and independent from public and collective obligations. No one is obliged to invite those not wanted. This individualistic and egalitarian principle permits -- paradoxically -- the breakdown of the principle of equality which dominates the political code adopted by the society.

To give a Brazilian example that might seem trivial but is in fact significant for my argument, aspirants to the prestigious Academy of Letters petition in an open candidacy, but the actual selection is resolved by way of a closed and secret election by its members. Similarly, in the United States, the Academy of Sciences and other highly prestigious institutions exercise the exclusive privilege of choosing members by means of invitation. The same occurs in other institutions: by electing or inviting its members, it can hierarchize and discriminate against the social totality without frontally assaulting the egalitarian ideology and the idea of citizenship as a levelling device.

Hence my suggestion made elsewhere[9] that it would not be absurd to see the United States as dominated by the real ethic of a secret society. In effect, it is only through exclusive groups (like clubs) formed with a base in the inalienable preferences of the individuals that a society mesmerized by the egalitarian creed can effectively discriminate.

Following a similar logic, the citizen in Brazil is the subject of impersonal (and universal) laws, as well as of the brutal power of the police, which serves to systematically differentiate him and exploit him ruthlessly, making him into an "equal but inferior" (*igual para baixo*), in a clear perver sion of liberal political concepts.[10] Consider for example, the arrival of a Brazilian in Brazil where, in an international airport, one immediately discovers the enormous disadvantage of Brazilian citizenship. One must wait in a long line, running the risk of being disgracefully and tragically accused by the police computer which operates with great precision and efficiency *against* the Brazilians. Here hierarchy is reversed, with the foreigners having the opportunity to receive much more attention and cordiality from the police and national customs agents!

All of this seems to indicate that in different historical and social situations the same notion of citizenship, and the same concept of the individual, can allow for substantially different social realities. And to complicate things more, revealing how these concepts are not watertight nor linear, one can reflect upon what Wanderley Guilherme dos Santos has called "regulated citizenship." This is a more or less wrong-headed form of citizenship which is: a) recognized and defined by a law granted by the state; but b) linked to a "system of occupational stratification" and "not a code of political values."[11] The result is a clear distinction between certain occupational categories which come to have more rights than others, that enjoy certain "universal rights" (such as vacations and rights to belong to a union) but which are still theoretically linked to the general idea of the worker-citizen. This demonstrates that the role of the citizen, as well as the political notion of citizenship, can be differentially applied in different societies and even within a single social system. What the Brazilian case undeniably reveals is that the notion of citizenship suffers a type of detour (*desvio*), whether from below or above, which impedes the complete realization of its universalistic and levelling political meaning.[12] But what is the social mechanism which allows such a variation to occur? Or better: why does the notion of citizenship suffer such variation in Brazil, when in societies such as England, France, the United States and Canada, it is so enviably stable?

The answer lies, obviously, in structural considerations, as well as in the historical and cultural processes which have shaped Brazilian society. In fact, historical and cultural processes reveal, as Richard Morse and others have noted,[13] the legacy of a colonial state which operated not on the basis of private agents, but through laws and institutions that the state itself created as its instruments of progress, change and control. In my own conception, it has to do with a mode of bureaucratic organization, where the whole predominates over its parts and *hierarchy* is fundamental to the definition of the role and meaning of the individual. This would certainly explain the so-called Brazilian and Latin American "individualism" (or "personalism"; or better still, "caudillismo") as a mode of reaction to the laws of the colonial state, in opposition to North-American individualism which is a creator of laws. Thus the historical-cultural process of Brazil (and Latin America) is one of having to open a social and political space for local and individual manifestations since everything is rigidly overseen and dominated by an enormous political, reli-gious and legal centralism. The historical North American experience is one of generating laws which can invent or save totalities greater than local systems. In Brazil, individualism is created with effort, as something negative and *against* the laws which emanate from the state and define the totality. In the United States, individualism is positive, and the thrust has been to create a *union*, a totality. Two different logics have permeated even the territorial formation of the two countries, in that Brazil has remained practically the same from the colonial period while the United States expanded its territory gradually.[14] In fact, the entire spectrum of social life in the two countries has followed radically different logics.

In structural terms what seems critical is the capacity to relate and to join tendencies which many times are separated by distinct historical and social traditions. Thus, in the United States the idea of community is founded on the equality and homogeneity of all of its members, here conceived as citizens. This is to say, the community can be seen as egalitarian because it is not made of families, kin groups and factions which objectively and effectively have different properties, styles, sizes and interests, but of individuals and citizens. In Brazil, by contrast, the community is necessarily heterogeneous, complementary and hierarchical. Its basic unity is based not on individuals (or citizens), but on relationships and persons, families and groups of relatives and friends. Thus in the United States the isolated individual counts as a positive unit from the moral point of view. In Brazil, the individual who is isolated without relations (the indivisible political entity) is considered highly negative, a loner, someone who, lacking ties and bonds, is a marginal human being in relation to the other members of the community. What is most striking in the Brazilian case is this capacity to relate in a common current not only persons, parties and groups, but also different social and political traditions. Thus while the community in America would be homogeneous, egalitarian, individualist and exclusive, in Brazil it would be heterogeneous, unequal, relational and inclusive. In one case, what counts is the individual and the citizen; in the other, what counts is the relationship.

This might explain the divergences and variations in the Brazilian notion of citizenship. For if the individual (or citizen) does not have a link with a person or an institution of prestige in society, he is treated as an inferior. As the old Brazilian saying goes, what controls him are the laws. But if those in a professional category (the workers as citizens and no longer as employees) have a strong link with the state (the government), then they can be differentiated and given privileged treatment. It is the relationship that explains the perversions and the variations of citizenship in the Brazilian case. This allows us to understand what happens to diverse occupational groups in Brazil, which form a clear hierarchy in terms of their proximity to power or, better yet, to that which represents the center of power.

I believe that the basic point of this perspective is the following: notwithstanding the Thomist and centralizing tradition existent in Brazil, one cannot exclude one other fundamental fact. Society also relates to these values liberal and Puritan traditions in which the individual and citizen are the most important unities. This means that to a centralizing and legalistic tradition we add another which is egalitarian, individualist and liberal. The result is a social system in which different conceptions of society, politics, economy and, naturally, citizenship, coexist. In a system where the key word is relationship, the dimensions and spheres of life with different values can coexist, however complementary among themselves. This raises a question: can we really speak of a single conception of citizenship as a hegemonic form of political participation, or do we necessarily have to discuss the hypothesis of a single society with multiple forms and sources of citizenship, as many as the spheres of action which exist in its environment?

To reach the core of this problem, we must re-examine several initial questions. I had never perceived the complexity of the term "citizen" (and the concept of the "individual"), until I began to write an essay on relations between individuals and laws in Brazil. For this, I chose to study the expression current throughout Brazil which is put aggressively: "do you know to whom you are speaking?" Everyone recognizes this type of questioning as unpleasant and authoritarian, being used in situations where the user wishes to break some rule to which in theory he is subject. A majority of Brazilians believes that the ideal situation for using this expression is when breaking a traffic law, when attempting, for example, to park illegally. The hapless policeman then triggers a "do you know to whom you are speaking?" response from the citizen who believes he is endowed with special rights, whether real or imagined.

When I began to list cases of the use of this expression, I discovered that it involved a typical scene. It always happened, as I indicated above, on an occasion when a universal law determined a type of behavior and a type of social role (that of the "citizen" and the "individual"), but when the person himself wished to be judged and perceived in another manner which necessarily bent (or permitted the softening) of the general law.

Facing me was a very rich drama revealing just how very complicated the role of the "citizen" is in Brazil.

While this role is embedded in the public ethic and extolled in public meetings as a part of party programs and electoral platforms, and, moreover, proclaimed in constitutions which say that all are equal before the law, making the citizen the basic unit on which the rights, laws and critical prerogatives of all Brazilians are founded, citizenship as a social role is not experienced in this manner in daily life. In effect, the word "citizen" is always used in negative situations in Brazil to demarcate the position of someone who is at a disadvantage or inferior. When one says: "the automobile belongs to that *citizen*; or, "the *citizen* will have to wait a bit;" or, "the *citizen* does not have all of his documents in order," one knows that a universalizing and depersonalizing treatment is being used not to solve a problem but to complicate or hinder the resolution of a problem. In the Brazilian social world, one always awaits with the best psychological and social expectations the ritual of recognition which humanizes and personalizes formal situations. In fact, the distinction of treatment by general rule (and its respective social roles) is embedded in our social conscience as a way of turning something down. Never does a negative situation occur using personal justification as a focal point. Rather, to the contrary, universal criteria are used for the negative attitude.[15] In this sense, it is common to overhear the following: "Well, if it was up to me I would accept your documents and explanations, but the *law determines* this type of process and I have no choice but to fine you!" The citizen is the entity subject to the law in Brazil, whereas the family and the ties of friendship and the webs of relationships which are highly formalized politically, ideologically and socially, are not governed by the law. This results as we shall see in a highly complex and correlative system of legal and social codes of behavior.

In a survey conducted by me together with my postgraduate students, the response to the question: "how would you classify a person who obeys the laws in Brazil?," was invariably negative. All, without exception, mentioned that whoever conducted himself this way was an inferior status person without resources. One informant provided the standard response to this question: "a person who obeys all the laws is a *babaca* (jerk)." That is to say, obeying the laws in Brazilian society conveys the impression of anonymity and great inferiority. Normally this signifies an absence of relations and these relations -- I repeat -- are what clothe a person with humanity, rescuing him from the condition of universality which is conveyed in the role of "citizen" and "individual."

For all of this, the hue and cry over citizenship (and of individualism) assumes particular forms in the Brazilian case. Moving against the grain of what one finds normally in the world of daily life this can acquire a violent significance from the political point of view. In fact, joining a party to demonstrate for one's rights as an employee, student, citizen or individual, could mean giving up one's most important social relations, above all the relations of *parentesco* (kinship), family and friendship. Hence, perhaps, the necessity to first construct the party (the framework), and then carry out the protest.

In any case, this act of clamoring for universal rights is very dangerous. It is just as dangerous to charge your boss for work completed as it is to assume the role of the citizen confronting the police in a display of public political participation, such as a rally. Here, procaliming that one is a Brazilian citizen can mean an arrest and even a few blows. In the same sense and surely by the same logic, I cannot ask to be paid for a job or speak of money to a friend, even if he owed me a set amount for work that I have done. In both cases, this would be tantamount to giving up relational identities, behavior which is always seen negatively in Brazil.

All this makes us understand why the Brazilians always navigate socially by making a personalized calculation of their actions. Thus, before going to some public agency, the norm and indeed "wisdom" dictates first discovering one's relations there. Once this is established, the situation at the agency changes radically. The upshot is that Brazilian social institutions are always subject to two types of pressure. One of them is the universalist pressure, which comes from bureaucratic norms and laws that define the existence of the agency as a public service. The other is determined by the webs of personal relations to which all are subjected and by the social resources which these networks mobilize and distribute.

Herein lies the difficulty of mounting a systematic and consistent criticism of any institution in the Brazilian case. In fact, if the criticism is made impersonally, demanding that the person or institution perform the services which they should perform, one always ruptures the linkages and ties of a personalist logic which dilutes it. Thus, if the telephone company was horrible to you but treated me well it is because, when all is said and done, "I have acquaintances and relatives inside;" or, as is actually said, "I have prestige in the company." And as social prestige is something which one locates in the fabric of relationships -- and in the relationships as much as in individuals -- a person can effectively put his networks at the disposition of a friend, so that all the social institutions suddenly become efficient. Evidently, this makes open social criticism not only complicated, but also suspect. Because he who criticizes "creates a scene," or is a "jealous sort" or "is spiteful." That is, the person without friends approaches the agency by the worst path, that of universalism and impersonality. Thus the ancient Brazilian expression: "for my friends, everything; for my enemies, the law!"

Another aspect that the expression "do you know to whom you are speaking" reveals is the perfect inversion of universalism, a type of logical and social reversal of everything which was said about the roles of "citizen" and the "individual." In fact, what allows this expression to be used, as well as determining its success or failure, is the possibility of claiming and establishing a linkage. Against the universal law I defend myself and make my will prevail not by using another universal law, but through a personal relationship -- a personal relationship that permits the bending or breaking of the law, highlighting its abstract impersonality in contrast to the reality and reasonableness of my uniqueness, or the singularity of my case. Not that the law is wrong in principle; it is just that it doesn't apply in my case (or in the case of those I protect). Therefore, the law should be forgotten or anesthetized and the particular case be resolved by means of a specific relationship.

To cite an historical example: just this occurred in 1676 when Jose de Freitas Serrão, a judge on the High Court of Bahia, refused an order to vacate houses he had rented and, later, would not let his landlord be heard before the court. Or take the case of Judge Caetano Brito de Figueiredo who borrowed heavily to make several investments and afterwards prevented his creditor from taking any legal action. Another judge protected his assassin nephew, and still another whose slaves were involved in a street brawl saw to it that they were freed. In our times the Vice Governor of Rio de Janeiro had his car towed for double-parking in Copacabana, only to have it returned so his driver could pay the fine.[16] What these cases reveal is the enormous relevance and depth of the use of personal relations for social navigation in Brazil. If colonial judges would use their authority to bend the laws of contract, so today officials at all levels use their position to bypass the universal laws which theoretically apply to everyone, just not to them....

In sum, we live in a society where there exists a type of battle between the public world of universal laws and contracts, and the private universe of the family, of godparents, relatives and friends. It is a society which possesses differentiated forms of definition for its members, according to the complex of relations that they can claim or demonstrate in specific situations. Thus, if I am assuredly a citizen on Independence Day and in the political rally, in no way do I want to be *only* a citizen when I am struggling with the police over a robbery, or when I need a bank loan, or have to explain my income tax return. In these situations, the first thing I do is be recognized but not as a citizen.[17] Rather, I hope to be *treated*, as we say in Brazil, with the maximum attention, consideration and tolerance. For this, before initiating official contact with any public agency, I contact someone who can mediate. Just as I do when I go to ask a favor from God, Our Lord, and make contact through my favorite saints, intermediaries between Heaven and mankind.

In other words, there is a form of universal citizenship, built on modern roles which are tied into the operation of a bureaucracy and a market; and also other forms of affiliation to Brazilian society -- other forms of citizenship -- that stem from the intimate, relational world of the *casa* (household). At heart, there is a Brazilian *nation* founded on its citizens, and a Brazilian *society* which functions through traditional mediations. The modern Western revolution which eliminated these structures of segmentation continues to operate socially and politically, being *also* part of the social system.[18] What still hasn't been done, it seems to me, is to recognize these traditional mediations as an important part of the social dynamic. Until this is done, they will continue to operate on an implicit level, with the same force they have always had, creating invisible pressures as true behind-the-scenes manipulators of the social processes.

With this in mind, the role of friendship, of godparenthood and the logic of personal relations in general needs to be seriously studied as a basic component of Brazilian society and not treated superficially at the anecodotal level. The double game called Brazilian "politics" can thus be easily understood. The public discourse is made in a liberal-universalist idiom and directed to the citizens. But political practice is made in another frame of reference and follows, as I am trying to reveal, another logic. Here, the frame is of friends and political supporters who, once in in power, will have it all! The dynamic is that of relational loyalties which are based on no legal or ideological commitment.

The result does not go unrecognized by the Brazilian masses who look on politics as fundamentally a dirty game, where everything exists except ethics. Hence the expression: "so-and-so is *very political*" to describe someone who knows how to take care of his personal interests. I have suggested in my work that this double game is complex and needs to be unveiled with some care. But, once inside this logic, what seems beyond doubt is that the classical and universal notion of the individual as citizen is counterposed to the idea of the person or *ser relacional* (relational being).

Thus in Brazil the first step in taking a person to court is his (or her) individualization. The tragic and dehumanizing rituals of solitary confinement and of extracting confessions by using torture (or other similar devices that simply disrespect basic human rights) could be seen as a way of isolating a person, by drastically and cruelly transforming him into an *individual*, that is to say, a being isolated from the web of relations which rule the world along with impersonal laws. Without this isolation (which obviously has different gradations in the Brazilian scene, according to the nature of the crime and the social position of the criminal), it is indeed complicated to try a person, because he never would be seen as being solely responsible for his actions. But I have to make myself clear with regard to this point: I am not saying that because of this torture, solitary imprisonment and other brutal forms of repression are justified in this society; or worse still, that fair trials would be impossible in Brazil. Obviously they are not. I am only saying -- and the work of Roberto Kant de Lima with the Brazilian judicial system from a similar perspective fully demonstrates this -- that from a social (or moral) point of view, it is only the person that exists in the majority of positive social contexts. Or, to say it in other words, only the "person" has a positive value in the Brazilian social scene. In fact, I would dare to reaffirm that one of our tasks in creating a more democratic society in Brazil will be to introduce fully and positively this conception of the individual (and of citizenship), taking it in its positive connotations.

Realistically, we know that it is almost impossible to judge a *person* in Brazil, for what is in the dock is a family, a kin group, a network of relations, a political party. In this sense the most visible social and political strategy in Brazil is looking for a relationship. Who you know versus who I know, is the fundamental fact in the Brazilian social calculus, being much more important than knowing what you do or where you were born. Or better yet, all this can be sorted out and done through finding someone who, being known to both parties, can serve as our mediator, cementing our relations.

Beyond relations and friendship, there exist only the laws which were invented to restrain or even to correct abuses of the networks of personal relations. In fact, perhaps it would be possible to show that the social and political ideal of justice that Stuart Schwartz indicates as being a mark of honor for the King in Iberian history and society, really starts from this ideal of social compensation. Thus, if nobility, clergy and *letrados* (the stratum or caste of judges, lawyers and functionaries) were able to enjoy powerful and peremptory personal relationships, in compensation the common folk and the poor could have bureaucratic institutions and the King's justice. It is necessary to point out that in Portugal the development of legal and bureaucratic structures took a radically different direction from those of France, Germany and England. In Portugal and Brazil, the purpose of universal laws was not to liberalize politics or economics but to achieve justice as manifested in the corrective, compensatory capacity of the state. In this sense, the letrados played an important role in the Portuguese and Spanish social dynamic, to the point of having (as Schwartz suggests) a marked opposition to the nobility. And as Raymundo Faoro has suggested, it is possible that this facilitated the absorption of commerce by the state and royal bureaucracy, which gave a unique shape to Portuguese history.[19] Another difference is that these general laws always came from the top down; they were not the result of local conflicts.

All this brings us to a central point, already highlighted several times: Brazilian society has diverse sources for the classification and affiliation of its members. Societies which went through the revolution of individualism instituted a hegemonic code of conduct, founded on the idea of the citizen, but in relational societies many codes of conduct operate simultaneously, not in competition, but complementing each other. Thus, what the one code negates, the other can facilitate. The result, as we see more clearly below, is a mutiplicity of codes and axes of classification which give the system a highly complex and peculiar dynamism. In essence, it is as if the society had various sources of citizenship, each one being basic and all operating to permit a series of social compensations. But to make this clear, it is necessary to start from the beginning, with a look at the Brazilian system of ritual.

In earlier work I have shown that Brazil has a complex and multiple vision of itself as a society. Thus, when I spoke of a "ritual triangle," a triangle of civic, religious and carnivalesque festivities, I did not speak only of three types of commemoration which can exist in all modern societies, but of something much more dense and profound. I noted that these forms of ritualization prompted three readings of the Brazilian world by Brazilians themselves, to use a good formulation of Clifford Geertz.[20] This indicated that the Brazilian ritual universe expressed a society with diverse images which are complementary between themselves. Thus, if the world of the carnaval and of religion presented us with an image of ourselves as masters of enormous confidence, creativity and hope in the future, the universe of civics and politics points us to a much more arduous road, a road full of pessimism and distrust. The fundamental point here is the positive value given by Brazilian ideology to all the angles of this social configuration. Thus it is not only the carnavalesque hope which is positive, but also the *malandragem* (rascality) and despair of politics which are virtually institutionalized as a form of reading or interpreting Brazil.

I don't believe that it would be like this in individualist countries, where a single vision of the world permeates the spheres of religion, of economy and of society as a whole.[21] But in Brazil, social life follows a rhythm composed of tensions and compensations. What I don't have in the public universe, in the *world of the street*, I can have galore in my *house*; and what I cannot have in *this world* I will certainly have in the other. The fundamental point here is not only that the society has a differentiated and complex vision of itself -- in a certain sense all societies have these visions -- but also that these spaces and dramatic planes express an internally divided, but complementary totality. In the Brazilian case, one cannot have a complete vision of society only with the house, with the street or with the other world. One must have the three versions (or readings) to be able to build the totality which is, then, perceived as Brazilian. These spheres are not in competition, as occurs with a party, club or factory in the individualist universe, but are in full complementary relation.

Thus, inside my web of kinship, godparenthood and friendship, inside the house, I am a person. I am a being divided and relational, whose social existence is legitimized by ties which I maintain with other persons in a system of transitivities and gradations. I live in this house because I am the son of "X" and I have the right to use the social resources allocated there because I am a member of the family "Y." It is not as an individual that I make up the family, but it is the family and the relations which are made through it which legitimize me as a member of that social space. Relations are what transform me from an individual to a person.[22] In this domain, I am also a unitary reality and socially irreproducible, because I can never be substituted. In the house, far from being indivisible, I am frankly divided by innumerable personal loyalties which are demarcated by kinship and by personal sympathy.

In Brazil no one escapes from the ties of the family and from those of some friendships, just as in the United States in the same sense, it is impossible to escape from your alma mater or from your social security number, or credit card. In fact, the comparison shows how the two systems operate, differentiating and "selecting" different aspects, and then emphasizing these to create their most legitimate forms and lasting affiliations. In America, social existence is practically impossible without a bank account, a credit card, and the social security number; but, in compensation, you can live without instrumental and imperative social ties. In Brazil, by contrast, there are millions who live without a bank account, INPS (health insurance) number or credit card. But no one exists in the full social sense without having a family and a net of imperative and instrumental personal ties. Side by side, these social configurations point up two ways of conceiving social reality, enabling us to see laws as a systematic method to allow social dynamics and social affiliations.

But what happens to me when I leave the house and go to the world of the street and the impersonal relations this implies? What happens when I am transformed into a citizen? When I leave for work and have to convert myself into an individual? What can be said is that in the street I have to think of radically different strategies. If looking out from the house my vision of Brazil is that "our society is one great big family," with a place for all, in the sphere of the street my vision of Brazil is very different. Here I am in "open combat" and life is a fight between strangers. I am also subject to the impersonal laws of the market and of citizenship which frequently say "I am nobody." This leaves me at the mercy of whoever might be manipulating the social order at that moment. I know also that in the impersonal universe of the street, the logic impels a systematic effort to destroy privileges. Thus, I perceive that universal law is a weapon to subdue groups and networks of relations, so they can be controlled legally and politically. One conclusion is obvious from all of this. If in the universe of the house I am a super-citizen, for there I only have rights and no obligations, in the world of the street I am a sub-citizen, in that the universal laws of citizenship always define me by my negative determinants: by my duties and obligations, by the logic of "you can't" and "you shouldn't."

How can I reconcile these two modes of living, which are so diverse (but compensatory and complementary), in the same society? The answer is found in the capacity to relate one system with another, preferably so that the negative experiences on one side can be transformed into positive experiences on the other. But the critical fact is that these spaces are different bases of affiliation to the same social reality, allowing its classification in a differentiated, but still complementary mode.

What all these points seem to indicate is that Brazil constitutes a society with a system endowed with multiple spheres of action and social significance. We know little about this system and we still do not understand its logic well. We do know, however, that its touchstone is the capacity for relating and from there to create an intermediate position, a relational perspective which is translated into a language of conciliation, negotiation, and gradation. I maintain that this is critical to explain the popularity of figures such as the malandro and the populist politician (*carioca* or *mineiro*), figures which always skillfully manipulate both sides. Given this fascination for relating, how else can we interpret Jorge Amado's delightful myth of Dona Flor and her two husbands (one being a malandro, the other a dull bourgeois)? His is of course the perfect literary myth for a society struggling with codes which are complementary and absolutely essential for social navigation.

These considerations are far from resolving all of the questions which I have raised throughout this work. But they do enable us to speculate with some degree of security on the way in which certain institutional arrangements are lived and perceived by the members of the system. It is not just a question of the way social and political institutions are legitimized, but of discovering the cultural profiles that a society makes out of certain basic notions in the Western political vocabulary. Not that we should stop studying the Brazilian political world through the prism of its structural and institutional logic. But it is equally necessary to pay more attention to certain unique social processes which have given societies such as the Brazilian a way of living together that bothers not only its most aware members but also upsets all the theories of social justice coming out of societies with a much more individualized social experience.

There is no Brazilian who does not know the value of social relations and hasn't utilized them all his life as instruments to solve problems. There is no Brazilian who has never used the expression "do you know to whom you are speaking?" when up against a universal law and at risk of having his moral self being transformed into a mere number or anonymous entity, open, thus to an unjust arrest or the sometimes brutal will of the organs of repression. In the same sense and by the same logic, there is no Brazilian who does not understand (as the sociologist Oliveira Vianna told us early on in 1923) that in the universe of the national public life, one can deny everything except a favor to a friend![23] Whether at the level of anecdote or as an irreducible fact of Brazilian uniqueness, social scientists should be preoccupied with the implications of all this and emphasize it in their work. Not to do this would be to continue doing studies of Brazilian and Latin American society that were purely normative or formalistic, and thus missing the twists and dilemmas of societies which, without abandoning the past, are already embracing the future.

In conclusion, I would like to suggest a few questions for future research into the transformation of peripheral societies where, as in Brazil, particularistic social patterns and distinct social spaces such as *the house*, the *street*, and the *other world* co-exist with universal values.

In this essay, I maintain that any one member of Brazilian society is simultaneously an individual and a person, being individualized (the citizen in Western legal thought) and relational (that is, an entity always composed of and perceived by his social links and by the groups he belongs to). To be considered an indivisible social entity is to be subjected to all the implications of the law, hence throughout Brazilian society the position of the *individual* is always disadvantageous. What are the political and legal implications for a society that operates at the juncture of a system composed of ideal norms and a legitimizing system of social practices based personal relations?

Constitutions and legal codes in semi-traditional countries, that is, societies with double or triple codes of social behavior, are frequently utopian in their aim to correct the "vices" and "errors" of society, and at the same time "create" the same society. This is a basic problem in the transformation of social dynamics in peripheral societies. Bear in mind also that what we are dealing with in the Brazilian case is a centralized system and not a society which legitimizes laws which come from the bottom up. And, moreover, that the legal-formal aspects of this centralization are subject to the implicit and certainly more powerful rules (because they operate unconsciously) of friendship, kinship and relations.

The great transformation of the West was the passage from a system of personal codes to a universal code, when the complex of special laws which operated in specific spaces and for single persons was liquidated. But this passage can follow various possible roads and Brazilian society has maintained its own social spaces which are very well marked: the *house*, the *street*, and the *other world*, domains where the laws penetrate differently, and with different intensity. Thus I can be one person in the house and another in the street, and still another at church. Brazil lacks the unity of social principles that typify societies which underwent the "puritan revolution," a movement which according to Max Weber and others tended to place religion in all places. In Brazil's multiple spaces the various "legal systems" are equally in force. The extraordinary thing about Brazil is that while history and society are perceived and analysed as legal-formal entities, the forms of relating by friendship, kinship and sympathy are not seen as something out of date or lapsed but rather as eternal, as a part of nature. Why should this be?

Certainly part of the answer lies in the fact the family never underwent a generalized and universal crisis as occurred in some other Western societies. This helps to explain the extremely unequal development of the country. Brazilian social history reveals a shocking maintenance of family unity, of kinship and of neighborhood, of the *house* in the almost Roman sense of the expression, at the expense of other *houses* which are the houses of our subordinates and thus can be destroyed.

In the Brazilian social dynamic, many traditional elements remain surprisingly intact. And this dynamic is maintained by a curious game. The discourse of the street is modern, because it is determined by economic logic and the legal code based on universal rights. But running along with it is a discourse of loyalties and friendships, speaking to the personal ties which still are not perceived as having serious social and political implications. Hence my suggestion that we need to look at this side of Brazilian life less anecdotally, as something basic to it. The truly transforming social movement will occur when we are open to the two sides of the question. This is no simple matter because the Brazilian social and political world is always seen from one side or the other, as if they were exclusive and were not profoundly related. Thus, we speak of "social classes" and of social movements, or of the *casa grande* society of traditional values, forgetting that Brazilian society contains, internally, two discourses or modes of perception of itself.

Among the problems needing basic research is the role of multiple, but complementary codes in developing societies. Modernization theories always assume that certain forces such as urbanization and industrialization condition social change to follow certain directions. That these forces do provoke certain changes, and a certain dynamism while raising the level of misery is not in doubt. The chapters in this book provide abundant evidence of this. But it is much less clear that these modernizing forces can liquidate traditional forms of negotiation, of confirmation, and of giving sense to the social world.

The fact that basic institutions such as *Umbanda* and *carnaval* are located are the juncture of the formal and the informal modes shows that is is where Brazilian society has given some of its most ingenious and resourceful solutions, while resisting the hegemony of an exclusive framework of values. This explains why these institutions have proliferated with such vigor.

Thus rationality is not the only force that operates in the multiple spaces that order the society. Umbanda waxes with industrialization because neither of the two institutions can penetrate all social life homogeneously. Nor need the values of Umbanda be updated to those of the factory, because the values of the factory are not expected to embrace those of the other world, which is the supernatural world of Umbanda. But why don't the modernizing forces triumph? Why this clear and almost chivalrous division between the world of religion and the world of action, the economy and industry?

This critical problem needs to be looked at, not as a study of so-called exotic systems (for example, Afro-Brazilian religions) in themselves, but in their political and social implications for the system as a whole. Similarly, the question of obedience to universal norms is perhaps the central problem for semi-traditional societies like Brazil. Why don't universal laws penetrate the house, and how does the society of the house penetrate the world of the street? How can universal rules be disobeyed without being modified, in consequence? These are essential questions for understanding the Brazilian system. Detailed studies of Brazilian voluntary organizations would reveal much about the relations between politics, politicians, ideologies and the laws of loyalty and friendship. And since politics lies at the juncture of formal and informal modes, at the crossroads of house and street, this too is ripe for rethinking and more investigation.

NOTES

1. To be brief, I will cite only T.H. Marshall's chapter, "Cidadania e classe social," in his *Cidadania, classe social e status* (Rio de Janeiro, 1967), where a history of the concept is presented, but at no time is sociologically examined. Numerous Brazilian political commentators and social scientists have addressed the same question in similar terms.

2. See his "The Modern Conception of the Individual," in *Contributions to Indian Sociology*, III (1965); *Homo Hierarchicus*, (Chicago, 1970); *Religion, Politics and History in India* (The Hague, 1970); and *From Mandeville to Marx: The Genesis and Triumph of Economic Ideology* (Chicago, 1977).

3. Steven Lukes, *Individualism* (New York, 1973), p. 79.

4. Dumont, *Contributions to Indian Sociology*, p. 19; also *Homo Hierarchicus*.

5. This is an important point in the theories of roles and social identities by Ralph Linton and Ward Goodenough. Goodenough takes complementarity (which he calls "matching identity") as a critical element in the definition of a "relation of identity," a key point in the description of important social situations. Thus I know that the "matching identities" father/ mother set the stage for kinship. See Goodenough, "Rethinking Status and Role," in *The Relevance of Models for Social Anthropology*, ASA Monographs, 1 (London, 1965), pp. 6-7.

6. In effect, Linton says that social statuses are "polar positions... in patterns of reciprocal behavior" (*The Study of Man*, [New York, 1936] pp. 113-114 as cited in Goodenough, pp. 6-7). It is significant that as far as I know, no theoretician of social identity has critically studied the role of "individual" and of "citizen." To the contrary: these concepts are always taken as axiomatic points of departure for the theory of social roles. Thus as "individuals" we "choose" our social roles, just as we "choose" our clothing and automobiles. This, I repeat, is taken as a truth which does not require sociological proof. But the fact is that in sociology, as in life, we are constantly discovering roles that "choose" their actors, turning the latter into instruments of the collectivity. To do sociology is to take into account the truths of society.

7. See Alexis de Tocqueville, *O antigo regime e a revolução* (Brasília, 1979); and René Remond, *O antigo regime e a revolução: 1750-1818* (São Paulo, 1976).

8. As Karl Polanyi instructs us in *The Great Transformation: The Political and Economic Origins of Our Time* (Boston, 1967).

9. Roberto da Matta, *Carnavais, malandros e herois* (Rio de Janeiro, 1979), p. 132.

10. See Da Matta, *Carnavais*; "As raizes da violência no Brasil," in *A violência brasileira* (São Paulo, 1982); and "A

questão da posse," in *Humanidades*, I:2 (1983), pp. 37-45.

11. See Wanderley Guilherme dos Santos, *Cidadania e justiça: A política social na ordem brasileira* (Rio de Janeiro, 1979), p.75.

12. *Carnavais*, pp. 184*ff*; and Mariza Peirano, "Documentos e identidade social: Reflexões sobre a cidadania no Brasil," *Serie Antropologia Social*, no. 30 (Brasilia, 1982) for similar considerations.

13. See Richard Morse, "The Heritage of Latin America," and Glen Dealy, "The Tradition of Monistic Democracy in Latin America, both in Howard J. Wiarda, ed., *Politics and Social Change in Latin America: The Distinct Tradition* (Amherst, Mass., 1974); also Dealey's *The Public Man: An Interpretation of Latin America and Other Catholic Countries* (Amherst, 1974), p. 1977. See also Manuel Paulo Merêa, *O poder real das cortes* (Coimbra, 1923); Philippe Schmitter, *Interest, Conflict and Political Change in Brazil* (Stanford, 1971); Vitorino Magalhães, *Estrutura da antiga sociedade portuguesa* (Lisboa, 1977); Simon Schwartzman, *Bases do autoritarismo brasileiro* (Rio de Janeiro, 1982).

14. Hence the importance of the ideology of the frontier is a dominant institution. Thus, in the United States the frontier is everything that is "new." The concept is not restricted to its geographic aspects. On this topic, see Otavio Velho, *Capitalismo autoritário e campesinato* (Rio de Janeiro, 1976).

15. In the context of this discussion it is important to recall the observations of Michel Crozier, *The Bureaucratic Phenomenon* (Chicago, 1964) on the bureaucratic systems of France, Russia, North America and England.

16. The colonial cases are taken from Stuart B. Schwartz, whose history of *Burocracia e sociedade no*

Brasil colonial (São Paulo, 1979) documents relations between persons and bureaucracy without discussing their full sociological and cultural implications. The contemporary examples are from *O Globo* (January 20, 1984) and from my *Carnavais*, chapter IV.

17. This is not to admire the surprise with which any Brazilian reacts to orderly queues and the respect for those first in line that characterizes England and the United States. In Brazil, the relationship allows one person to wait in line for another, or to hold his seat at the movies. The profession of *despachante* (fixer) institutionalizes this *apadrinhamento para baixo* (protecting or sponsoring towards below) as mentioned in *Carnavais*, p. 183. Erico Verissimo, who was an excellent observer of American life, comments on just this in two of his books: "Now and then we hazard an excursion to the drive-in restaurant and we have to wait for ten, fifteen or twenty minutes in line. These lines are a living example of North American democracy. If the soldier arrives before the corporal, the corporal before the sargeant, and the sargeant before the captain, there is no law which could change this order. The officer awaits his turn with equanimity, knowing that all the *citizens have equal rights according to the Constitution of the United States, and the fact that they are soldiers does not stop them from being citizens....*" (in *A volta do gato preto* [Porto Alegre, 1957], p. 81. My emphasis). See also Caetano Veloso's song: "London, London, where there is joy in discovering the citizen interacting civilly with the police, but in London..."

18. These observations refer to the famous 1920 article of Marcel Mauss on "La nacion," *Obras* III (Barcelona, 1972 ed). In a critical passage he says that, "to begin with, one cannot have a nation without a certain level of social integration, meaning that the nation should have abolished all segmentation such as clans, tribes, kingdoms and feudal dominions." And, he adds, "this integration is such that in the advanced nations no intermediary between the nation

and the citizen exists." (Quotes on p. 290).

19. Schwartz, *op. cit.*, and Faoro's classic *Os donos do poder; Formação do patronato político brasileiro* (Porto Alegre, 1975).

20. See Clifford Geertz, *The Interpretation of Cultures; Selected Essays* (New York, 1973).

21. The point of departure for this perspective on dual ethics *versus* unitary or hegemonic ethics is found in Max Weber, *A ética protestante e o espírito do capitalismo* (São Paulo, 1967 ed.). See also Dealey's *The Public Man* for an interpretation that has many points in common with mine, but that in my opinion fails to evaluate the implications of complementarity and hierarchy in the Iberian social world. Thus the problem is not only to underscore the differences between the public and the private spheres, but to discover that they (like the *house* and the *street*) are profoundly related, just like two sides of the same coin. See my *A casa e a rua* (São Paulo, 1985).

22. *Carnavais*, p. 174*ff.*

23. F.J. Oliveira Vianna, *Pequenos estudos de psicologia social* (São Paulo, 1923).

About the Contributors

Maria Hermínia Tavares de Almeida, political sociologist, University of Campinas, and Director, Nucleus for Studies on Public Policy at the University of Campinas

Thomas E. Bogenschild, anthropologist, Ph.D. candidate in Latin American Studies, University of California, Berkeley

Regis Bonelli, economist, Instituto Universitario de Pesquisas do Rio de Janeiro (IUPERJ)

Renato R. Boschi, political scientist, IUPERJ

Barbara Geddes, political scientist, University of California, Los Angeles

Carlos Hasenbalg, sociologist, IUPERJ

Pedro S. Malan, economist, Executive Director, The World Bank

Roberto da Matta, anthropologist, Museu Nacional, Rio de Janeiro

Edson de Oliveira Nunes, political scientist, Director, Brazilian Institute of Geography and Statistics (IBGE)

Ben Ross Schneider, political scientist, Ph.D. candidate, University of California, Berkeley

Nelson do Valle Silva, sociologist, IBGE

John D. Wirth, historian, Stanford University, recently Director of the Stanford-Berkeley Joint Center for Latin American Studies and currently Chairman, Department of Spanish and Portuguese

Index

For Product Safety Concerns and Information please contact our EU
representative GPSR@taylorandfrancis.com
Taylor & Francis Verlag GmbH, Kaufingerstraße 24, 80331 München, Germany

www.ingramcontent.com/pod-product-compliance
Lightning Source LLC
LaVergne TN
LVHW011109300926
849160LV00008B/321
9780367304119